Lecture Notes in Artificial Intellig

Edited by J. G. Carbonell and J. Siekmann

Subseries of Lecture Notes in Computer Science

Paolo Bresciani   Paolo Giorgini
Brian Henderson-Sellers   Graham Low
Michael Winikoff (Eds.)

Agent-Oriented Information Systems II

6th International Bi-Conference Workshop, AOIS 2004
Riga, Latvia, June 8, 2004 and New York, NY, USA, July 20, 2004
Revised Selected Papers

 Springer

Series Editors

Jaime G. Carbonell, Carnegie Mellon University, Pittsburgh, PA, USA
Jörg Siekmann, University of Saarland, Saarbrücken, Germany

Volume Editors

Paolo Bresciani
Institute for Scientific and Technological Research (IRST), Trento, Italy
E-mail: bresciani@itc.it

Paolo Giorgini
University of Trento, Department of Information and Communication Technology
Trento, Italy
E-mail: paolo.giorgini@dit.unitn.it

Brian Henderson-Sellers
University of Technology, Sydney
Faculty of Information Technology, Sydney, Australia
E-mail: brian@it.uts.edu.au

Graham Low
University of New South Wales
School of Information Systems, Technology and Management
Sydney, Australia
E-mail: g.low@unsw.edu.au

Michael Winikoff
RMIT University, School of Computer Science and Information Technology
Melbourne, Australia
E-mail: winikoff@cs.rmit.edu.au

Library of Congress Control Number: 2004106088

CR Subject Classification (1998): I.2.11, H.4, H.3, H.5.2-3, C.2.4, I.2

ISSN   0302-9743
ISBN-10   3-540-25911-2 Springer Berlin Heidelberg New York
ISBN-13   978-3-540-25911-4 Springer Berlin Heidelberg New York

Springer is a part of Springer Science+Business Media

springeronline.com

© Springer-Verlag Berlin Heidelberg 2005
Printed in Germany

Typesetting: Camera-ready by author, data conversion by Scientific Publishing Services, Chennai, India
Printed on acid-free paper   SPIN: 11426714   06/3142   5 4 3 2 1 0

Preface

Information systems have become the backbone of all kinds of organizations today. In almost every sector – manufacturing, education, health care, government and businesses large and small – information systems are relied upon for everyday work, communication, information gathering and decision-making. Yet, the inflexibilities in current technologies and methods have also resulted in poor performance, incompatibilities and obstacles to change. As many organizations are reinventing themselves to meet the challenges of global competition and e-commerce, there is increasing pressure to develop and deploy new technologies that are flexible, robust and responsive to rapid and unexpected change.

Agent concepts hold great promise for responding to the new realities of information systems. They offer higher level abstractions and mechanisms which address issues such as knowledge representation and reasoning, communication, coordination, cooperation among heterogeneous and autonomous parties, perception, commitments, goals, beliefs, intentions etc., all of which need conceptual modelling. On the one hand, the concrete implementation of these concepts can lead to advanced functionalities, e.g., in inference-based query answering, transaction control, adaptive work flows, brokering and integration of disparate information sources, and automated communication processes. On the other hand, their rich representational capabilities allow for more faithful and flexible treatments of complex organizational processes, leading to more effective requirements analysis and architectural/detailed design.

The Agent Oriented Information Systems (AOIS) workshop series focusses on how agent concepts and techniques will contribute to meeting information systems needs today and tomorrow. To foster greater communication and interaction between the Information Systems and Agents communities, the AOIS workshop is organized as a bi-conference event. It is intended to be a single "logical" event with two "physical" venues. This arrangement encourages greater participation from, and more exchange between, both communities.

AOIS 2004 was the sixth edition of the workshop. The first part was hosted on the 8th of June at CAiSE'04 – the 16th International Conference on Advanced Information Systems Engineering – in Riga (Latvia). The second part was held on the 20th of July at AAMAS'04 – the 3rd International Joint Conference on Autonomous Agents and Multi-Agent Systems (AAMAS'04) – in New-York (USA). The workshop received in total 36 submissions, 23 of which were accepted for presentation. These papers were reviewed by at least 3 members of an international programme committee composed of 31 researchers. The submissions followed a call for papers on all aspects of agent-oriented information systems and showed the range of results achieved in several areas, such as methodologies, applications, modelling, analysis and simulation.

This volume contains the revised versions of 14 selected papers presented at the workshop and an invited paper by Terry Halpin who gave a keynote speech at the CAiSE event. The papers are grouped into four categories: *information systems, analysis and modeling, methodologies* and *applications.*

We believe that this carefully prepared volume will be of particular value to all readers in these key topics, describing the most recent developments in the field of agent-oriented information systems.

We thank the authors, the participants and the reviewers for making AOIS 2004 a high-quality scientific event.

March 2005   Paolo Bresciani
                                                           Paolo Giorgini
                                               Brian Henderson-Sellers
                                                           Graham Low
                                                      Michael Winikoff

Organization

Organizing Committee

Paolo Bresciani (AOIS@CAiSE Co-chair)
Institute for Scientific and Technological Research (IRST)
Trento, Italy
Email: bresciani@itc.it

Paolo Giorgini (AOIS@AAMAS Co-chair)
Department of Information and Communication Technology
University of Trento, Italy
Email: paolo.giorgini@dit.unitn.it

Brian Henderson-Sellers (AOIS@CAiSE Co-chair)
Faculty of Information Technology
University of Technology, Sydney, Australia
Email: brian@it.uts.edu.au

Graham Low (AOIS@CAiSE Co-chair)
School of Information Systems, Technology and Management
The University of New South Wales, Sydney, Australia
Email: g.low@unsw.edu.au

Michael Winikoff (AOIS@AAMAS Co-chair)
School of Computer Science and Information Technology
RMIT University, Melbourne, Australia
Email: winikoff@cs.rmit.edu.au

Steering Committee

Yves Lespérance
Department of Computer Science
York University, Canada
Email:lesperan@cs.yorku.ca

Gerd Wagner
Department of Information and Technology,
Eindhonven University of Technology, The Netherlands
Email: G.Wagner@tm.tue.nl

Eric Yu
Faculty of information Studies,

University of Toronto, Canada
Email: eric.yu@utoronto.ca

Program Committee

Table of Contents

Applications

An Agent-Based Collaborative Emergent Process Management System

Aizhong Lin, Igor Hawryszkiewycz, and Brian Henderson-Sellers

Faculty of Information Technology,
University of Technology, Sydney,
POBox 123, Broadway,
NSW 2007, Australia
{alin, igorh, brian}@it.uts.edu.au

Abstract. An emergent process is a process whose goal and activities to achieve the goal are unable to be specified in advance but emerge over time as knowledge gained from the activities performed earlier shapes the subsequent goal and activities. Collaborative emergent process management needs functions to support the representation and storage of emergent process instances, process automation and knowledge sharing. Traditional process management systems lack the full functionality of collaborative emergent process management. Our research provides an agent-based collaborative emergent process management system that provides the full functionality needed for managing emergent process instances collaboratively. This paper presents the system including the management model, system architecture, major components, key modules and an application.

1 Introduction

An *emergent process* is a process whose goal and activities to achieve that goal are unable to be specified in advance but emerge over time as knowledge gained from the activities performed earlier shapes the subsequent goal and activities. A research project is an example of an emergent process. Emergent processes have the following distinctive features. Firstly, an emergent process may not have a predefined goal, or its goal may mutate over time. Secondly, an emergent process does not have a predefined solution. The solution of each emergent process instance differs from the solutions of other emergent process instances. Thirdly, an emergent process is a knowledge-driven process. The process knowledge gives direction to the current process. Next, an emergent process will not terminate until a satisfactory conclusion is reached - achieving a business goal is not the termination condition of an emergent process. Finally, an emergent process is the intertwining of two process stages - process definition (also called process modelling) and process enactment (also called process execution). In the process definition stage, process participants determine or change the process goal and activities. In the process enactment stage, process participants perform the activities and harvest the knowledge.

Managing emergent processes requires a management system equipped with the functions to support the representation and storage of emergent process instances, support process enactment, support the intertwining of process definition and

P. Bresciani et al. (Eds.): AOIS 2004, LNAI 3508, pp. 1–18, 2005.
© Springer-Verlag Berlin Heidelberg 2005

enactment, and support process knowledge management and sharing. Traditional process management, which focuses on managing routine processes, is inadequate for managing emergent processes because (1) early systems [1,2] do not provide a mechanism to bridge process definition and process enactment, and (2) recent systems (such as workflow management systems) lack the capability to support the evolution of process goals and activities.

Our research contributes an agent-based collaborative emergent process management system to support emergent processes by interacting with human process participants to define and change goals and activities; perform process activities; and manage and share process knowledge. The system consists of two components: a process workspace manager and a personal process agent framework. The process workspace manager resides on a server to manage process workspaces that are used to represent and store emergent process instances. The personal process agent framework is used to construct personal process agents that run on a client allowing process participants to define or change process instances (including goals and solutions), achieve goals or execute activities, support interactions between process participants, and manage and share process knowledge. An experimental emergent process management system has been implemented as demonstrated here.

2   The Management Model

An emergent process instance can be represented by a meta-model (Figure 1). An *emergent process meta-model* defines a collection of elements (such as process goal, process activity, process constraint) and their relationships (such as activity "achieves" a goal) used in emergent processes.

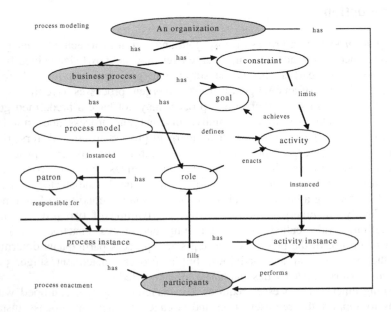

Fig. 1. The meta-model to represent emergent process instances

An emergent process instance (left arrow in Figure 2) can be defined (create, change, or mutate the goals, activities, constraints) by process participants who can also achieve goals or perform activities defined in the instance. Process participants can perceive the changes that take place in the process instance and harvest process knowledge from performing the process instance (right hand arrow in Figure 2). The newly gained process knowledge combined with existing knowledge is used to define process goals and activities (back to the left arrow).

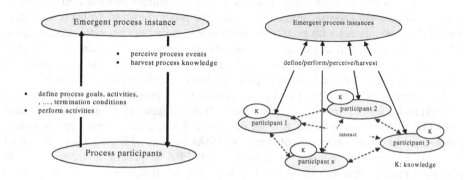

Fig. 2. The management model   **Fig. 3.** The detailed management model

During the enactment of an emergent process instance, distributed process participants interact with each other. Figure 3 expands the system architecture shown in Figure 2 for managing emergent business processes. From these two figures, process functions can be summarized as:

- *define*:   create, modify or mutate process elements
- *perform*:   execute activities to achieve process goals
- *perceive*: perceive changes in process instances
- *harvest*:   harvest process knowledge from emergent process instances
- *manage*:   manage process knowledge and the path of changes for process instances
- *interact*: support interactions between process participants

3   The System Architecture

The emergent process management model determines the emergent process management system architecture. To convert the management model to the system architecture, two decisions have to be made. Firstly, a process workspace component is developed to represent and store instances of emergent processes. The process workspace component consists of

- *a process workspace (PW) model* is a set of process elements, a set of relationships between process workspaces and a set of links each of which connects a process workspace to another process workspace.

- *a directed process workspace graph (DPWG)* contains a set of related process workspace to represent a process instance.
- a process workspace library (PWL) contains a set of directed process workspace graphs in an organization.
- a process workspace manager (PWM) is a software component that manages a PWL. The management functions provided by PWM include the creation, retrieval, modification, deletion and access control of a single PW in the PWL.

Secondly, software agents are developed to assist human process participants to define and perform process instances, to perceive process events, to harvest process knowledge and interact with each other. Each agent, called the personal process agent (PPA), works on behalf of one and only one human process participant. It is situated in a specific process environment (such as an organization) and is capable of autonomous and flexible actions to respond to changes in the process environment.

The management system has two components: a process workspace manager (PWM) and a set of personal process agents (PPAs) (Figure 4). The PWM maintains DPWGs, each of which contains a set of related PWs, used to represent and store emergent process instances (top of Figure 4). PPAs (middle of Figure 4) are employed to assist the work of human participants. Each PPA is generated from a generic personal process framework. An agent has process functions to define process elements and relationships for process instances in PWs, to perceive the events that have taken place in PWs, to achieve goals or execute activities defined in PWs, to harvest process knowledge from activities performed and to interact with other PPAs.

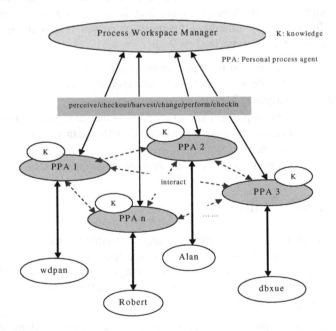

Fig. 4. The architecture of an emergent process management system

The system architecture is a hybrid, combining three traditional architectures: client/server, peer-to-peer and producer/consumer. Firstly, the client/server architecture is necessary in this system architecture because:

- An emergent process instance should be accessed by all participants who have permission to work on it.
- The process instance should appear the same to all participants at all times.

Secondly, the producer/consumer architecture is necessary to:

- Produce: any human participant may define or change (produce) process goals or activities and advertise process knowledge in the process instance.
- Consume: any human participant may perform process activities or achieve process goals.

However, this producer/consumer architecture extends traditional producer/consumer architecture in two respects:

- In a traditional producer/consumer architecture, producers and consumers play different roles. A producer is not a consumer and a consumer does not have to be a producer. In our producer/consumer architecture, however, a PPA can be both producer and consumer, i.e., a PPA may produce goals or activities for others to consume, and consume goals or activities produced by others, even by itself.
- In a traditional producer/consumer architecture, producers do not have to wait for the results of consumers. In this architecture, however, producers may expect the results from consumers to produce new goals or activities.

Finally, the peer-to-peer architecture is needed because:

- Participants in a group are naturally distributed.
- The relationships between human participants are peer to peer because no participant can control other participants. No participant can directly access knowledge owned by other participants.

4   The Implementation of the Emergent Process Management System (EPMS)

Based on the system architecture, the management system is implemented with two components: the process workspace manager (PWM) and the PPA framework.

4.1   Support Techniques

The emergent process management system is implemented as shown in Figures 5 and 6. Figure 5 illustrates the technical support of the PWL (Process Workspace Library) and the PWM. The PWL is built on two technologies: Folders/Files management technology and PWXML (Process Workspace XML – designed by the first author as part of his PhD). Folders/Files management is used to manage folders and files in which each folder is a DPWG (Directed Process Workspace Graph) and each file is a PW. Based on standard XML [3], PWXML is used to represent the PW, each PW being saved as a .xml file in a folder. A PWXML Document Type Definition defines the syntax and semantics of the PWXML. SAX (Simple API for XML) and DOM (Document Object Model) are used to assist the conversion from a XML format stream to an object and vice versa. The PWM employs SAX and DOM to parse or generate an XML stream from or to the PWL. The PWM is a Java Servlet program that extends the Sun Servlet module, running on an Apache HTTP server that has a fixed IP address or a universal domain name.

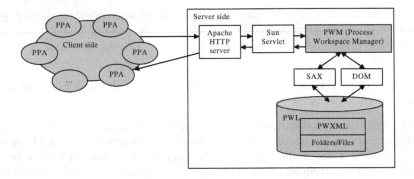

Fig. 5. The technical support of PWM and PWL

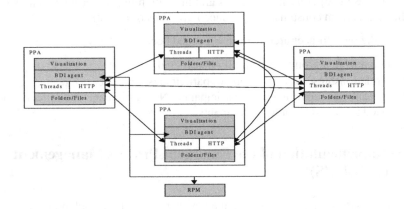

Fig. 6. The technical support of a PPA

On the other hand, the technical support for a PPA is illustrated in Figure 6. Firstly, Folders/Files management in a PPA is used since a PPA has to manage its private abilities (functions) and knowledge. Some systems may use databases to maintain data records; however, in our system, we prefer the use of XML files. The benefits of using XML to maintain data records are that (1) the data records are application independent because XML has an application-independent data format; (2) an XML format file is an object-oriented database; and (3) removal of third party database products avoids possible licensing problems. Secondly, Thread and HTTP are major technologies we use in a PPA. Because of the use of threads (a thread activates itself in a period of time, say every two minutes), a PPA can automatically do things (such as perceiving events and performing activities). With the use of the HTTP protocol (communication channel between PPAs), a PPA can communicate with another PPA via an individual communication channel without considering any block such as a firewall. Thirdly, BDI (Belief, Desire, and Intention) agent technology is employed in the PPA to realize deliberative reasoning to achieve goals or perform activities for a research project, BDI being a cognitive model of problem solving in humans [4]. In our PPA, we use the concepts of "goal" and "action" to replace the concepts of "desire" and "intention" respectively. From the beliefs (generated from the perceived events or messages), a PPA can reason about the goals to "achieve" and, from this, what actions to take. Finally, visualization technology is supported in a PPA since it uses visual interfaces to interact with its human user so that the user can conveniently and efficiently give inputs to the PPA and understand its outputs.

4.2 The Major Components

The major components in the emergent process management system are a PWM (Process Workspace Manager) and a PPAF (Personal Process Agent Framework). The PWM is a server side application that can manage the PWL (Project Workspace Library) and provide services to reply to the requests from individual PPAs. The PPAF is a generic process framework that provides infrastructure (such as knowledge management, communication and interaction, deliberative reasoning and process assistant visualization) for process problem solving. Human process participants can configure the PPAF (by setting the private personal information) to a specific PPA. After a PPA has been generated from the PPAF, the human process participant can transmit private knowledge to the PPAF. Here, we describe the implementations of the major components: the PWM including the PWL, the PPAF and, in turn, a PPA.

4.2.1 The Process Workspace Manager - PWM

The PWM consists of *one table, two threads, and eight services*. The table is the "default index table" that maintains the identifiers and names of all PWs in the PWL. The two threads are "index_by" and "perceived_by". The thread "index_by" automatically builds temporary index tables according to the keywords (such as PPA name) in each time period (say two minutes). The thread "perceived_by" automatically detects the changes (events) of every PW in each time period. The eight services are:

- *checkout*:   check a process workspace out, which will block others from changing it
- *checkin*:   check a process workspace in, which will replace the original
- *browse*:   send the process workspace to a client
- *perceive*:   detect the events in a process workspace
- *broadcast_new_PPA*: tell others a PPA is joining
- *naming*:   give a unique name for an object in a workspace
- *knowledge_moniker*: map a piece of knowledge to its accessible place
- *plan_moniker*:   map a plan to its accessible place

When the PWM is started, it provides a user interface, which has a visual view to display the PWL. For example, it could list all the research projects and PWs in our example PWL application. Clicking the right mouse button in each research project node activates a popup menu. We can open the process instance to view the detailed information such as name, patron, created date and so on. Alternatively, we can view the PWDG of the research project.

When clicking the "view process workspace graph" menu item of the popup menu, a DPWG is displayed (Figure 7). This graph can not only show all PWs of an emergent process instance, but also show the relationships between the PWs. For example, from the picture, we know that process workspace PW12 has evolved from PW1 and PW2, but is not used to generate other PWs. This interface can show all PWs indexed by their identifiers and names or by other keywords such as the name of the participant. It can list all events that are indexed by using the participant's name. It can show the checkout PWs, goals and activities.

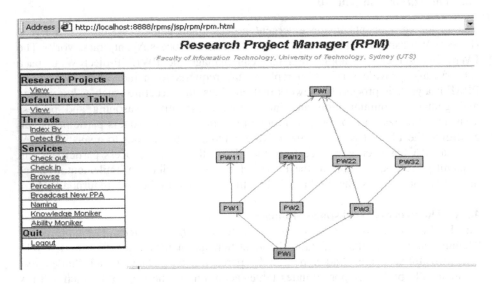

Fig. 7. The display of the directed process workspace graph (DPWG)

4.2.2 The Personal Process Agent Framework - PPAF

The PPAF has a set of basic process functions defined in the management model (Section 2). Those functions are divided into four layers, each of them being responsible for relatively independent functions (left hand panel of Figure 8). For example, the management layer is responsible for knowledge management (creation, modification, sharing and deletion); the collaboration layer is responsible for communication and interaction between PPAs; the automation layer is responsible for perceiving events and performing activities; and the assistance layer for process changes (creation, modification and deletion of process elements and relationships).

When a PPA is generated for a human participant, it exists in the EPMS (Emergent Process Management System) persistently until its user kills it. From its creation, the user can start a PPA, suspend it and recover it until it is killed. Once started, a PPA keeps working using its own BDI model [4] via threads. If suspended, all its running states are kept so that they can be restored when the PPA is recovered.

4.2.2.1 The Assistance Module

The assistance module implements the "define" function for the agent user to create, change or delete process elements and their relationships (Figure 8) in a PW. A visual interface is provided for the "define function" to show a PW including its goals, activities, constraints, artifacts and participants. When right-clicking the mouse button, a popup menu is activated, listing the actions that the agent user is permitted to do. For example, an agent user can create a new element, open an element or delete an element. The agent user can also create a relationship between two elements, open a relationship or delete a relationship. In addition, it can "checkout" a process element to change its attributes (e.g. changing the element name, type), to perform or to "check in" a process element to the PWM that saves the new element in the PW.

When a process element or a relationship is changed, two versions of the element (the content "before changed" and "after changed") are kept in the element version list of the PW. When saved, the "perceived-by" thread of the PWM detects the changes of the element, generates a new event and adds that event to the event queues of the PPAs involved in this PW. After that, the old version of the changed elements or relationships is saved to the old version of the PW by the PWM.

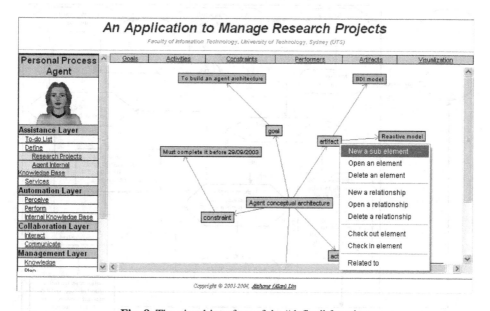

Fig. 8. The visual interface of the "define" function

4.2.2.2 The Automation Module

The automation module is the most important module of the PPAF. It is built to implement the automation of goal achievement or activity enactment. It realizes the "perceive" function and "perform" function of the PPAF. Figure 9 is the flowchart of the automation module, also showing connections to the PWM and other PPAs. When changes occur in the PWL, these are managed by the PWM and collaborations happen between PPAs. The automation module has two parallel threads to perceive events (changes) from the PWM and to receive messages incoming from other PPAs. The detected events are put in the event queue with the detection time-stamped and the messages are recorded in the message queue with a "receive" time-stamped.

An event is a data structure that contains not only the changed process element but also the changing time and modifier. For example, it contains the "goal x has been changed", the time the change occurred, the participants who changed the element, as well as the objective of the new goal "got_fund_support". From the objective of the element, if it is a goal or an activity, the automation module knows who is the "expected_participant". If this PPA is the expected participant, it begins to retrieve the plan repository to find the appropriate plan, to fetch the parameters from an artifact element and to realize the automation. If no private plan is available to do the automation, the PPA can search the sharable plan advertised in the plan_moniker of the PWM. If one is found, this PPA initializes an interaction (a negotiation) and then sends a "request" message to the owner of the plan to request sharing of the plan. If nothing is found, the automation module submits the event to the To-Do list and the agent user can decide what to do for this event. The agent user may simply drop the event by doing nothing or build a new plan to respond to such an event.

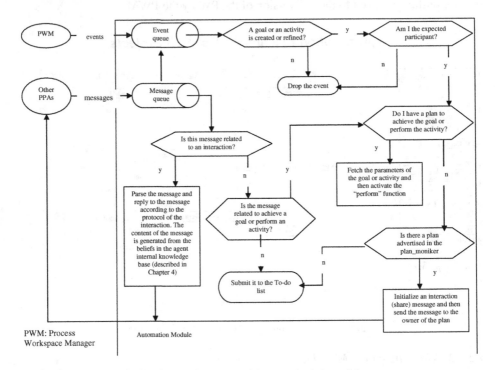

Fig. 9. The flowchart of the automation module

A message could contain structured (a defined .xml format) or unstructured (such as a normal email) information. Unstructured information is directly submitted to an unknown message list (works as an email manager) and the agent user handles the unknown messages. The agent user may reply to it or just delete it, or do something else. For structured information, the automation module can parse it. If the message is related to an interaction (e.g. another PPA makes a request to share plans), the automation module can automatically reply to the message according to the interaction protocol and the beliefs about itself and the requester.

4.2.2.3 The Collaboration Module

The collaboration module of the EPMS realizes the collaborative functions of the PPAF. The collaboration module is supported by four layers of protocols as shown in Figure 10. The Network Layer is the Transport Control Protocol (TCP). When a PPA is started, it firstly creates a server socket in a default port (the default port number is 51666). If the default port number is not available (it may be used by another application), the number is automatically increased by one and further attempts made until a number becomes available. Then the PPA reads the IP address of the computer on which it resides and sends a message to the RPM to inform the registration of itself. The contents of the message contain the PPA name, IP address, server socket port number, PPA email address and a description. When the RPM receives a registration message, it activates its "broadcast_new_PPA" service to tell all other registered PPAs about the joining of a new colleague.

The Content Layer uses the PWXML protocol. When a message is sent from one PPA to another, the contents of the message are converted to a PWXML string or stream. The receiver PPA can parse the stream and understand the contents according to the DTD of the XML attached in a specific field (ontology) of the message. So the receiver knows what it should do next according to its understanding of the message. The Content Layer is supported by the Network Layer because the contents are sent from one PPA to another PPA via a socket (the sender PPA creates a socket that connects to the receiver's server socket).

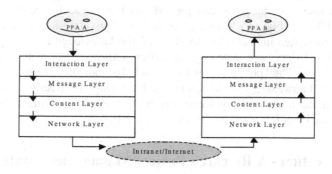

Fig. 10. The collaboration module is supported by four layers of protocols

The Message Layer uses the Agent Communication Language (ACL). According to FIPA [5], the content of a message can be wrapped by using the ACL protocol. ACL works as an envelope and consists of fields such as performative, sender, receiver, content and so on. The contents of the message are placed in the field of content so that the Message Layer is supported by the Content Layer. A user interface is provided by the emergent process management system for the Message Layer. This interface is built for the agent user to send an ACL message to another PPA manually.

The protocols provided in the Interaction Layer are the Delegation protocol and the Negotiation protocol. They are applied to the Interaction Layer to constrain the messages for a delegation or a negotiation in an acceptable pattern. The implementations of the protocols are their Finite State Machines (FSM). The delegation FSM constrains the performatives of delegation messages and the negotiation FSM constrains the performatives of negotiation messages so that the receiver of a message can understand the message according to the protocols. Any message that is not defined in the FSMs is not considered as a message of interactions. An interaction message is wrapped by an ACL protocol in which the ontology field is the name of the interaction protocol (delegation or negotiation).

4.2.2.4 The Management Module
The Management Module of the EPMS is built in PPAF, when a PPA is generated from the PPAF, to assist the agent user to manage (create, open, modify, advertise and delete) private knowledge. The human interfaces provided by the management module are visualized interfaces.

Knowledge added by the agent user is categorized into three different types: "public", "group" and "private". If the knowledge is "public", it is automatically advertised to the knowledge_moniker and accessible to all PPAs even if they are not registered in a process. If it is "group", it is automatically advertised to the knowledge_moniker but only the group members have permission to access it directly, other PPAs having to negotiate with the owner in order to share it. If the knowledge is "private", the agent user has to decide whether to advertise it to the knowledge_moniker of if PPAs working in the same group are to be permitted access.

To add knowledge to the PPA, the agent user has to fill out a knowledge record - a data structure. The attributes included in the knowledge record are identifier, category identifier (because knowledge is categorized, such as law, financial, …), name, created date, URL, public to ("public", "group", or "private") and description. The URL of the knowledge indicates the location of the knowledge and the protocol to access the knowledge. The category identifier indicates to what category the knowledge belongs. The "public to" of the knowledge indicates if this knowledge is advertised to the knowledge_moniker and if the knowledge is directly sharable or can be shared after negotiation. Knowledge can be harvested from the history of the process performed, but is not yet implemented in the EPMS.

5 An Application - A Research Project Management System

Research projects in universities need to be managed so that project members working in those projects may achieve common goals, join research activities, share research plans and knowledge, share resources and share results. The managed research projects can also be used by researchers to harvest process knowledge. A research project is an example of an emergent process instance. Firstly, a research project may have an initial goal and a series of briefly defined activities to achieve the goal, but the goal and activities are not completely specified in advance. They may be changed, refined or mutated over time. Secondly, there is no predefined process model that specifies a plan to achieve the project goal. Each instance of a research project has to find its own individual solution. If we knew precisely how to carry out research in advance, it would not be research. Next, the growing body of knowledge drives a research project from its start to its termination. In any stage in a research project, the knowledge obtained from previous activities governs the subsequent activities. Finally, a research project may be terminated after obtaining a satisfactory conclusion even if the initial research goal has not been achieved.

The EPMS is used to manage research projects. Firstly, the EPMS supports the representation (process modelling: using a DPWG) and storage of the research project evolution by controlling PW versions. The representation can be dynamically and collaboratively accessed and modified by a team of research members. Secondly, the EPMS supports executions of activities for research projects (process enactment: using PPAs). A PPA can autonomously check out an activity from a PW for execution and the results of the execution may cause a change to the PW. Finally, the EPMS keeps track of the research project evolution after the research project is completed. A visual interface is provided by the EPMS for researchers to review the project and a process knowledge harvest function is provided to harvest process knowledge from the completed research projects.

In this research project management application (RPMA as shown Figure 11), PWs are used to maintain project activities and project documents. The PWM manages the PWs. Each project member is equipped with a PPA to monitor the progress of research projects. A PPA supports interactions between project members.

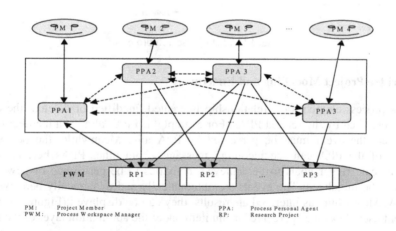

| PM: | Project Member | PPA: | Process Personal Agent |
| PWM: | Process Workspace Manager | RP: | Research Project |

Fig. 11. Project members perform project activities

5.1 Project Modelling

A project member creates a research project by creating an interface. A default PW is then created for this project, with a default member group, a default role "patron" and a default member of the project member who takes the role of "patron". When "open", the list of all projects of this member can have items appended, modified or deleted.

When a project from the project list is "open", the user can see all their PWs in a list view (Figure 12) or a visual view (Figure 8). When a PW is opened, a visual view of the workspaces is displayed, as in Figure 12. New elements or relationships can be added to the workspace by clicking the menu item in the popup context menu. Existing elements or relationships can be modified or deleted.

An Application to Manage Research Projects
Faculty of Information Technology, University of Technology, Sydney (UTS)

Personal Process Agent

> Hi, alin, this is the list of your research projects!

Add a new research project

#	name	goal	patron	date	open	remove
1	Agent in LiveNet	To build agents in LiveNet	alin	2003-09-16	open	remove
2	Component for Active Knowledge Portal	to build reusable agents	alin	2003-10-24	open	remove
3	Visual Component for Research Project	To build a management solution on visual	alin	2003-09-17	open	remove
4	Visual Component for Research Project	to build component for visual input and	alin	2003-09-26	open	remove
5	Emergent Business Process Management	To build a management solution	alin	2003-09-16	open	remove
6	Web Service Technology	To investigate the technologies of web s	alin	2003-10-23	open	remove
7	Reusable Components for Portals	to build reusable components	alin	2004-01-15	open	remove

Add a new research project

Assistance Layer
To-do List
Define
Research Projects
Agent Internal
Knowledge Base
Services
Automation Layer
Perceive
Perform
Internal Knowledge Base
Collaboration Layer
Interact
Communicate
Management Layer
Knowledge
Plan

Copyright © 2001-2004, Aizhong (Alan) Lin

Fig. 12. A list of research projects

5.2 Bridge Project Modelling and Enactment

When a process element or a relationship is created, modified or deleted, the event can be perceived by the related PPAs. For example, if PPA "alin" is a member of the workspace, the event must be perceived by PPA alin. Meanwhile, the perceiving function of the PPA can see incoming messages from other PPAs because those messages can trigger goals to be achieved, activities to be performed or new inter-actions to be initialized. The events are automatically and dynamically perceived by the PPA. Meanwhile, as intermediate results, they can be displayed (Figure 13) when the agent user clicks the "perceive" menu item under the automation layer of the PPA.

5.3 Project Enactment

If an event is generated because of a change (created or refined) in a goal, the goal is automatically matched to the goals of existing plans of the PPA. If there is a process plan that can achieve the goal, the plan is executed (if more than one plan can achieve the goal, the PPA chooses the plan that has the highest success rate to achieve the goal). If there is no such process plan, the PPA checks the plan_moniker in the PWM.

If there is no matched plan in the moniker, the event is converted to a to-do item and is submitted to the agent user. Otherwise, this PPA initializes a negotiation interaction with the owner of the plan in order to obtain permission to use that plan.

An Application to Manage Research Projects
Faculty of Information Technology, University of Technology, Sydney (UTS)

Personal Process Agent	This is the list of events related to you							
	7 create a plan delegate_interaction_plan			plan	working	view	remove	
	8 Created a new performer "alin"	Agent in LiveNet	Agent conceptual architecture	performer	working	view	remove	
	9 create a plan publish_papers_plan			plan	working	view	remove	
Assistance Layer	10 Created a new performer "alin"	Emergent Business Process Management	Emergent Process Meta Model	performer	working	view	remove	
To-do List	11 Created a new goal "Must complete it before 29/09/2003"	Agent in LiveNet	Agent conceptual architecture	goal	working	view	remove	
Define Research Projects Agent Internal Knowledge Base	12 create a artifact An Agent-based Collaborative Architecture	Agent in LiveNet	BDI agent architecture	artifact	working	view	remove	
Services	13 create a artifact Published Papers	Agent in LiveNet	BDI agent architecture	artifact	working	view	remove	
Automation Layer Perceive	14 create a artifact An Agent-based Active Portal Framework	Agent in LiveNet	BDI agent architecture	artifact	working	view	remove	
Perform Internal Knowledge Base	15 Create a plan share_document_plan			plan	working	view	remove	
Collaboration Layer Interact	16 Created a new artifact "BDI model"	Agent in LiveNet	Agent conceptual architecture	artifact	working	view	remove	
Communicate	17 create a constraint Time Constraint	Agent in LiveNet	BDI agent architecture	constraint	working	view	remove	
Management Layer Knowledge Plan	18 create a artifact Submitted Papers	Agent in LiveNet	BDI agent architecture	artifact	working	view	remove	

Copyright © 2003-2004, Zizhong (Alan) Lin

Fig. 13. The events of the PPA "alin"

5.4 Browse Project

The agent user or other permitted project members can browse a research project at any time after it is created. They can view their records and the relationships between them. Because the interface is visualized, the relationships between PWs and the relationships between process elements are explicitly expressed (Figure 14).

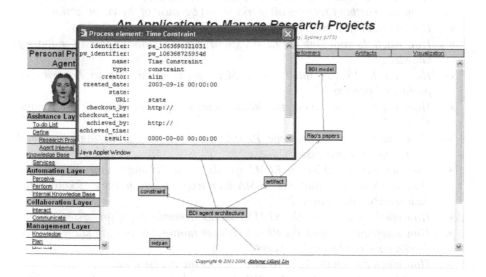

Fig. 14. The visual interface of the whole copy of a research project

5.5 The Result Analysis

The application results are analyzed by asking some questions to the users who were required to use the application. A group of researchers (four Ph.D students and three research assistants) were invited to assess the RPMA casually for three months. Each of them finally was required to complete an online survey (shown in Figure 15) with the following thirteen questions:

Research Project Management Application Survey

From your qualitative assessment, compared with the research project management dealt with by human:

1   How much do you think the RPMA speeds up the awareness of partners' work?

○ No idea   ○ Very negative   ○ Negative   ○ Normal   ○ Positive   ◉ Very positive

2   How much do you think the RPMA speeds up the understanding of what has happened (without reading all workspaces) because of the visualization?

○ No idea   ○ Very negative   ○ Negative   ○ Normal   ○ Positive   ◉ Very positive

3.   How much do you think the RPMA speeds up the response to events?

○ No idea   ○ Very negative   ○ Negative   ○ Normal   ○ Positive   ◉ Very positive

4.   How much do you think the RPMA speeds up access to the latest versions of knowledge?

○ No idea   ○ Very negative   ○ Negative   ○ Normal   ○ Positive   ◉ Very positive

5.   How much do you think the RPMA speeds up access to histories of performed processes?

Fig. 15. The survey of the RPMA

- *How much do you think the RPMA speeds up the awareness of partners' work?*
- *How much do you think the RPMA speeds up the understanding of what has happened (without reading all workspaces) because of the visualization?*
- *How much do you think the RPMA speeds up the response to events?*
- *How much do you think the RPMA speeds up access to the latest versions of knowledge?*
- *How much do you think the RPMA speeds up access to histories of performed processes?*
- *How much do you think the RPMA speeds up interaction of knowledge sharing?*
- *How much do you think the RPMA speeds up the gathering of related information for processes?*
- *How much do you think the RPMA speeds up the "change" of processes?*
- *How much do you think the RPMA increases the proficiency of knowledge management and sharing?*
- *How much do you think the RPMA enables streamlining of processes?*
- *How much do you think the RPMA reduces multiple sources of knowledge --- "write once read many" concept?*
- *How much do you think the RPMA reduces the access times?*
- *How much do you think the RPMA saves the time and cost – travel and subsistence, paper, postage, quality time, paper storage capacity?*

The final result shows that the overall assessment of the RPMA. To all questions, more than sixty percent of the users give "positive" or "very positive" answer except for the question 10. Considering the users are not paid testers, the results that can claim to be objective. Later, sixty students who are going to study a subject of one of the current authors will be invited to form several groups to assess the RPMA casually.

6 Related Work

To manage emergent processes, different systems or researchers have made various suggestions. Several related works [1,2,6] discuss the research of business process (re)engineering. However, they focused on the management of routine processes (the process has fixed goals or predefined solutions) rather than on emergent business processes.

LiveNet [7] provides a web-based client/server architecture to support emergent process management. It uses a workspace model to maintain the elements such as goal, activity, artifacts, roles, participants and actions to support process participants' collaboration and knowledge sharing. However, its functions focus on supporting public work rather than personal work.

ADEPT [8] provides an agent-based (pure distributed) architecture to support business process management. Each agent is assigned services that can perform tasks of processes. Since different agents may be assigned different services, they have to negotiate with each other to share them when performing a social task. We do not see that this architecture supports the "emergence" of process goals and activities.

Debenham [9] proposed a hybrid three-layer BDI process agent conceptual architecture to achieve emergent process goals. Each process agent works for one and only one human process participant. It lacks functions to support human process participants involved in emergent processes.

WORKWARE [10] provides a solution for managing emergent workflow. In WORKWARE, workflows are no longer process definitions separated from process enactment as in traditional approaches; they provide instead active support for planning, performance and coordination of work based on a (more or less complete) explicit process model. Consequently, they broaden the scope by including support for more forms of coordination, with less structured process models. They also incorporate planning as part of the process by integrating process definitions. This approach does not, however, provide process enactment.

7 Conclusion and Future Work

The management solution for emergent processes proposed here combines a process workspace (PW) that maintains process elements and their relationships for emergent process instances plus process agents that automatically perceive changes in PWs and perform activities defined in PWs. The system thus supports intertwined process modelling and enactment. Moreover, the system supports process participant collaborative work using the functions of knowledge sharing. Our further work will focus on (1) providing process knowledge harvesting functions that support agent users to collect process knowledge from processes performed earlier and (2) providing a visual plan generator to help process participants to build new plans for personal process agents at run-time.

Acknowledgements

We wish to thank the Australian Research Council for funding. This is Contribution number 04/33 of the Centre for Object Technology Applications and Research.

References

1. Van Der Aalst W. M. P.. "Formalization and Verification of Event-driven Process Chains". *Information and Software Technology*, 41 (10): 639-650, 1999.
2. Marca D. and McGowan C.. "IDEF0: Business Process and Enterprise Modeling", *Eclectic Solutions,* 1992
3. Extensible Markup Language (XML) 1.0 (Second Edition). *W3C Recommendation* 6 October 2000. http://www.w3.org/TR/REC-xml
4. Bratman M. E.. *"Intentions, Plans, and Practical Reason"*. Harvard University Press: Cambridge, MA, 1987
5. FIPA specification. *"Agent Communication Language"*. http://www.fipa.org/specs/fipa00003/OC00003A.html
6. Georgakopoulos D., Hornick M., and Sheth A.. "An Overview of Workflow Management: From Process Modeling to Workflow Automation Infrastructure", *Distributed and Parallel Database* 3(2) 119-153, April 1995.
7. Hawryszkiewycz I. T.. "Knowledge Sharing through Workspace Networks". *Proceedings of the Special Interest Group on Computer Personnel Research (SIGCPR99)*, April 1999, New Orleans (ISBN 1-58133-063-5), pp. 79-85.
8. Jennings N. R., Norman T. J., and Faratin P.. "ADEPT: An Agent-based Approach to Business Process Management". *ACM SIGMOD Record* 27 (4) 32-39. 1998.
9. Debenham J. K.. "Three Intelligent Architectures for Business Process Management". *Proceedings 12th International Conference on Software Engineering and Knowledge Engineering SEKE 2000*, Chicago, 6-8 July 2000.
10. Jørgensen H. D. and Carlsen S.. "Emergent Workflow: Integrated Planning and Performance of Process Instances". *Workflow Management '99*, Münster, Germany, 1999.

Mobeet: A Multi-agent Framework for Ubiquitous Information Systems

Nobukazu Yoshioka[1], Akihiko Ohsuga[2], and Shinichi Honiden[3]

[1] National Institute of Informatics
[2] Corporate Research & Development Center, Toshiba Corporation
akihiko.ohsuga@toshiba.co.jp
[3] National Institute of Informatics and the University of Tokyo
{nobukazu, honiden}@nii.ac.jp

Abstract. In recent years, the rapid development of network infrastructure and the spread of terminals capable of network access have made it possible to access networks at any place and at any time. Ubiquitous information systems, in which necessary information can be accessed easily and safely at any place, are becoming an important issue. It is, however, hard to design such distributed systems when the user uses many kinds of terminals and migrates with these. That is, traditional approaches to development of distributed systems have problems when the systems are used in a ubiquitous environment. This paper proposes a new framework for ubiquitous information systems. The framework includes three kinds of agents: User Interface Agents, Programmable Agents and Service Mediation Agents. We can easily design ubiquitous information systems by ensuring that these agents collaborate. In addition, in cases where distributed systems must be implemented on various networks and terminals, it gives a high degree of flexibility to the systems. We also evaluate the framework's flexibility.

1   Introduction

In recent years, the rapid development of network infrastructure and the spread of terminals capable of network access have made it possible to access networks not only when you are home or at your office, but also when you are away. In addition, network connections by cell phones or smart appliances have made it possible for users who have not used PCs to use services or share information through networks. The environment in which necessary information can be accessed easily and safely at any place is called "ubiquitous information system"(UIS). The foundation for UIS is being formed in society. Under such background conditions, various services have appeared on networks and a massive amount of information continues to be transmitted. Because of the standardization of web services and the spread of broad-band networks by which we can always connect our PC to the Internet, general users who previously had difficulty providing services themselves are now beginning to be able to provide those services.

P. Bresciani et al. (Eds.): AOIS 2004, LNAI 3508, pp. 19–35, 2005.

However, such web services include a mixture of services with varying degrees of reliability and quality, and using them well has become difficult. Furthermore, conventional web services are constructed based on the assumption that they will be accessed through one PC, and are not prepared for the type of usage that takes into consideration the above described network environments. Specifically, users who traverse broad-band connections at home, portable terminals away from the home or office, hot spot wireless services and LANs at the office, have problems with today's services, such as the presence of restrictions of available places or terminals, or no availability of continuous services when they change their location from one to another.

In this paper, we propose a new framework for development of flexible distributed systems in order to solve these problems using agent technologies. This framework achieves UIS by asynchronous communications between three kinds of agents, i.e. the user interface agent (UIA), the programmable agent (PA), and the service mediation agent (SMA).

The organization of this paper is as follows. Section 2 introduces a web information search system as an application example of the framework proposed in this paper. Section 3 summarizes the problems and challenges relating to UIS as mentioned above. Section 4 describes the details of this framework and section 5 describes the implementation of the framework. Section 6 explains how to assemble a web information search system using this framework. Section 7 evaluates this framework and then discusses the relationship with conventional systems. Section 8, the last section, summarizes this paper.

2   Application Example: Web Information Search System

For the purpose of describing and evaluating our framework, this paper discusses a web information search system as a typical application example of UIS.

Here, a web information search system is a system that uses keywords specified by the user to search for related information on the web. Specifically, this system uses a natural language analysis service, a synonym search service, some search engines, web servers, HTML converter, content compression service etc. on the internet. A natural language analysis service is a service that takes natural language text as an input and returns the parts of the speech and the relationship between the words; the HTML converter is a service that takes an HTML file as an input and converts the content into plain text, PDF, CHTML format etc. We assume that some search engines and HTML converter services exist on the Internet. The server instability and usage situations of the user are the determining factors as to which ones will be used.

Typical operations for this system are as follows. When the user requests a search in the natural language form, a natural language analysis service is used to extract keywords from this natural language expression and then a synonym search is done to find related keywords. The search engine is used to find pages related to these keywords and the links from this page are followed with filtering to acquire those that meet the conditions. Finally, the HTML converter is used to convert the acquired contents to an appropriate format for a user's terminal and search options, and they are put together, compressed and then returned to the terminal.

When doing this, the user can continue the information search by using multiple terminals, such as portable terminals and PCs. In order to make this possible, it is necessary that searching and filtering can be performed on the server side. Furthermore, the results need to be retained after the completion of the search until the user requests their retrieval. Also, the user's usage situation and request can change while the information search is still being performed and the system needs to be able to cope with such changes. For example, after searches have finished, the system needs to respond to further filtering requests or changes in search conditions. Therefore, we cannot use only notification mechanisms, such as e-mail, but also need communication mechanisms with the user's terminal and the system.

3   Challenges Pertaining to UIS

This section analyses the problems arising when a conventional method is used to develop a distributed system that meets UIS, and clarifies the challenges that should be overcome by the framework to resolve such problems.

Generally speaking, the following problems arise when using a client/server model (abbrevated to C/S) system to develop software for UIS as mentioned in section 1.

Problem 1: It is difficult to accommodate and port to various terminals.
Problem 2: It is difficult to cope with changes in the location and data structure of the service.
Problem 3: It is difficult to select an appropriate service each time.
Problem 4: It is not easy to add new type of services.
Problem 5: It is difficult to cope with situations in which the user environment or the service is unstable. In addition, in such situations, the usability of the software becomes poor.
Problem 6: Since there is no mechanism for automating the processes according to the situation, usability becomes poor for a terminal with a limited interface.

These problems are caused by the fact that the software on the client side includes the details of access to services on the server in addition to the user interface.

Problem 3 and the changes in the location of services mentioned in problem 2 can be resolved by separating the service selection portion from the client by using a Broker pattern [3] or a facilitator that mediates an appropriate service. However, the other problems cannot be coped with by just separating the service selection component as an independent structure.

In order to use different services and terminals depending on locations and situations, the following problems need to be resolved.

Problem 7: It is difficult to create functions to cope with various situations in advance.

Problem 8: It is difficult to cope with changes in situations on the user's side.

Problem 9: It is impossible to cope with changes in the terminal that the user is using. Therefore the process cannot be continued over multiple terminals.

For problem 9, a directory service can be used to determine which terminal the user is using. However, even in such a case, the process cannot be continued on multiple terminals.

Furthermore, the following problems need to be resolved in order to use services without worry.

Problem 10: When the user wants to reuse existing local services, such as intranet services, in ubiquitous open environments, it is difficult to add security functions to the services.

Problem 11: It is difficult to protect user information.

The Three-tier Model [1, 2] is a software structuring method that separates the logic portion that implements the software functions from the client portion for the purpose of overcoming various problems arising in the C/S system. In this model, the structure of the program in the distributed system is divided into three layers, i.e. the client layer, the domain layer and the database layer (Figure 1 (a)). The client layer is a program that directly receives instructions from the user, and the domain layer is a program that processes and manages applications and transactions. This layer also executes the processing requested by the user and mediates between the user and the data to be processed. The database layer manages various data, such as customer information and employee information, and directly accesses the data when requested by an application.

Some of the aforementioned problems can be resolved by using this Three-tier Model architecture. Having the logic portion be independent increases the portability of the client portion, which makes it possible to solve problem 1. Also, the introduction of the intermediate layer increases the degree of independence

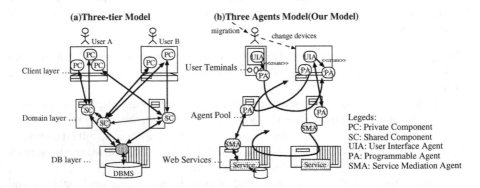

Fig. 1. Three Tree-tier Model and Three Agents Model

between the client and the service, which, compared with conventional ways, makes it easier to do things such as coping with the changes in the service structure in problem 2, adding new services in problem 4 and adding security functions in problem 10. However, the other problems 5-9 and problem 11 cannot be dealt with by conventional structuring alone.

In order to solve these problems, a framework that overcomes the following challenges is needed.

Challenge 1: It can cope with the instability of terminals and servers.
Challenge 2: It can easily accommodate various situations.
Challenge 3: It has a mechanism for automation/substitution of processing according to the situation.
Challenge 4: It can cope with changes in the situation on the user's side.
Challenge 5: It can continue processing over multiple terminals.
Challenge 6: It has a mechanism for protecting user information.

4   Multi-agent Framework: Mobeet Framework

4.1   Overview

The framework proposed in this paper is configured with three kinds of agents (Figure. 1 (b) and Figure. 2). These software agents are expanded versions of the components in the three layers of the Three-tier Model described in section 3. In this paper, agents corresponding to these layers are called the User Interface Agent (**UIA**), the Programmable Agent (**PA**) and the Service Mediation Agent (**SMA**). An overview of each agent is given below.

UIA: The UIA provides an interface for the user. In addition, it detects the user's situation and copes with his/her various situations. Upon receiving the user's request, it considers the situation at the moment and outputs a script that carries out the user's processing. For the purpose of achieving these functions, the UIA contains a logic language processing system (hereafter referred to as "inference engine"). In order to cope with various situations, the system designer describes behaviour of the agent corresponding to such situations by using logic language rules (hereafter referred to as "reasoning rules").

This inference engine is capable of outputting a script and the UIA can execute this script. Using this capability, it inspects the current situation and the user's request as a goal, carries out inference and can output a script as a sequence of actions to achieve the goal. For example, in the case of the web information search system wherein the user's request is a restaurant search, it infers that restaurants serving lunch in the vicinity should be searched for, and then outputs a script for this search. The output script is executed as a PA described below.

The reasoning rules defined at the UIA are event driven so as to be able to cope with changes in the situation. That is, in addition to when there is a direct request from the user, relating rules are reevaluated when the values

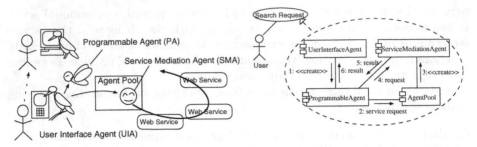

Fig. 2. Overview of a framework   **Fig. 3.** Collaboration between Agents

of the predicate defining the situation have changed. This mechanism makes a system autonomous in coping with changes. Using this mechanism, for example, when a user in the outdoors goes back to his company office in the middle of an information search, the system may sends the results to the company's computer.

PA: The script (PA) output from the UIA is executed as a mobile agent migrating between hosts. The PA copes with terminal instability and changes in the using terminal of the user. This is because the agent can execute the actions after migrating from the UIA onto a server host called an "agent pool". The PA communicates with other agents by using the Agent Communication Language (ACL [4, 5]). This allows for an increase in independence between the agents and prevents unnecessary leakage of user information by increasing the autonomy of each agent.

SMA: The SMA is an agent that actualizes the request from the PA. This agent is dynamically synthesized at the agent pool to cope with diverse services and requests. Components that describe logic for using web services are registered in the agent pool and the agent pool responds to requests from the PA by synthesizing an SMA that is a group of components that meet the request. For example, upon receiving a web information search request in the form of a natural language input from the PA, the agent pool synthesizes an SMA to actualize the request by combining components that generate search keywords from the natural language and components that search web information using the search keywords.

Thus synthesized, the SMA is then executed by the framework. Multiple components having the same specifications can exist; the mechanism is such that an error resulting from calling a component will lead to calling another component having the same specifications. For example, when there is no response from a search engine and an error occurs, this mechanism automatically copes with this error by calling a component that uses a different search engine.

Figure 3 is a UML representation of the collaboration between these three agents and the agent pool. All the agents have a mechanism for sending/receiving asynchronous messages and can communicate with each other by using the ACL. Typical operations for this framework are as follows.

1. The user sends a search request to the UIA. Using this as a goal, the inference engine of the UIA is called. In the case of a web information search, the goal is a search request whose arguments are the search keywords
2. The framework of the UIA defines the current state as a predicates and then infers the goal. At this time, a script (PA) is output from the executed reasoning rules and is then executed. (Corresponding to 1 in Figure 3)
3. The PA sends a request to the agent pool. (Corresponding to 2 in Figure 3)
4. The agent pool generates an SMA according to the PA's request. (Corresponding to 3 in Figure 3)
5. The PA makes the actual request for the SMA generated by the agent pool. (Corresponding to 4 in Figure 3)
6. The SMA coordinates web services to perform the service and return the result back to the PA. (Corresponding to 5 in Figure 3)
7. The PA sends the result from the SMA to the UIA specified by the user. (Corresponding to 6 in Figure 3)
8. The UIA presents the result to the user in the manner suitable for the situation of the user and the terminal.

By communicating with each other, these three kinds of agents can flexibly cope with changes in the user environment.

4.2   The User Interface Agent Copes with Situations

The UIA has the role of accommodating users in different and various situations and coping with changes in their situations, as well as the role of protecting user information.

The user's situation depends on time and location, as well as the terminal environment, such as network connection situations. For the purpose of using these environments to infer the user's intention, the framework is equipped with a mechanism that monitors the terminal environment and provides information in the form of predicates. Specifically, the time, location and network connection situation can all be looked up as situation dependent predicates (environment predicates).

For the purpose of calculating the user's intention and situation from the terminal environment, the framework is equipped with an inference mechanism using a logic language. Its reasoning rules include scripts that are output when the applicable conditions and rules are met.

The format of a rule is "Head :- Guard | Body {Script}.". The grammar of the head and the body in the rule is the same as that of the Prolog. The guard part is the same as the GHC (Guarded Horn Clauses [6]) of the parallel logic language, and the conditions for applying this rule are described as an arithmetical equation.

The inference engine is activated when a new goal is thrown with a request from the user or when a new goal from the PA is thrown. After reasoning, all the scripts related to the applied rules are combined to constitute a new PA. In addition, whenever this framework changes the environment predicates, inference is performed so that the behaviour can be determined in response to changes in the situation.

4.3   Execution of the Request by the Programmable Agent

The PA executes the request from the user while coping with instability in the user's terminal. It also copes with switching the terminal that the user is using. In order to do this, a script contains instructions for autonomously migrating between hosts.

Potential causes of terminal instability include power loss and network disconnection due to changes in the location of users. For example, in the case of a web information search, the user may turn off the portable terminal or the network may be disconnected because the terminal has changed its location. In order to cope with such instability, the PA transfers the necessary information to the agent pool after receiving it from the UIA. The PA then executes the given request.

The script includes an abstract service request to realize user requests. What actualizes the abstract service is an SMA, which is explained in section 4.4. For this purpose, the script is equipped with functions to search for necessary services and obtain their addresses. The actual search for services and the generation of the agent (SMA) that executes the service is performed by the agent pool. The PA searches for necessary services and asks the SMA thus found to perform the service by sending a request message in the ACL. For this purpose, the script is equipped with commands for communicating with any agent using the ACL.

The PA uses the ACL to send user information to the SMA. By using different performatives, the user information presentation request from the SMA can be expressed not only as an unconditional request but also as a conditional request specifying added benefits obtained by presentation. In response to the user information presentation request, the PA can communicate an intention of rejection by using "refuse" as well as an intention of presentation by using "inform".

4.4   Actualization of the Service by the Service Mediation Agent

The SMA is synthesized by the agent pool and executed automatically. In the case of a web information search, various requests are possible depending on, for example, whether the related information is specified by a natural language or by a string of keywords. If all services are fixed in advance to cope with such diversity, it is not possible to flexibly cope with request changes and additions. In view of this, the present framework copes with this problem by defining a necessary service as a group of components (service components), synthesizing it by automatically combining these components, and then executing them one after another. To this end, for each service, the input specifications and the output specifications are defined as types with a meaning, in addition to the service name to be implemented. When a service search request comes from the PA, the service that is suitable for the request is synthesized from a group of components having the specified service name.

For example, in the case of a web information search service, the service component for generating keywords from a natural language is defined by the following specifications:

```
Service name: Information search
         Input: String:Natural language text
         Output: list of String:Keywords
```

This means: the input/output specifications are defined in the "type:meaning" format, the input of the aforementioned component is String type natural language text and the output is keyword expressed as a String type list.

When components with such specifications are found, the agent pool collects a group of service components that can provide output from the input specifications of the service requested by the PA and designates this as the SMA. These service components are assembled by using one or more web services.

The SMA is executed by the framework in the following manner. First, the framework receives data from the PA that meets the input specifications of the service and executes a component that uses the data as input specifications. When the output of the component is calculated, another component that has the necessary inputs is executed. Finally, when all the outputs requested by the PA are obtained, the obtained values are returned to the PA by using the ACL. If the service components to be executed run out before all the outputs are obtained, then an ACL failure message is sent.

Each service component can use the API for migration in order to cope with instability in the services used. The migration request in a service component implies migration of the group of components that constitutes the SMA, and the execution of the components is continued at the migration destination. Instability of services can be due to instability in the server or instability in the network; in the former case, the service is called remotely. In the latter case, after the migration of components, the service is used locally.

4.5   Coping with Changes by Means of Inter-agent Communications

When the situation of the user changes, the UIA detects the change and alters the request that is already being executed. The PA responds to this change by altering its own behaviour using the re-inference (re-planning) function. The change is propagated by the ACL.

An example of a change in the user situation is a change due to a locational change of the terminal when the user who has been away comes back to the office. This change can be inferred by the change in the environment of the terminal that the user is using.

The UIA has the function to infer the user's situation when the environment, such as the time and location, has changed. Specifically, a change in the environment results in redefinition of the environment predicates and the reasoning rules are reevaluated. Based on this inference, a new script corresponding to the change is generated to cope with the change. The generation mechanism is the same as the case of new PAs described in section 4.2.

This coping action includes altering the request as well as altering parameters such as search options. For example, when the user comes back to the office, changes are made so the user can view the search results at the terminal in the office. Such changes in the request are managed by using the PA's re-planning function as described below. That is, the new request is sent by means of the ACL to the already executing PA; upon receipt of this, the PA activates the inference engine, using this request as a new goal (re-planning). If this inference needs user information, migration to the terminal occurs. The inference for the new goal is conducted here and a new script is output. This script becomes the definition of the new behaviour of the PA.

5   Implementation of the Framework

The framework is implemented by using Plangent [7] for the UIA and PA, and using Bee-gent [8] for the SMA. Although Plangent has a unique feature which is that it generates scripts being agent behaviour from Prolog programs, the scheme of our framework cannot be implemented in its original form by Plangent. Specifically, Plangent has limitations in terms of the activation of the inference engine and the description of the reasoning rules. The following is the format for rules (action definitions) in Plangent.

```
action(_,_,_,[script],[Precond], [Postcond], [Manifestation]):-Body.
```

Here, the list of postconditions (Postcond) corresponds to the goals and the inference engine is done in such a way that the preconditions (Precond) are met. The body part is the same as common Prolog. The user information called "info file" can be accessed at the manifestation string to view/update the information.

The inference engine of Plangent is not event driven; it is driven when a goal is put in. Furthermore, since the guard cannot be described, the rules to be inferred cannot be determined without a goal. In order to cope with this, a dummy goal "response" is given when the situation changes[1] so as to activate the inference engine. Also, conditions corresponding to the guard are described at the beginning of the body of this predicate so that an appropriate action definition can be selected.

In addition, Plangent does not support ACL. Therefore, a mechanism for sending/receiving an ACL used by Bee-gent is prepared, so that the ACL can be read/written from inside of a script and also from the UIA to communicate any other agents.

A Plangent script has a function to rewrite itself (newgoal), which can be used to cope with changes in the user's situation. When a notification of changes in the user's situation is received while the script is executed, the situation is

---

[1] Changes in the environment are checked at a time interval in the UIA.

written on the agent's own information (agent info) and the newgoal is executed to regenerate itself.

The service components of this framework are made to correspond to state classes in Bee-gent. Bee-gent has a mechanism that executes a specific state (mental state) when necessary conditions are satisfied. Using this mechanism, all the service components are defined as mental state classes, and the input/output specifications of the framework are made to correspond to preconditions/postconditions of Bee-gent. The planner of Bee-gent is used to implement the SMAs operations. For each mental state class, this planner mechanism can set goals for which the class is activated and for the goals to be executed next. The number of state classes that can be executed simultaneously is set to 1, so that state classes having the same precondition are selected one after another by changing the priority (utility value) for goal selection.

For the purpose of picking up a group of SMA service components, the input/output specifications of each state class are managed by a definition file that is different from Bee-gent. In the external command of Plangent, for a service search, this file is looked up and necessary service components are collected to generate Bee-gent mediation agents.

6   Implementation of a Web Information Search System

Using the framework described in section 4, a prototype for a web information search system was implemented. An overview of the implementation is described below.

The action definition of Plangent can be used to define rules for inferring the user situation and rules for generating scripts. Figure 4 is a portion of the action

```
info (_,_,_,[goAgentPool(AgentID), webSearch(AgentID, SmartOption,Results),
         convert(AgentID, Results,'CHTML',CPages), sendResults(AgentID,CPages,UAgentID)],
     [],[search(Option)],            %% precondition is null, postcondition is search
     [assert(info(agent, dummy, dummy, searchOption(SmartOption), unknown)] %% agent knowledge
):- place(outdoor),agent(AgentID),masterAgent(UAgentID),outdoorOption(Option,SmartOption).
outdoorOption(O1,O2) :- timeIsNoon, ... %% check the user situation and generate options
timeIsNoon:- info(form,_,_,environment(time,[Hourl_]),Hour >= 11, Hour < 14. %% General Rule
```

Fig. 4. An Example of Action Definitions using Plangent

```
webSearch($myname, @option, $results) {
   @inputs=(getKeyword(@option), "String:KeyWords","List:SearchOption");
   @outputs=("Contents:WebPages");
   $agentName = lookup("SearchWebInfo", @inputs, @outputs);
   sendMessage("request", $agentName, $myname, @option);
   waitMessage();
   @mes = receiveMessage($agentName); ...
```

Fig. 5. An Example of Script Definitions using Plangent

Table 1. An Example of Service Parts

Component:	KeywordGenerator
Service:	SearchWebInfo
Input:	String:NLang
Output:	String:KeyWords

Component:	SearchEngine B
Service:	SearchWebInfo
Input:	String:KeyWords
Output:	List:URL

Component:	SearchEngine A
Service:	SearchWebInfo
Input:	String:KeyWords
Output:	List:URL

Component:	ExtractWeb
Service:	SearchWebInfo
Input:	List:URL, List:SearchOption
Output:	Contents:WebPages

definition. The user's situation in terms of whether or not he is away from the office is inferred by "place" in the body of this definition; if the user is away, "outdoorOption" sets optimum options. When this action definition is applied, a PA calling "goAgentPool", "webSearch", "convert" and "sendResults" is output. This PA migrates to the agent pool (goAgentPool), searches web information (webSearch), converts the results to the terminal's format (convert) and sends them to the UIA (sendResults). Figure 5 shows how the action for searching web information (webSearch) is actually defined. In this script definition, "lookup" external command is used to search for an SMA that executes the service of a web information search.

A web search engine service, a content conversion service that converts the HTML to various formats, and data compression service are newly assembled for this system. Web services used for the web information search service are of four kinds, i.e. a natural language analysis service, a synonym search service, a search engine and a web server. Specifically, these web services are used to prepare the SMA's service components. Table 1 shows definition examples of the input/output specifications of the SMA service components. Among these, the service component that generates keywords from a natural language (KeywordGenerator) is implemented by combining two web services, i.e. a natural language analysis service and a synonym search service.

7 Discussion

7.1 Evaluation of the Framework

This section describes how the framework presented in this paper meets the challenges mentioned in section 3.

Meeting challenge 1: This framework can cope with instability on the terminal side by transferring the PA to an appropriate server. This transfer control needs to be described in the PA generation rules that the UIA possesses, and the programmer has to specify it explicitly. Instability on the service side is handled by transferring the SMA or replacing the service component to be executed. Specifically, it is possible to cope with network instability by transferring the SMA to the host providing the service or to a host experiencing stable communications. Upon error termination of the service component calling the service remotely, the framework can execute an alternative component and thus cope with a service down in a semi-automated manner.

Meeting challenge 2: This framework copes with diverse requests by dynamically generating the request details and the usage order of the services. Since the response to the user's requests are defined and added by the reasoning rules, the existing definitions do not have to be changed for a new request.

There can be multiple combinations of services for the same request; this can be handled by SMA's service component selection mechanism by means of automatically calling different service components having the same input type. The addition of a new service can be handled by simply registering its components without altering existing components.

Meeting challenge 3: This framework contains an inference engine in the UIA as a mechanism for automating various processes according to the situation. Also, predicates for checking the terminal environment are made available for evaluating the situation.

In order to carry out processing in the place of the user, a script is output as the result of the inference and then made executable. Using this mechanism, batch processing, such as format conversion of all the collected texts at once, can be performed. If this processing fails, another processing can be selected by means of re-planning. However, when the reasoning rules for the selection are on the terminal side, returning to the terminal is required. If the terminal is not connected at that time in this case, the processing cannot be continued. That is, the managing method for the reasoning rules of the UIA is limited.

Meeting challenge 4: In order to cope with changes in the situation on the user side, situations and instructions corresponding to them are described as reasoning rules and asynchronous communications between agents are made possible. For such reasoning rules, the event driven logic language is adopted to allow inference responsive to the situations. Also, the ACL is made available for sending/receiving messages for smooth cooperation between the agents. Furthermore, re-planning is introduced to the PA as a mechanism to alter its behaviour in response to changes.

When re-planning involves the necessity to cancel existing processing, scripts have to be carefully custom-made. For example, when there is an interdependent relationship between a series of PA requests, such as in transaction processing, it is difficult to define the precise scripts.

Meeting challenge 5: In this framework, the PA is designed as a mobile agent and continuous processing over multiple terminals is achieved through the PA carrying around the processing states. For example, the PA that makes a search request is generated at the portable terminal and placed on standby on the server side; another PC can call this PA back and the results can be viewed at another terminal. This way, the user side can provide processing, such as filtering of the search results, in the form of a script.

Meeting challenge 6: This framework supports the use of the UIA's inference engine to infer the user situation and supports flexible exchanges of user information by means of the ACL. Because of these, the system can be designed in such a way that user information is treated appropriately.

When user information is needed to use a service, an information query message from the SMA to the PA can be used. Although this is not used in the example, for nonessential information, the message "user information will be requested if you need to know this information" can be expressed by using a query-if message. In response to a query, the example is implemented in such a way that the PA returns messages such as "inform" or "refuse". However, a scheme, such as content language, for this purpose is not defined, which increases the programmer's burden if complex information needs to be exchanged.

In addition, the framework uses user information defined at the UIA to derive appropriate actions for the user at the terminal side, thus maintaining higher security of user information compared with the case in which the same processing is done at the server side.

7.2   Functional Comparison with Conventional Methods

In this section, we compare our framework with a PAC agent framework [9] from the viewpoint of the UIS.

The PAC agent framework is a framework for a distributed system that configures the system with three kinds of agents, i.e. the Top-level, Intermediate-level, and Bottom-level. These agents cooperate with each other by using three interfaces called "Presentation", "Abstraction" and "Control" to constitute a flexible distributed system. These three interfaces increase independence between the agents and secure flexibility in terms of portability and configuration. Figure 6 shows the structure of this framework. The top-level agent accesses the repository and is in charge of data exchanges necessary for the system. The bottom-level agent allows users to display and manipulate the results, and the intermediate-level agent mediates between the bottom-level agent and the top-level agent and sends necessary data from the top-level to the bottom-level.

In principle, this framework is designed to provide various displays and manipulations to one resource, and the three kinds of agents constitute a tree-like structure with the top-level being the root. However, this structure does not allow flexible responses in application domains where various services exist. Even if the Broker pattern is used to introduce a mechanism for selecting appropriate services, flexibility such as altering the procedures for cooperation between services cannot be implemented. Our framework dynamically derives the behaviour of the SMA by synthesizing components and selectively executes the components. This makes it possible to cope with a diversity of services and instability in the servers.

The PAC agent does not specifically prescribe where each agent is executed, how cooperation is done, and a mechanism for autonomy inside an agent. Therefore, when assembling a flexible system by making the agents cooperate with each other, it is hard to design it. In addition, the instability of servers or clients and dynamical changes of user's situation are not taken into consid-

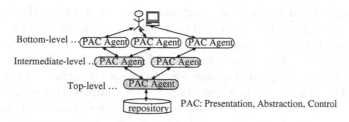

Fig. 6. PAC Agent Framework

eration; i.e. there is no support for these in the framework. In comparison, our framework focuses on a domain of UIS; it prescribes not only the roles of the three kinds of agents but also the mechanisms to perform these roles. Specifically, a combination of an asynchronous communication mechanism, ACL, inference engine, agent transfer mechanism, PA's re-planning mechanism etc. allows this framework to easily cope with cooperation between the agents, instability in the servers and changes in situations.

7.3   Related Work

Our framework provides more flexibility than a conventional C/S system, Three-tier Model or PAC Model. There are other architecture styles and design patterns of these models. Some patterns are proposed for flexibility. For example, Broker pattern, Reflection pattern, Client-Dispatcher-Server pattern and so on are described in [3]. In addition, Strategy pattern is described in [9]. In contrast, we can regard our framework as a pattern for ubiquitous environment. Our framework is more flexible than use of only conventional patterns. In addition, the conventional patterns, such as the Broker pattern, are used as complementary to our framework.

BDI agents and distributed multi-agent systems have been proposed to cope with changes of environments flexibly [10, 11, 12]. For each BDI agent, environments can be modelled in its Belief and its behaviour is derived using an inference engine. In addition, agents in distributed multi-agent systems can negotiate each other for the coordination flexibly. However, it is difficult to design a system responding to various changes because we need to make each agent with high intelligence individually. On the other hand, our framework consists of three kinds of agents having each role and the agents cooperate with each other keeping each role to realize flexibility. Consequently, it is easier to make a design plan and to design the system using our framework than is the case with other multi-agent systems.

Some mobile agent platforms [13, 14] have been proposed for mobile computing, especially for resource-limited devices. LEAP is a FIPA-compliant agent platform sufficiently lightweight and powerful to execute both on mobile devices and on enterprise servers. The extentions also have been proposed for nomadic users [15], for ad hoc networks [16] and for handheld devices [17]. Although these platforms and extensions are for ubiquitous computing infrastructures, no support for application level design using such agents is provided. However, we can adapt the platforms for UIA's mobility to support nomadic applications.

Automated or semi-automated composition mechanisms of Web Services have been proposed [18, 19, 20]. Narayanan and Mcllraith [18] use DAML+OIL, which is a description logic-based language, for describing the formal semantics of Web services. The mechanism described in [18] can compose the sequence of Web services satisfying a user's goal using each service semantics. We can use such mechanisms to synthesize SMAs. In other words, our framework is consistent with Web Services as service parts of SMA.

8   Conclusions

In this paper, we have proposed a new multi-agent framework to make ubiquitous information service available easily. This framework is for distributed system consisting of three kinds of agents: UIA, PA and SMA. The UIA monitors the client environment and copes with changes in the situation on the user's side. The PA is a mobile agent that is created from reasoning rules and executes a series of requests from the user. The SMA is an agent that is composed from service components based on specification of a requirement to provide a service for a PA. PA responds to change of user terminals and instability of user environment, and SMA responds to instability of the server side.

Further work includes construction of various systems for UIS to elaborate our framework and CASE tools to develop the system easily.

References

1. C.A.Aarsten,D.Brugali and G.Menga: "Patterns for Three-Tier Client/Server Applications", Proc. of PloP 1996 (1996).
2. R. Hirschfeld: "Three-Tier Distribution Architecture", Washington University Tech. Report No. wucs-97-34 (1997)
3. F.Buschmann, R.Meunier, at.el.: Pattern-Oriented Software Architecture: A System of Patterns, John Wley&Sons,Ltd. (1996)
4. T.Finin, R.Fritzson, D.McKay and R.McEntire: "KQML as an Agent Communication Language", Proc. of CIKM'94, ACM Press, pp.456–463 (1994)
5. Agent Communication Language, http://www.fipa.org/repository/aclspecs.html.
6. J.Tanaka,K.Ueda,T.Miyazaki,A.Takeuchi, Y.Matsumoto, and K.Furukawa: "Guarded Horn Clauses and Experiences with Parallel Logic Programming",Proc. of Fall Joint Computer Conference '86, IEEE Computer Society Press, pp. 948–954 (1986)
7. Plangent, http://www.toshiba.co.jp/plangent/index.htm.
8. Bee-gent, http://www.toshiba.co.jp/beegent/.
9. E.Gamma, R.Helm, R.ohnson and J.Vlissides: Design Patterns: Elements of Reusable Object-Oriented Software, Addison Wesley Longman, Inc. (1997)
10. J.M. Bradshaw (Ed.): Software Agents, MIT Press (1997)
11. M.J.Wooldridge: "Agent Theories, Architectures, and Languages: A Survey", LNAI, Vol.890, Springer-Verlag, pp.1–32 (1994)

12. A. S. Rao: BDI Agents: From Theory to Practice, Proc. of ICMAS-95, pp.312–319 (1995)
13. F. Bergenti and A. Poggi: "LEAP: A FIPA Platform for Handheld and Mobile Devices", Intelligent Agents VIII, LNAI, Vol.2333, Springer-Verlag, pp.436–446 (2002)
14. M. Laukkanen, S. Tarkoma and J. Leinonen: "FIPA-OS Agent Platform for Small-Footprint Devices", Intelligent Agents VIII, LNAI, Vol.2333, Springer-Verlag, pp.447–460 (2002)
15. M. Laukkanen, H. Helin, H and Laamanen, "Supporting Nomadic Agent based Applications in the FIPA Agent Architecture", Proc. of AAMAS'02, ACM Press, pp.1348–1355 (2002)
16. J. Lawrence, "LEAP into Ad-Hoc Networks", Workshop on Ubiquitous Agents held in AAMAS'02 (2002)
17. G. Caire, N. Lhuillier and N. Lhuillier, "A communication protocol for agents on handheld devices ", Workshop on Ubiquitous Agents held in AAMAS'02 (2002)
18. S. Narayanan and S.A. McIlraith, "Simulation, verification and automated composition of web services", Proc. of WWW'02, ACM Press (2002)
19. D. Wu, B. Parsia, E. Sirin, J.A. Hendler and D.S. Nau "Automating DAML-S Web Services Composition Using SHOP2", Proc. of ISWC 2003, pp.195–210 (2003)
20. E. Sirin, J.A. Hendler, B. Parsia, "Semi-automatic Composition of Web Services using Semantic Descriptions", Proc. of WSMAI 2003, pp.17–24 (2003)

The Analysis of Coordination in an Information System Application - Emergency Medical Services

Wei Chen and Keith S. Decker

Department of Computer & Information Sciences,
University of Delaware,
Newark, DE 19716, USA
{wchen, decker}@cis.udel.edu

Abstract. There is an inevitable need for collaboration and coordination among response organizations during the occurrences of emergencies. We attack the coordination problem by analyzing intelligent agents' organizational behaviours and exploring a set of coordination mechanisms. This paper studies the application of our coordination research to a small-scale Emergency Medical Services (EMS) information system with response agencies modeled as organizations of autonomous agents. Due to the excessive amount of information and the dynamic change in the environment, the information decision process has become the backbone of EMS. The significance of our extended set of GPGP coordination mechanisms is examined under various environmental settings in this application domain. This paper models the coordination among three organizations during emergency responses to a set of small scale, concurrent incidents, like ambulance calls, police calls and mixed calls with potential needs of transporting the emergency victims to appropriate medical facilities. An EMS agent framework is implemented, an integrated coordination algorithm is introduced, early experimental results are presented and finally appropriate decisions are suggested for the response organizations. This paper also briefly discusses the extension for the management of emergency incidents to larger scale disasters.

1 Introduction

Our recent work has been involved with the reconceptualization and formalization of the Generalized Partial Global Planning (GPGP) approach [1] to coordination for intelligent agents. This approach is focused on the recognition of well-defined *coordination relationships* (*interdependencies*) and the application of *coordination mechanisms* chosen from a large enumerated space of potential mechanisms. To demonstrate that this approach is truly a general one, we have applied it to several application areas, such as Bioinformatics, Internet information gathering and EMS [2, 3]. In this paper, we focus on modeling the coordination relationships present in EMS information systems and examining the performance of elements in the space of coordination mechanisms.

Lots of attention has been focused on the research of response to disasters and other large-scale emergent situations (e.g., earthquakes, hurricanes and terrorist attacks), which require highly intensive communication, coordination and immediate responses to the changes of the environment. Aiming to simulate an entire disaster is one

P. Bresciani et al. (Eds.): AOIS 2004, LNAI 3508, pp. 36–51, 2005.

candidate approach; however, this kind of top-down simulation is very complicated and it is sometimes impossible to evaluate the research results unless one is faced with real disasters. In this paper, we will focus at a lower level of granularity, where an EMS system is a basic unit under the "big picture". The extension from EMS to disasters will be briefly discussed in Section 6.

Emergency Medical Service, EMS, is defined as a comprehensive, coordinated arrangement of health and safety resources designed to provide expedient care to victims of sudden illness and injury. It covers all phases of care from first response to discharge from a medical facility, and it includes prevention and education as well[1]. An integral part of this system, prehospital EMS (often called out-of-hospital EMS), plays a critical role in the effectiveness, efficiency, safety and quality[2] of the entire system [4]. This paper focuses on *prehospital EMS*, which is generally defined as the response process from the start of incident to the hospitalization of victims. In EMS systems, events happen rapidly and unexpectedly; resources move accordingly in the same fashion; decision making is highly time-critical based on involving response organizations, institutions and even geographical cites. Information flow among the related entities needs to be highly effective; however, communication channels could be impaired radically based on certain environmental changes, such as traffic jams and power failures. Thus, effective coordination is key to EMS systems. This paper models the coordination process in EMS and tries to figure out the best coordination mechanisms.

There has been previous work about EMS. However, it either merely concentrated on conceptual analysis without presenting much data [5], or just provided simple simulation results based on fixed, limited environmental settings according to the available technologies at the time [6, 7] without potential extensions. Adequate amount of simulation results were provided in [8]; however, there is a lack of analysis of response organizations' task structures that deduce helpful rules as explained later in this paper. Several modern approaches [9–11] focused on system development and ignored the effect of the actual coordination processes carried out by different emergency response agencies. Although the most important goal of an entire EMS process is *to save victims' lives*, different response agencies prefer their respective interests under this big goal. For example, independent ambulance service companies try to minimize their costs, police have to organize and control the overall situation (e.g., patrolling, clearing roads/traffic or responding to police calls) instead of accompanying the victims all the time, and hospitals have to care about the availability of open beds. Notably, an EMS system is a perfect domain that well fits computational organization theory [12]. The different response organizations by nature share the characteristics of heterogeneity, goal-orientation, adaptiveness etc. However, the purpose of this paper is not to study and improve the EMS organizations or the EMS models themselves; instead, the objective is to demonstrate the application and the performance of our extended set of GPGP coordination mechanisms in this special information system—EMS.

---

[1] For example, police are educated/trained with CPR.

[2] Each of these system evaluation factors has a corresponding definition in the EMS model introduced in Section 5.

Section 2 will introduce the GPGP approach in an abstract way. Section 3 will describe our EMS model. An experimental framework, which allows an analysis of the performance of various coordination mechanisms, will be demonstrated in section 4. Both analytical and quantitative results are explained in section 5. Finally, conclusions and future work are stated in section 6.

2   An Extended Set of GPGP Coordination Mechanisms

Coordination in multi-agent systems is defined as *managing interdependencies between activities* [13] and it addresses the special issues arising from the interdependency relationships among multiple agents' tasks. Assuming that each agent is capable of reasoning locally about its schedule of activities and possible alternatives [14], the key to handling the interdependency is *removing the uncertainty* in agents' task execution behaviours. GPGP is one possible approach [1] for coordination reasoning and it is based on TÆMS (Task Analysis, Environment Modeling, and Simulation) [15], an abstract modeling representation that represents task interdependencies quantitatively. We define an *interdependency*, or coordination relationship, as a relationship between a local and non-local task (NLT) [3] where the execution of one changes some performance- or utility-related characteristics associated with the other. Interdependencies are often associated with the processes of information exchange. Thus, this definition of coordination also holds in information systems, especially when involving information extraction, gathering or searching processes performed by multiple information wrappers. For example, cooperative searching peers within a P2P information system provide services or referral and learn about each other through caching [16].

The above definition of interdependency gives rise to the following questions: (1) how to represent the dependencies, and (2) how to manage the dependencies? For the first question, in order to represent and reason about the features of agents' tasks and their system environments, such as worth-oriented goals, contingencies and the uncertainties that arise when agents' plans distributed over multiple agents [4], we developed an Extended Hierarchical Task Networks (Extended HTN or EHTN) model [17, 18] to represent interdependencies. EHTN represents the changes in utility-based characteristics of tasks, the impact of information flow on task enablement and the contingent impact of task outcomes on control flow. We have proved an *expressiveness theorem* which states that our EHTN is strictly more expressive [2, 17] than the traditional HTNs. For the second question, we developed an extended set of GPGP coordination mechanisms [3] to manage the interdependencies. Each of these extended mechanisms consists of two parts: *a pattern-directed re-writing of the EHTN* and *a coordination communication protocol* specific to the mechanism. This extension of GPGP means a much larger number of coordination mechanisms and the introduction of task structure alteration in coordination process based on our new task representation. EHTN provides a quantitative definition of a vector of measurable, utility-influencing characteristics, a method that specifies how these characteristics accumulate as actions and explicit task relation-

---

[3] A local task only belongs to its owner agent; a non-local task belongs to a remote agent.

[4] Traditional HTNs can not represent these terms and features due to the lack of expressiveness.

ships indicating how task progress affects primitive action characteristics elsewhere in the task structure. Based on EHTN, the extended GPGP approach addresses the coordination problem: utilizing these task features, which are uniquely available to the knowledge representation method of our EHTN, to further modify the agents' task plans and to enable the communication among agents for coordination purpose.

We recast these GPGP mechanisms using our EHTN and proved that the GPGP coordination processes for those coordination problems that can be represented with our EHTN are deterministic. Using EHTN, we are able to represent a *coordination strategy problem*:

$$\text{Given } k \; nlts \in \text{NLT in } E \text{ and } M, \text{ find } m_i \in M \tag{1}$$
$$\text{corresponding to } nlt_i, \text{ that maximizes } EV(E, m_i, ..., m_k).$$

The above equation addresses an important question: which mechanism to use under a certain environmental condition; and it provides a method to choose the appropriate coordination mechanism m_i from the mechanism set M to maximize the user's evaluation function EV [5], given k non-local tasks (NLT) in a coordination environment E. We are also able to project an *integrated coordination problem* that includes planning and scheduling processes as explained in [2, 17]. The integrated coordination problem points out that the key of a coordination process is to remove the uncertainty in the involved agent's task plans in order to get better schedules. The term, *integrated*, means that planning and scheduling are incorporated together with coordination to form an *expanded coordination process*, which will be described in a later paragraph when explaining Figure 1. As a solution to the projected problem, an integrated coordination algorithm is presented as follows. $GPGP_{Detect}$ is a method that detects the coordi-

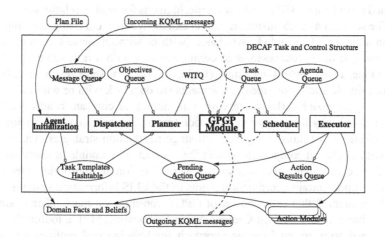

Fig. 1. DECAF agent architecture

---

[5] An evaluation function can be either preset by developers or dynamically selected according to the rules learned from the changing environments.

nation points within an input plan; *Branch* figures out the task branch of the execution path that contains a selected target coordination point; *ApplyMechanism* applies a mechanism to a selected coordination point. Further explanation can be found in [17].

Given: (P, M, R)

Input: P, an uncoordinated plan with uncertainty represented using EHTN; M, the extended set of GPGP coordination mechanisms; R, the role of this agent involved in a particular coordination process.
Output: S, a coordinated schedule with uncertainty removed.

1. Apply the function GPGP$_{Detect}$ to P to discover a set of k Coordination Points, $CP = \{nlt_i \mid i = 1, \ldots, k\}$;
2. While $(CP \neq \phi)$
   - Select a coordination point $nlt_i \in CP$ and $CP \leftarrow CP - \{nlt_i\}$;
   - if (nlt_i is *avoidable*)
      $P \leftarrow P - \text{Branch}(nlt_i)$;
      continue;
   - else
      select $m_j \in M$ according to Equation 1;
      $P \leftarrow \text{ApplyMechanism}(P, \{nlt_i\}, m_j, r)$;
3. Generate a better schedule, S, based on a selected utility function;
4. Return S.

An extended set of coordination mechanisms were developed around the common coordination relationship of "enablement". Each mechanism has different requirements in terms of the information needed by each party, the risk involved etc. [2, 3]. We have catalogued seventeen GPGP coordination mechanisms for *enable* relationships as listed in [3]. The seventeen mechanisms are not an exhaustive list; and many are simply variations on a theme. They include avoidance (with or without some sacrifice), reservation schemes, simple predecessor-side commitments (to do a task sometime, to do it by a deadline, to an earliest-start-time (EST), to notify or send result directly when complete), simple successor-side commitments (to do a task with or without a specific EST), polling approaches (busy querying, timetabling, or constant headway), shifting task dependencies by learning or mobile code (promotion or demotion), various third-party mechanisms, or more complex multi-stage negotiation strategies. These mechanisms exist as optional components within the coordination module of every intelligent agent[6]. Thus, each agent can choose one, or a combination of, appropriate mechanisms for its needs upon certain coordination points in the EMS information systems.

We implemented this extended set of GPGP coordination mechanisms using DE-CAF (Distributed, Environment-Centred Agent Framework) [19], a toolkit that allows a well-defined software engineering approach for building real multi-agent systems. The internal structure of a DECAF agent with newly designed *GPGP (Coordination)*

---

[6] This set of domain-independent mechanisms are "hard-coded" within every agent; whether to apply a certain mechanism or not is based on an agent's own estimation of the current environment, i.e., selection of a particular mechanism for a particular relationship is dynamic.

Module is shown in Figure 1. These internal components work together to keep track of an agent's current status: plan selection, scheduling, execution etc. The selected components, the planner, the GPGP (coordination) module and the scheduler, are integrated as an expanded coordination structure. The relationships among these three adjacent components are as follows: The planner provides uncoordinated plans (with uncertainty) to the GPGP (coordination) module; the coordination module takes uncoordinated plans as input, applies one or a combination of appropriate GPGP coordination mechanisms to this input and outputs coordinated plans as the input to the scheduler; the scheduler uses the coordinated plans to produce better schedules. The arrow from the scheduler to the coordination module indicates that the coordination module takes advantage of the local scheduler's scheduling ability to evaluate/estimate the features of remote agents' actions by asking "What-If" questions. The relationships among these agent components further illustrates the aforementioned integrated coordination algorithm.

Further information about all the extended set of GPGP coordination mechanisms and the actual application of these mechanisms can be found in [2, 3, 17].

3 EMS Model

We do not intend to simulate the exact real world EMS. The objective of this paper is to demonstrate the effectiveness of our extended set of GPGP coordination mechanisms in this selected information system, EMS. This EMS model is similar to the real EMS systems under certain assumptions and selected environmental settings.

In order to suit our model to larger-scale disasters with more participating agencies, we add a police department into the traditional EMS model. Police carry out the tasks of clearing traffic jams on the road and controlling police calls, which are both common during disasters. We remove fire departments from the model to simplify the system, since fire trucks have similar behaviour patterns as ambulances.[7]

Based on real world facts [20], an *agency assumption* holds in the model: police cars belong to police station, ambulances belong to independent ambulance companies, and there is no supervision relationship among different response agencies. According to the assumption, we describe a *vehicle behaviour pattern* as follows: A police car starts from its police station, patrols around the local area randomly until an incident call and continues the patrol after dealing with the incident. An ambulance waits in its ambulance station for an incident call, finds its way to the incident site, transports the victims to an appropriate medical facility and returns to the ambulance station for a next call.

In practice, an EMS response process includes patient flow, equipment flow and information flow [4]. In this paper, we regard patients and equipment as part of the information flow resources that help make proper decisions. Figure 2 depicts the infor-

---

[7] Fire departments are capable of putting out fires and other specialized tasks, e.g., removing victims from severely damaged vehicles, and cannot be replaced by ambulances or other response organizations; i.e., there is an important functional distinction among different response organizations. The removal of fire department from this model is just for simplification purposes.

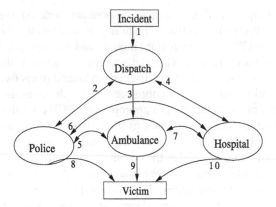

Fig. 2. An EMS system information flow chart

mation flow of the EMS model. First, incidents are reported to the dispatches. Then, the incidents are responded to by police departments, ambulance companies and hospitals, each made up of equipment and personnel trained for this purpose. In the model, a police car agent represents the role of a police department. Similarly, an ambulance agent represents an ambulance company. The police department and ambulance company may have multiple vehicles. There are also hospitals and corresponding dispatches: ambulance dispatch, police dispatch and 911 dispatch. [8]

A typical EMS process is described as follows: A 911 call, activated by an incident, comes in and the 911 dispatch screens the call; the 911 dispatch contacts an appropriate response agency or multiple agencies based on the type of the incident; the dispatch of each agency broadcasts the incident to the response vehicles and sends appropriate vehicles to the incident site; the response vehicle finds its way to the incident site; proper treatment is provided and the incident is under control; if there is any victim who needs further medical care, the victim will be transported to a proper medical facility by an ambulance; if the incident updates to require additional care, other appropriate response vehicles will be dispatched to the site as well; all the response vehicles then find their ways back to their base stations or continue to respond to other emergency calls.

4   Framework

We implemented a framework for modeling the EMS system using DECAF [19]. The framework has also been applied to domains like Internet information gathering in bioinformatics [3]. This framework supports and is able to produce dynamically changing environments for selected applications. EMS is a perfect example of high-volume communication, high-velocity and coordination-intensive information systems, where

---

[8] In the real world, some of the 911 (the emergency telephone number in the USA) dispatches are the same thing as police and ambulance dispatches; while in most cases, they are not. We model them as separate roles in this paper.

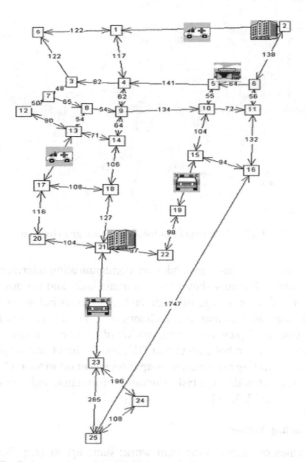

Fig. 3. A snapshot of the EMS framework demonstration program

coordination occurs both vertically within a response organization and horizontally across organizations routinely.

The EMS framework is simplified to include limited types of agents. A snapshot of the framework program is shown in Figure 3: two police cars and two ambulances move around in the local area map in response to incident calls and find their ways back and forth from their base stations or their current patrol locations to incident sites. The indexed boxes are corners and intersections; the arrow lines represent directed roads and streets; a number along with an edge stands for the length of the road and street. The system map in Figure 3 is the actual local street map of the University of Delaware and the vicinity with minor modifications.

The coordination points within EMS are the interdependencies (information exchanges) among the tasks of all these agents. Different types of agents have different tasks; the tasks for the same type of agents share the same structures. Because of space constraints, we only show the task structures of these agents: ambulance, police car, and hospital in Figure 4. The three tree structures represent the tasks that the response agents need to do. The top level nodes are root tasks; the leaf nodes represent the action each

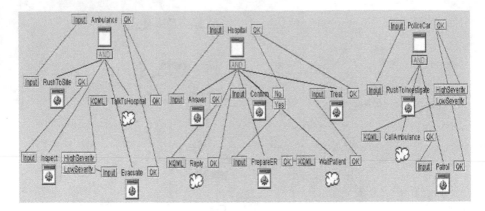

Fig. 4. EMS task structures for Ambulance and Hospital

agent has to execute; the cloud-shape nodes are communication interfaces for receiving and sending messages. Figure 4 shows only the main tasks and actions in a simplified version. The root nodes are the agents' main tasks; the nodes below are executable actions; the cloud nodes are communication channels among local and non-local agents' tasks; the task structure depicts the decomposition of the corresponding root tasks into executable actions. The symbols, Input and OK, are the input and output of a task or action. The links connecting the input and output represent information flow. The meanings of various types of nodes, the task structural information and task decomposition are further discussed in [2, 3, 19]

4.1   Participating Agents

There are two kinds of agents in the framework: static agents (e.g., hospitals, ambulance stations, police stations, dispatches) and mobile agents (e.g., police cars and ambulances). The static agents are able to communicate with each other, but cannot move along the roads; the mobile agents are capable of both. Next is a brief description of each kind of agent.

A hospital receives victims from incidents and manages open beds. An ambulance station is a base for ambulances and is represented by a coordinate in the map. A police station is also represented as a coordinate. The coordinate of a base station represents the start point of a vehicle. There are three kinds of dispatches: police dispatches, ambulance dispatches and 911 dispatches; in this model, a 911 dispatch is implemented as a DECAF agent, which screens incidents and sends notifications to the dispatches of other response agencies. Upon receiving the notification, the police and ambulance dispatches inform the incident to their vehicles and send an adequate number of them to the incident site. The tasks of ambulances and police cars are shown in Figure 4, conforming to the behaviour pattern explained in the previous section.

4.2   Input Factors

We define an event, or an accident, that causes a 911 emergency call as an *incident*. There are various types of incidents requiring different kinds of response organizations.

Coordination during the response processes involves all types of participating agents. An incident is represented as

incident(time, type, severity,location, duration, number, victims[number].(life, life_function)).

Time means the start of an EMS process [9]. There are three types of incidents in the model: *Ambulance call*, which requires ambulances only; *police call*, which requires police only, is modeled as a traffic accident and requires the police to clear the road; *mixed call*, e.g., a big traffic accident with injury or ambulance call and also requires the police to clear the blocked road. *Severity* indicates whether there is any injury in the incident and the level of the injury: ($severity = 0$) means no injury; ($severity = 1$) means low severity injury and no ambulance needed; ($severity = 2$) means high severity and an ambulance is needed to transport the victim to a hospital. *Location* means the spot on the roads and streets in the local area map where the incident happens; it is represented with coordinate $Incident.Location(x, y)$. *Duration* indicates how long an incident lasts, that is, how long the emergency vehicles are kept on the incident site. *Number* represents the number of the victims of an incident; if the number is greater than a single ambulance's capacity, multiple ambulances may be dispatched. The compound variable, *victim*, is one of the major resources in the system. *Victim[number].life* represents the victim's initial life value immediately following the incident and this value drops according to the victim's *life function*. Life function indicates how a victim's life value drops as time goes on after the incident. If *life* drops to zero before entering an appropriate medical facility, it indicates the death of this victim. There are two kinds of life functions defined: linearly and exponentially decreasing functions due to the time change, t,: (1) $f_1 = (1 - t)$ and (2) $f_2 = (2 - e^t)$.

Incident Generation is complicated. In order to simplify the system without losing generality, a stand-along *incident generator* is developed to produce incident instances. A 911 dispatch receives a new incident from the incident generator and then activates the response process.

4.3   Output Evaluations

There are three main evaluation factors for EMS: *response time* for quality control, *survival rate* for effectiveness control and *coordination efficiency* for efficiency control.

The most critical measurement of the performance of an EMS is its *response times*:

$$\text{Response Time} = \text{Call Evaluation} + \text{Caller Interrogation} + \text{Unit Dispatch Time}$$
$$+ \text{Launch Time} + \text{Routing Time}.$$

The duration of a response time can be defined in different ways. In our EMS model, the start of a response time is *when an emergency call is received*; and the end time is *when any appropriate agency first arrives at the incident site*. *Survival rate* evaluates the effectiveness of EMS and reflects the overall system performance. However, there may be multiple coordination points in an entire EMS response and the analysis of our coordination mechanisms may be not directly related to this factor. Besides the response time,

---

[9] What happens before EMS response is not of our interest. Thus, time means the start of an EMS response process, not the start of an incident.

there are other important factors that determine the survival rate: the *routing time* and the victim life function etc. Survival rate is affected by various factors, e.g., response time, availability of the resources, victims' life functions and traffic patterns at the times of the incidents, etc. A victim's life function and the potential traffic condition is out of the control of EMS. However, these factors still matters, e.g., the police's clearing the blocked road provides shorter *routing time* for ambulances. *Coordination efficiency* is another important factor, which reflects the level of the occurrences of coordination processes within EMS:

$$\text{Coordination Efficiency} = \frac{\text{Coordination Time}}{\text{Entire EMS Response Time}}.$$

The importance of this measurement lies in that coordination efficiency indicates whether it improves resource allocation and reduces cost, i.e., whether energy, funding and time are saved for actual emergency control and not wasted on indirect expenses.

There are other factors for evaluating EMS, e.g., location of a base station, dispatch accuracy (reflecting how misunderstood, faulty, or missing information impairs correct dispatch), which will not be discussed here.

5   Experimental Results

5.1   Quantitative Results

The average EMS response time under different sets of environmental factors were recorded for performance analysis. Due to the paper length constraint, we only show one set of quantitative results, the average EMS response time, which indicates the quality of EMS systems, based on the following input parameters: the selection of one to three police cars, the selection of one to three ambulances, two hospitals, a fixed 0% communication error rate, constant traffic factors (we assume that an EMS response process is finished before the change of traffic patterns), randomly generated and potentially concurrent incidents, and four different GPGP mechanisms: *Reservation, Demotion, Sending_Result*, and *Polling*. The content and the application of these mechanisms will be introduced in the next subsection. Here, the coordination point, to which we apply the four mechanisms, is the information exchange process starting from the dispatch of the selected response vehicles until the first arrival of any one of them. The results are as shown in Figure 5. From this figure, Reservation and SendingResult mechanisms share similar performance. Polling uses a little bit more time because of extra communication handling. Demotion has two thresholds: the *location repeat rates*[10] of 0.2 and 0.4. If (location repeat rate < 0.2) that indicates this spot is safe, the application of the Demotion mechanism results in more time for the agents to respond to the EMS requests; if ($0.2 \leq$ location repeat rate ≤ 0.4), Demotion's performance is similar to other mechanisms; if (location repeat rate > 0.4) that implies this spot is problematic, Demotion outperforms others, where routine patrolling is needed. Notably, the decreasing trend of the average EMS response time for Demotion in Figure 5 is not as steep

---

[10] Defined as the rate of incident happening at previous locations.

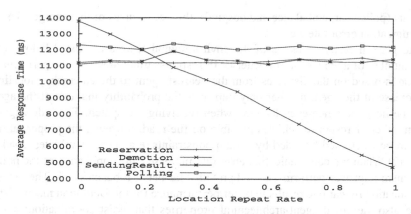

Fig. 5. Performance of coordination mechanisms on changing locations

as the the decrease of the task execution time in Figure 4 in [3]. The reason lies in the different behaviours of police cars and ambulances: ambulances have the advantage of starting from their own stations (locations) using the previous cached route if the emergency location is repeated, while police cars need to re-calculate the route because of their random patrolling tasks. More quantitative results are in [2].

5.2 Analytic Results—Mechanisms and Domain Task Situations

This section discusses in what situations a certain coordination mechanism is better than the others, or a certain set of mechanisms more effective than the rest of them. Analytic results provide general guidance to dynamic environments. Our final objective is to discover the relationships between these GPGP coordination mechanisms and the different settings of environmental factors, which is exactly what the *coordination strategy problem* addresses in [3, 17]. If this problem is solved, every agent is capable of selecting the best coordination behaviours using different GPGP coordination mechanisms within the changing environments. As a result, the optimal solution for the entire system can be achieved by distributing coordination intelligence to every agent; scaling-up is easy when the agents make decisions independently [21].

In order to answer a broader range of questions and be ready for new environmental instances, we must make general statements and detect some patterns from these experimental results. We normalize data in a proper format and feed the data to the C5.0 decision tree learning algorithm[22]. Based on the resulting decision tree, C5.0 forms rules representing different paths in the tree from the root to a leaf node for the classification of success (higher than a threshold) or failure (lower than a threshold). Thus, each rule explains a classification for future test cases. In this approach, we map the dense (or continuous) attribute values into a set of discrete categories. For example, the traffic factor associated with each edge can be normalized into the set of $\{Low, Medium, High\}$, instead of the continuos range of $[0, 1]$. The performance evaluation is whether the response time is good (or short) enough. The inputs to the decision-tree algorithm are the normalized values of the changing environmental factors described above: GPGP coordination mechanisms, the number of the various types of agents (police car, ambulance and hospital), the occurrences of the emergencies and communication error rate etc.

The general analytic results of the environmental factors are listed below: (1)A larger number of agents result in better EMS response time; however, the performance increase is based on the distances from the nearest agent to the emergency locations; the increase of the agent number only improves the probability that one of the agents might be near the emergency location when receiving a dispatch. This rule suggests large number of response vehicles possible on the road; however, the proper number needs to be calculated bounded by certain constraints, e.g., cost of vehicles, road capacity. (2) When the communication error rate increases, the application of the polling mechanism improves performance and provides far better robustness. (3) The increase of the location repeat rate results in better performance for the Demotion mechanism.

We also identified agent-architectural properties that assist coordination: a local scheduler reasoning about non-local commitments and a way to generate such commitments by "what-if" questions. Indeed, viewing the eventual end-product of coordination mechanisms as information for better schedules gives a consistent and general way of combining different coordination mechanisms. The most difficult aspect of the implementation of an information system is to develop a proper agent architecture so that well-represented, pre-planned activities can be analyzed and possibly altered before they are executed.

Next, we briefly explain the performance of the four selected mechanisms tested in the EMS system.

For *Avoidance and Sacrifice Avoidance* mechanisms, there is a situation that a victim only has a trivial injury. Therefore, there is no need to send any ambulance. The task of basic medical treatment carried out by the police can be regarded as a local alternative and it is different from the non-local task that needs coordination, which is the police calling an ambulance for this treatment. We can design the task structure of a mobile agent with not only the task of its specialty, e.g., the police clearing the traffic, but also the alternative task of calling an ambulance. Under this task design, we conclude that: when police training cost is low, this mechanism is good; when ambulance operation cost is high, this mechanism is economical; when all ambulances are busy, e.g., during disasters, this mechanism is especially excellent.

For *Coordination by Reservation*, the coordination point is the communication between ambulances and hospitals. Reservation of a hospital is the process to apply *Coordination by Reservation*. An ambulance either reserves an open bed in a hospital after an initial exam of the victim or simply transports the victim to a nearest hospital without reservation, which potentially does not have any open bed at the time of their arrival[11]. We conclude that *coordination by reservation* is generally better than without coordination; this mechanism is bad only if a reservation process costs too much time or there is an impaired communication channel. Compared with the transportation time, the reservation time in EMS is negligible.

---

[11] In large-scale emergencies, ambulances in neighbouring cities could be used and the number of open beds in hospitals could be decreased, which is exactly the situations that reservation is vital.

For *Demotion*, we state that it is efficient for saving most lives possible and it fits the fact that demotion has already been applied in the real world. For example, policemen have already been trained with CPR (cardiopulmonary resuscitation) and basic first aid, which is what autonomous agents choose to do based on the experiments for saving more lives. Although extra training and cost are needed, it is still a matter of life and death if policemen can do it to save a victim/patient in emergency, instead of doing nothing and simply waiting for the arrival of an ambulance. It looks similar to the situation for *Avoidable Mechanisms*, but they are different in that (1) it is from an ambulance's view, instead of from a policeman, and (2) before training, policemen could not do CPR; thus the first aid is not an alternative task to choose. Most importantly, there are tasks that can be actually "demoted" to the police. In the real world, paramedics will be in an ambulance and accompany patients in the ambulance all the way to the hospital. Paramedics are capable of high-level emergency care[12]. If we demote the relative high-level emergency care to the police, *Demotion Shift* needs to be applied. Here we have to point out that in reality CPR and the similar first aid skills have been widely distributed to almost all emergency responders already and this fact proves our research result. We conclude that the demotion of the medical treatments by a non-ambulance agent is effective; the effectiveness also depends on the frequency of the need for the medical treatments during incidents; in our EMS model, it changes the life function from a non-linear into a linear decrease.

For *Polling*, it can be applied to all kinds of dependencies. The reasons of using polling in the real world are the vagueness of cellular phone signal, temporary unavailability of hospital personnel, communication overfill during disasters etc. We conclude that: Polling is robust in dynamic environment with unpredictable communication quality, but a waste of communication resource in all other cases because of the extra communication load.

6   Conclusion and Future Work

We have introduced an extended set of GPGP coordination mechanisms, which are formally represented by our highly expressive EHTN. A coordination strategy problem and an integrated coordination problem are presented, together with an integrated coordination algorithm. We also briefly introduced a high-volume communication, high velocity and coordination-intensive information system—EMS, projected an EMS model and implemented a framework using DECAF. Experimental results, including quantitative and qualitative results, have been presented and briefly analyzed. The framework is flexible and extensible to new technologies, such as wireless communication, telemedicine etc. Our extended GPGP coordination mechanisms are demonstrated as significantly helpful in coordination- and communication-intensive environments like EMS. Certain rules have been projected, e.g., CPR should be demoted to the responders, whoever first reaches the incident site, usually the police, which reflects the actual real-world situation of today.

---

[12] There are different levels of medical treatment. Current medical training for police is the lowest.

The EMS framework is flexible and extensible. We have concentrated on the relatively small incidents in this paper; these incidents are basic elements of what happens during much larger emergencies or disasters. The increasing complexity during a disaster other than an incident lies in the following facts: a disaster requires much more emergency responders and more types of response agencies; communication channels may be damaged, overly used or even totally unavailable; the hierarchy of resource management for a disaster contains more layers than for an incident, e.g., at the highest level a command centre is created for coordinating the entire response operation. A viable way to extend our existing system to deal with the increased complexity of handling disasters is through a model extension. For example, we modify the model by increasing the types and the capacity of the current incident parameters to include special disaster features, e.g., more victims, more quantity and types of responders; the complex disaster response management hierarchy could introduce extra layers of dispatches and special coordinators. Additional constraints are easy to be incorporated as well, e.g., road capacity, the availability of response organizations in nearby cities etc. The key idea of the extensibility of our framework is that a disaster consists of a series of incidents that happen in a condensed manner and each incident needs to be handled in the same fashion in micro-situations. Different kinds of agents are easily added into the EMS Coordination system. For example, in many areas, helicopters are available for the transportation of emergency victims. This kind of extra transportation vehicles can be represented with an extra route from the emergency site to a trauma centre; and this route is associated with a very small value meaning that the transportation by a helicopter is faster, with less traffic concern, but higher cost. For another example, the incident types can be extended as well: a fire incident will cause the immediate response from fire trucks and firefighters, which are new types of agents in the system.

Based on the flexibility and extensibility of this framework, our future work is: (1) introducing more heterogeneity into the EMS model, e.g., new types of response agencies (firefighters and physicians) for EMS and non-DECAF agents (an applet in a web browser for real time, public EMS queries) for the framework; (2) developing separate user/programmer interfaces—the user control of the coordination configuration and the application of this framework into different local settings. From a system's point of view, this project will lead to a user-centred approach: a user, or an EMS system inspector, or a response organization manager, inputs his targets (maximizing survival rate, minimizing cost, or the combination of them, etc.) to the EMS model; the coordination component associated with every responder automatically selects the best coordination mechanism(s) to apply to certain coordination points in its task structure; thus, finally the EMS system is adapted to the user's request.

As the technologies are advancing every day, the communication channel becomes much more capacious, clear and reliable. For example, a new GRYW (Grayling Wireless) communication system has been designed for high profile markets, e.g., small scale firefighting teams. For this small scale team coordination, communication is not a barrier any more; each firefighter's individual ability becomes the bottleneck of the system. We can easily extend our flexible framework to incorporate this new technology by applying *Demotion Shift* mechanism for the agents' individual tasks; and *Polling* becomes unnecessary, which implies that each firefighter should receive higher-level medical training in order to save more lives.

References

1. Decker, K., Li, J.: Coordinating mutually exclusive resources using GPGP. Autonomous Agents and Multi-Agent Systems **3** (2000) 133–157
2. Chen, W.: Designing an Extended Set of Coordination Mechanisms for Multiagent Systems. PhD thesis, Computer and Information Sciences, University of Delaware (2005)
3. Chen, W., Decker, K.: Applying coordination mechanisms for dependency relationships under various environments. In: Proceedings of Workshop in AAMAS02: MAS Problem Spaces and Their Implications, Bologna, Italy (2002)
4. Sachs, G.M.: Officer's Guide to Fire Service EMS. Fire Engineering (1999)
5. Clark, T., Waring, C.: A simulation approach to analysis of emergency services and trauma center management. In: the 1987 Winter Simulation Conference. (1987)
6. Iskander, W.H.: Simulation modeling for emergency medical service systems. In: Proceedings of the 1989 Winter Simulation Conference. (1989)
7. Parker, W., Johnson, R.: Simulation of a coordinated accident rescue system. In: the fourth annual conference on Applications of simulation. (1970)
8. Christie, M., Levary, R.: The use of simulation in planning the transportation of patients to hospitals following a disaster. Journal of Medical Systems **22** (1998) 289–300
9. Wears, R., Winton, C.: Simulation modeling of prehospital trauma care. In: the 1993 Winter Simulation Conference. (1993)
10. Giiler, N., Ubeyli, E.: Theory and applications of telemedicine. Journal of Medical Systems **26** (2002) 199–220
11. Nagatuma, H.: Developing of an emergency medical video multiplexing transport system. Journal of Medical Systems **27** (2003) 133–140
12. Carley, K., Gasser, L.: Computational organization theory. In: Multiagent Systems: A Modern Approach to Distributed Artificial Intelligence. MIT Press (1999)
13. Malone, T., Crowston, K.: The interdisciplinary study of coordination. In: ACM Computing Surveys. (1994) 87–119
14. Garvey, A., Humphrey, M., Lesser, V.: Task interdependencies in design-to-time real-time scheduling. In: AAAI93. (1993) 580–585
15. Decker, K.S.: TÆMS: A framework for environment centered analysis and design of coordination mechanisms. In O'Hare, G., Jennings, N., eds.: Foundations of Distributed Artificial Intelligence. Wiley Inter-Science (1996)
16. Udupi, Y., Yolum, P., Singh, M.: Trustworthy service caching: Cooperative search in p2p information systems. In: aois2003. (2003)
17. Chen, W., Decker, K.: Managing multi-agent coordination, planning, and scheduling. In: Proceedings of the Third Autonomous Agent and Multi-Agent Systems, New York, USA (2004)
18. Erol, K., Hendler, J., Nau, D.: HTN planning: Complexity and expressivity. In: AAAI94. (1994) 1123–1128
19. Graham, J., Decker, K., Mersic, M.: DECAF a flexible multi-agent system architecture. Autonomous Agents and Multi-Agent Systems **7** (2003) 7–27
20. Bureau of Labor Statistics: Occupational outlook handbook, 2002-2003 edition (2003) http://www.bls.gov/oco/.
21. Durfee, E.: Scaling up agent coordination strategies. IEEE Computer **34** (2001) 39–46
22. Quinlan, R.: Improved use of continuous attributes in c4.5. Journal of Artificial Intelligent Research **4** (1996) 77–90

Market-Based Recommender Systems: Learning Users' Interests by Quality Classification*

Yan Zheng Wei, Luc Moreau, and Nicholas R. Jennings

Intelligence, Agents, Multimedia Group,
School of Electronics and Computer Science,
University of Southampton, UK SO17 1BJ
{yzw01r, L.Moreau, nrj}@ecs.soton.ac.uk

Abstract. Recommender systems are widely used to cope with the problem of information overload and, consequently, many recommendation methods have been developed. However, no one technique is best for all users in all situations. To combat this, we have previously developed a market-based recommender system that allows multiple agents (each representing a different recommendation method or system) to compete with one another to present their best recommendations to the user. In our system, the marketplace encourages good recommendations by rewarding the corresponding agents according to the users' ratings of their suggestions. Moreover, we have shown this incentivises the agents to bid in a manner that ensures only the best recommendations are presented. To do this effectively, however, each agent needs to classify its recommendations into different internal quality levels, learn the users' interests and adapt its bidding behaviour for the various internal quality levels accordingly. To this end, in this paper, we develop a reinforcement learning and Boltzmann exploration strategy that the recommending agents can exploit for these tasks. We then demonstrate that this strategy helps the agents to effectively obtain information about the users' interests which, in turn, speeds up the market convergence and enables the system to rapidly highlight the best recommendations.

1 Introduction

Recommender systems have been widely advocated as a way of coping with the problem of information overload. Such systems help make choices among recommendations from all kinds of sources for users who do not have sufficient personal experience of all these alternatives [1]. Many recommender systems have been developed but they are primarily based on two main kinds of filtering techniques: *(i) content-based filtering* recommends items based on their objective features (such as the text content of a Web document), whereas *(ii) collaborative filtering* recommends items based on their subjective features (e.g., the fact that a user with similar tastes likes them). However, both kinds of techniques have their weaknesses. The former cannot easily recommend non-machine parsable items (such as audio and video items), whereas the latter fail

---

* This research is funded in part by QinetiQ and the EPSRC Magnitude project (reference GR/N35816).

P. Bresciani et al. (Eds.): AOIS 2004, LNAI 3508, pp. 52–67, 2005.

when there are an insufficient number of peers to accurately predict a user's interests. Given this, it has been argued that there is no universally best method for all users in all situations [2].

In previous work, we have shown that an information marketplace can function effectively as an overarching coordinator for a multi-agent recommender system [3, 4]. In our system, the various recommendation methods, represented as recommender agents, compete to advertise their recommendations to the user. Through this competition, only the best recommendations (from whatever source) are presented to the user. Essentially, our system uses a particular type of auction (generalized first price sealed bid) and a corresponding reward regime to incentivise the agents to align their bids with the user's preferences. Thus, recommendations that the user considers good are encouraged by receiving a reward, whereas poor ones are deterred (by paying to advertise their recommendations but by receiving no reward). In short, the market acts as a feedback mechanism that helps agents to correlate their own *internal ratings* of recommendations (i.e. the relevance rating computed by whatever recommendation algorithm they use) to the desires of the user.

While our system works effectively most of the time, an open problem from the point of view of the individual recommender agents remains: *given a set of recommendations with different internal rating levels, in what order should an agent try to advertise them so that it can learn the user's interests as quickly as possible, while still maximizing its revenue?* Thus, for example, the agent could bid the items that have never been advertised to the user, which would allow it to learn the user's interests quickly but would also result in it losing money. Conversely, the agent could always bid those that have been highly rewarded, so ensuring a good return, but it would take a very long time to learn the extent of the user's interests. While this problem is couched in the context of our specific system, this is a general problem that all recommender systems face. Thus, even though they may not have a currency or an explicit reward, they still need to determine the user's preferences as quickly as possible, while still making good suggestions, in order to make effective recommendations.

To overcome this problem, we have developed a *quality classification* mechanism and a reinforcement learning strategy for the agents to learn the user's interests. Intuitively, to make good suggestions, an agent needs to classify its recommendations into different categories based on some specific features of the recommendations and then suggest the right categories of items to the user according to his interests. In our context, each agent classifies its recommendations into different quality levels (e.g. very good, good, bad etc) based on its internal belief about their relevance to the user's context. Then, to assist an agent to direct the right categories of recommendations to the user, we developed a concomitant reinforcement learning strategy. This strategy enables an agent to relate the user's feedback about its recommendations to its internal quality measure and then to put forward those recommendations that are consistent with this. This is important because the more effectively an agent relates its recommendations to the user's interests, the better it serves the user and the more rewards it receives.

Against this background, this paper advances the state of the art in the following ways. Firstly, a novel reinforcement learning strategy is developed to enable the agents to effectively and quickly learn the user's interests while still making good recommendations. Secondly, and perhaps more importantly, we demonstrate how our learning strategy, coordinated through the marketplace, can be viewed as a quality classification problem and how the marketplace assists the classification and aligns the right recommendations to the right people. Third, from an individual agent's point of view, we show the learning strategy enables an agent to maximize its revenue. Finally, we show that when all agents adopt our strategy, the market rapidly converges and makes good recommendations quickly and frequently.

The remainder of this paper is structured in the following manner. Section 2 briefly recaps the basics of our multi-agent recommender system and highlights the problem an individual agent faces in it. Section 3 details the design of our learning strategy. Section 4 empirically evaluates this design. Section 5 outlines related work in terms of reinforcement learning and market-based recommendations. Section 6 concludes and points to future work.

2   The Quality Classification Problem for Market-Based Recommendations

Different recommendation methods use different metrics and different algorithms to evaluate the items they may recommend. Thus, the internal rating of the quality of a recommendation can vary dramatically from one method to another (e.g. some may think it is very relevant for the user, others may think it moderately relevant, while yet others may believe it is irrelevant). Here, we term this internal evaluation the method's *internal quality* (INQ). However, a high INQ recommendation from one method does not necessarily mean the recommendation is any more likely to better satisfy a user than a low INQ item suggested by another. Ultimately, whether a recommendation satisfies a user can only be decided by that user. Therefore, we term the user's evaluation of a recommendation the *user's perceived quality* (UPQ).

With these concepts in place, we now briefly outline our market-based recommender in the order of the market processes (see the circled numbers in Figure 1) as follows. Firstly, when the market calls the agents for a number (S) of recommendations, each agent submits S items and bids a price for each of them. Secondly, the market ranks all recommendations in decreasing order of their prices and displays the S items with the highest bid prices to the user. Consequently, each agent with displayed items pays an amount of credits (equal to how much it bids) for each of the corresponding displayed items for the advertisement. Thirdly, the user then visits a number of the displayed items and gives a rating (i.e. UPQ) to each visited item based on his satisfaction. Fourthly, the market rewards the agents with positive UPQ recommendations an amount of credit that is proportional to their UPQ values (see [3] for the details and the proof that this mechanism is Pareto optimal with respect to the group of rewarded agents and maximizes their social welfare). Thus, the system completes one round of operation and proceeds with another following the above four steps.

In this context, the role of the reward mechanism is to provide the agents with incentives to align their bidding behaviour with the interests of the user. From the point of view of an individual agent, however, it needs to learn which recommendations the user prefers. To do this, agents classify their recommendations into a predetermined number

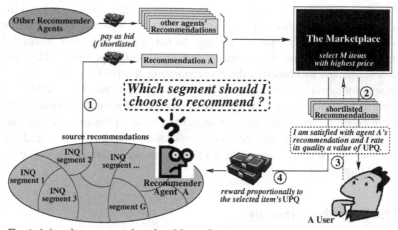

The circled numbers represent the order of the market process.

Fig. 1. An Agent's Learning Problem

(G) of categories (or segments) based on their INQs (e.g. in the simplest case, where $G = 2$, an agent could classify bad recommendations as those with an INQ of less than 0.5 and those with an INQ between 0.5 and 1.0 as good) and then they relate these INQs to the UPQs. Intuitively, the more the user is satisfied with a recommendation, the more reward the corresponding agent receives. Thus, an agent that has sufficient experience of the user's feedback can learn the user's interests by correlating its recommendations (and their corresponding INQ segments) to the rewards (that reflect their UPQs) they receive [4]. This, in turn, enables a self-interested agent to consciously make recommendations from those INQ segments that correspond to high UPQs so that it can best satisfy the user and, thus, gain maximal revenue. To effectively compute the agents' revenue, we define an agent's *immediate reward* (made from a recommendation displayed to the user in one auction round) as the reward it received minus the price it has paid for the advertisement[1]. With this, what an agent needs to do is to learn how much immediate rewards, on average, it can expect for items in each category (i.e. each INQ segment). We term this average immediate reward for each INQ segment an agent's *expected revenue*. Thus, a self-interested agent can maximize its revenue by frequently bidding recommendations from the segments with high expected revenue. Therefore, an agent's recommending task can be seen as a quality classification problem and it needs to align the user's preferences with its INQ segments (reflected by expected revenue) and meanwhile make maximal revenue.

However, when an agent starts bidding in the marketplace, it has no information about how much revenue it can expect for each segment. Therefore, the agent needs to

---

[1] Agents pay nothing for items they put forward that are not displayed to the user (this occurs when other agents are willing to pay more to advertise their recommendations). By definition, an immediate reward may be either positive or negative. If a displayed recommendation is not selected by the user or if it has paid too much to display an item, the corresponding agent's immediate reward is negative since it has paid for the display and received less reward.

interact in the marketplace by taking actions over its G segments to learn this information (as per Figure 1). In this way, an agent can produce a profile of such information from which it can form an optimal strategy to maximize its overall revenue. In this context, the agent's learning behaviour is on a "trial-and-error" basis. The agent bids its recommendations and receives the corresponding feedback in a manner that good recommendations gain rewards, whereas bad ones attract a loss. This kind of trial-and-error learning behaviour is exactly what happens in Reinforcement Learning [5]. Thus, to be more concrete, an agent needs an algorithm to learn the expected revenue over each segment. In addition, it also needs an exploration strategy to make trials on its G segments such that it strikes a balance between learning as quickly as possible, while still maximizing revenue.

3   The Learning Strategy

This section details the design of an agent's learning algorithm and exploration strategy in sections 3.1 and 3.2 respectively. The overall strategy is then pulled together in section 3.3.

3.1   The Q-Learning Algorithm

In previous work, we have proved (theoretically and empirically) that our marketplace enables an agent to relate the rewards it received to its G INQ segments [4]. Building on this basis, the contribution of this paper is in how to learn the expected revenue that is likely to accrue over its G segments. Such a strategy is desirable because high expected revenue on a specific segment implies that more rewards can be expected if it repeats bidding on that segment in future. Therefore, this subsection aims to address the problem of producing the expected revenue profile over an agent's G segments.

In detail, an agent needs to execute a set of *actions* (bidding on its G segments), $(a_1, a_2, \cdots, a_G)$, to learn the expected revenue of each segment ($R(a_i)$, $i \in [1..G]$). Specifically, an action a_i that results in its recommendation being displayed to the user must pay some amount of credit. Then, it may or may not receive an amount of reward (depending on whether its recommendation satisfies the user). We record the tth immediate reward that a_i has received as $r_{i,t}$ ($t = 1, 2, \cdots$). From a statistical perspective, the expected revenue can be obtained from the mean value of the series of discrete immediate reward values:

$$E[R(a_i)] = \lim_{t \to \infty} (\frac{1}{t} \sum_t r_{i,t}) . \tag{1}$$

In this context, the Q-learning technique provides a well established way of estimating the optimality [5]. In particular, we use a standard Q-learning algorithm to estimate $R(a_i)$ by learning the mean value of the immediate rewards:

$$\hat{Q}_i := (1 - \frac{1}{t}) \cdot \hat{Q}_i + \frac{1}{t} \cdot r_{i,t} , \tag{2}$$

where $\hat{Q}_i$ is the current estimate $R(a_i)$, and $\frac{1}{t}$ is the learning rate that controls how much weight is given to the immediate reward (as opposed to the old estimation). As $\frac{1}{t}$

decreases, $\hat{Q}_i$ builds up an average of all experiences, and the odd new unusual experience, $r_{i,t}$, does not significantly affect the established $\hat{Q}_i$. As t approaches infinity, the learning rate tends to zero which means that no learning is taking place. This, in turn, makes $\hat{Q}_i$ converge to a unique set of values that define the expected revenue of each segment.

PROPOSITION: *As $t \longrightarrow \infty$, $\hat{Q}_i$ converges to $E[R(a_i)]$.*
PROOF: We use $Q_{i,0}$ to represent the initial value of $\hat{Q}_i$, and $\hat{Q}_{i,t}$ to represent the local estimation to $R(a_i)$ when a_i has been experienced t times. $\hat{Q}_i$'s updates go:

$$\hat{Q}_{i,1} = 0 \cdot \hat{Q}_{i,0} + 1 \cdot r_{i,1} = r_{i,1}$$
$$\hat{Q}_{i,2} = \tfrac{1}{2} \cdot r_{i,1} + \tfrac{1}{2} \cdot r_{i,2} = \tfrac{1}{2}(r_{i,1} + r_{i,2})$$
$$\hat{Q}_{i,3} = \tfrac{2}{3} \cdot \tfrac{1}{2}(r_{i,1} + r_{i,2}) + \tfrac{1}{3} \cdot r_{i,3} = \tfrac{1}{3}(r_{i,1} + r_{i,2} + r_{i,3})$$
$$\vdots$$
$$\hat{Q}_{i,t} = \tfrac{1}{t}(r_{i,1} + r_{i,2} + \cdots + r_{i,t}) = \tfrac{1}{t}\sum_{j=1}^{t} r_{i,j}$$

As $t \to \infty$, $\lim_{t\to\infty}(\tfrac{1}{t}\sum_{j=1}^{t} r_{i,j})$ statistically defines $E[R(a_i)]$. ∎

This proof exemplifies how newly experienced immediate rewards, combined with the learning rate, produce convergence. With the Q-learning algorithm in place, an agent needs an exploration strategy to execute actions to build up its $\hat{Q}$ profile.

3.2   The Exploration Strategy

We assume all agents are self-interested and want to gain maximal revenue as they bid. However, before $\hat{Q}_i$ converges, it is difficult for an agent to know how much can be expected through each action and, therefore, which action it should choose. It is faced with the classic dilemma of choosing actions that have a well known reward or choosing new ones that have uncertain rewards (which may be higher or lower than the well known actions). To this end, the agent needs an exploration strategy over its G segments to build up its $\hat{Q}_i$ in an effective way so that it can know how much return can be expected from each segment.

In general, there is a fairly well developed formal theory for exploration strategies for problems similar to that faced by our agents [6]. However, the standard methods require very specific conditions (detailed in section 5) that do not hold in our context[2]. Specifically, the number of times that an agent can interact with the marketplace is not limited. Thus, the agent can gather as much information as it wants in order to form its expected revenue profile. Knowing how much can be expected through each action, an agent can use a probabilistic approach to select actions based on the law of effect [7]: *choices that have led to good outcomes in the past are more likely to be repeated in the future.* To this end, a *Boltzmann exploration* strategy fits our context well; it ensures

---

[2] In fact, it is hard to find the absolutely best strategy for most complex problems. In reinforcement learning practice, therefore, approaches tend to be developed for specific contexts. They solve the problems in question in a reasonable and computationally tractable manner, although they are often not the absolutely optimal choice [6].

the agent exploits higher $\hat{Q}$ value actions with higher probability, whereas it explores lower $\hat{Q}$ value actions with lower probability [6]. The probability of taking action a_i is formally defined as:

$$P_{a_i} = \frac{e^{\hat{Q}_i/T}}{\sum_{j=1}^{G} e^{\hat{Q}_j/T}} \qquad (T > 0). \tag{3}$$

where T is a system variable that controls the priority of action selection. In practice, as the agent's experience increases and all $\hat{Q}_i$s tend to converge, the agent's knowledge approaches optimality. Thus, T can be decreased such that the agent chooses fewer actions with small $\hat{Q}_i$ values (meaning trying not to lose credits) and chooses more actions with large $\hat{Q}_i$ values (meaning trying to gain credits).

In general, however, we have observed that the learning algorithm of equation (2) accompanied with the exploration strategy of equation (3) has a problem of producing bias from the optimal and very little work has been done to address this. This problem occurs when an agent obtains a very small negative $\hat{Q}_i$ value for a particular action in its first few trials[3]. If this happens, a bias from the true expected revenue of this action may occur (since the action may in general produce positive $R(a_i)$) and the agent will seldom choose it. This kind of bias is a particular problem in our system, because a user may not always visit all displayed items and, thus, some good recommendations may be skipped and, therefore, be deemed as bad ones. To avoid such bias, T needs to be assigned a very large value in the beginning of learning to limit the exploration priority given to those actions with very large $\hat{Q}$ values. However, controlling T in terms of producing the unbiased optimal strategy is hard to achieve, since different actions' $\hat{Q}$s converge with different speeds and their convergence is difficult to detect. Even with other exploration strategies, such biases still exist since no exploration can avoid such unlucky trials at the beginning of learning. To this end, we developed an algorithm that takes positive initial $\hat{Q}_i$ values into account to overcome this problem. We detail this in the next section.

3.3   The Overall Strategy

To overcome the impact of bias in the beginning of learning, we use positive initial $\hat{Q}$ values (i.e. $\hat{Q}_{i,0}$) and make them affect the learning. Thus, instead of algorithm (2), we use the following learning algorithm:

$$\hat{Q}_i := (1 - \frac{1}{t_0 + t}) \cdot \hat{Q}_i + \frac{1}{t_0 + t} \cdot r_{i,t} \ . \tag{4}$$

The difference between (2) and (4) is that the former does not take $\hat{Q}_{i,0}$ into account, whereas the latter does. Specifically, algorithm (4) assumes that each action has been experienced t_0 (t_0 is positive and finite) times and each time with a feedback of $\hat{Q}_{i,0}$ ($\hat{Q}_{i,0} \gg 0$) before the agent starts learning. This, in turn, removes the problem discussed in section 3.2. Indeed, if an action causes a negative immediate reward in the

---

[3] A negative immediate reward means punishment and an erroneous action. A reward of zero means that the action has received no feedback. Thus, actions with negative, zero and positive feedback are differentiated and exploration priority should be given to the latter two.

beginning, it does not force its $\hat{Q}_i$ to become negative. In this way, all actions will still be allocated a relatively equal opportunity of being explored as an agent begins learning. As the agent continues to interact with the marketplace, its $\hat{Q}_i$s update gradually to different levels and these levels still make its exploration follow the law of effect. Thus, the agent's exploitation tends to optimality with its $\hat{Q}$ values tending to converge. Additionally, by initializing $\hat{Q}$ with positive values, the exploration does not need a sophisticated control on T, since a relatively small positive value is sufficient and is easier to control. Moreover, the change from (2) to (4) does not affect the convergence.

PROPOSITION: *Given $\hat{Q}_i$'s definition by algorithm (4), its convergence to $E[R(a_i)]$ is independent of its initial value $\hat{Q}_{i,0}$ and initial time t_0.*
PROOF: $\hat{Q}_i$'s updates go:

$$\hat{Q}_{i,1} = \frac{t_0}{t_0+1} \cdot \hat{Q}_{i,0} + \frac{1}{t_0+1} \cdot r_{i,1}$$
$$\hat{Q}_{i,2} = (1 - \frac{1}{t_0+2})(\frac{t_0}{t_0+1} \cdot \hat{Q}_{i,0} + \frac{1}{t_0+1} \cdot r_{i,1}) + \frac{1}{t_0+2} \cdot r_{i,2}$$
$$= \frac{t_0}{t_0+2} \cdot \hat{Q}_{i,0} + \frac{1}{t_0+2} \cdot (r_{i,1} + r_{i,2})$$
$$\hat{Q}_{i,3} = (1 - \frac{1}{t_0+3})(\frac{t_0}{t_0+2} \cdot \hat{Q}_{i,0} + \frac{1}{t_0+2} \cdot (r_{i,1} + r_{i,2})) + \frac{1}{t_0+3} \cdot r_{i,3}$$
$$= \frac{t_0}{t_0+3} \cdot \hat{Q}_{i,0} + \frac{1}{t_0+3} \cdot (r_{i,1} + r_{i,2} + r_{i,3})$$
$$\vdots$$
$$\hat{Q}_{i,t} = \frac{t_0}{t_0+t} \cdot \hat{Q}_{i,0} + \frac{t}{t_0+t} \cdot \frac{1}{t} \cdot \sum_{j=1}^{t} r_{i,j}$$

Since t_0 is finite, $\lim_{t \to \infty} \frac{t_0}{t_0+t} \longrightarrow 0$ and $\lim_{t \to \infty} \frac{t}{t_0+t} \longrightarrow 1$.
Thus, $\lim_{t \to \infty} \hat{Q}_{i,t} \longrightarrow \lim_{t \to \infty} (\frac{1}{t} \sum_{j=1}^{t} r_{i,j}) = E[R(a_i)]$.   ∎

This proof shows that algorithm (4) also produces unbiased learning. Thus, we will use (4) and (3) for our agents and the overall strategy is detailed in Figure 2.

4   Evaluation

This section reports on the experiments to evaluate the learning strategy we have developed. The experimental settings are discussed in section 4.2, before the evaluations are presented in section 4.3. First, however, we discuss the criteria with which we can evaluate our design.

4.1   Evaluation Metrics

To evaluate the learning strategy we use the following evaluation metrics (the first two are concerned with an individual learner's performance and the second two are concerned with the performance of the collective of learners):

Convergence to Optimality: Many learning algorithms come with a provable guarantee of asymptotic convergence to optimal behaviour [5]. This criterion is included here to evaluate the quality of learning itself; it is important because if an algorithm does not converge, the agent will have no incentive to follow its behaviour.

Individual Rationality: All component recommenders in our system are self-interested agents that aim to maximise their revenue by bidding their recommendations [3]. Thus,

```
THE MAIN STRATEGY:
  for i = 1 to G do {
      Q̂_{i,0} = Q_{init};                                      // Initialize Q̂_i and Q_{init} ≫ 0
      t_i = 0;                                                 // Initialize t_i
  }
  do {
      for i = 1 to G do
          P_{a_i} = ExploreProbability( i, Q̂_1, Q̂_2,···, Q̂_G ); // Equation (3)
          a_k = ActionSelection( P_{a_1}, P_{a_2}, ···, P_{a_G} ) ★;   // k ∈ [1..G]
          t_k = t_k + 1;                                       // a_k has been experienced t_k times
          r_{k,t_k} = ImmediateReward( a_k );                  // compute immediate reward
          Q̂_k = UpdateQ( Q̂_k, t_k, r_{k,t_k} );                // Equation (4)
  } while (true)


★ METHOD ACTIONSELECTION:
  ActionSelection( P_{a_1}, P_{a_2}, ···, P_{a_G} ){
      double boundary[0..G];                                  // probability boundary for G segments
      for i = 0 to G do
          boundary[i] = 0;
      for i = 1 to G do                                       // compute the G actions' probability boundary
          for j = 1 to i do
              boundary[i] = boundary[i] + P_{a_j};
      double Rand = UniformRandom0to1() ♠;                    // generate a probability
      for k = 1 to G do
          if ( boundary[k − 1] ≤ Rand < boundary[k] )
              return a_k;                                      // select a random action based on its probability
  }
♠ UniformRandom0to1() returns a random value that follows a uniform distribution within the range [0, 1.0).
```

Fig. 2. The Learning Strategy

if an agent can make a profit by participate in a particular encounter it will do so. Thus, such individually rational mechanisms are important because, without them, there is no motivation for the agents to participate in the system.

Quick Market Convergence: If the prices of the displayed recommendations reach a steady state after a number of consecutive auctions, the market is convergent. In the analysis of our recommender system, we proved that convergence is necessary to ensure only the best items are displayed and that they are shortlisted in decreasing order of UPQ [4]. Therefore, a market that converges quickly means that it starts satisfying the user quickly. This is clearly important since a user will stop using a recommender if it takes too long to produce good suggestions.

Best Recommendation's Identification: A good recommender system should be able to identify the best recommendation (the one with the highest UPQ) quickly and suggest it frequently [8]. This is important because, otherwise, if the best recommendation cannot be identified and displayed, the user will stop using the system.

4.2   Experimental Settings

Having previously shown that our marketplace is capable of effectively incentivising good recommendation methods to relate their INQs to the UPQ [4], we will not discuss how the agents do this. Rather, here, we simply assume that there are four good recommendation methods (able to correlate their INQs to the UPQ) and four poor ones (unable to do so). Given a specific recommendation (Rec), the correlations of its UPQ to a good method's INQ (INQ_g) and to a poor one's (INQ_p) are described in equations (5) and (6) respectively ("$\not\cong$" means "has no relation to"):

$$UPQ(Rec) = INQ_g(Rec) \pm 0.1 \cdot random() \tag{5}$$

$$UPQ(Rec) \not\cong INQ_p(Rec) \tag{6}$$

where $random()$ returns a random value that follows a uniform distribution within the range [0, 1.0). This random value can be seen as the noise (or bias) between the INQ and the UPQ. All UPQ and INQ values are fixed within [0, 1.0). These values are chosen based on the experience of our previous work [4]. In each auction round the market-place calls for ten bids. We use an independent-selection user model to decide which recommendations displayed to the user will be rewarded [9, 4]. In this model, selecting one item is independent of selecting another and all recommendations with a UPQ higher than a particular threshold will be rewarded. Here, we set this threshold to 0.75. To correlate their INQs to the UPQs, all agents divide their INQ range into $G = 20$ equal segments. We assume that all agents share the same set of recommendations and each agent has at least ten items in each segment. Before starting to bid, Q_{init} is set to 250, $T = 200$ and $t_0 = 1$ for all agents. All agents are initially endowed with same amount of credit (65536). At the beginning, each agent will bid the same (128) for items from any segment, since it does not know which segments are more valuable than others.

4.3   Learning Strategy Effectiveness

Having outlined the configuration of the agents, this section details the evaluations. Among all the properties that we want the learning strategy to exhibit, convergence is the most important. Indeed, in its absence, an agent loses its basis to reason. Thus, we will start with experiments on the convergence of $\hat{Q}$ values.

Convergence to Optimality: To evaluate an agent's $\hat{Q}$ value convergence, we arranged 300 consecutive auctions. Among the eight agents, the first four employ the good rec-ommendation method and the last four employ the poor one. We find that, with a good method, an agent's $\hat{Q}$ values always converge such that high INQ segments' $\hat{Q}$s (cor-responding to high UPQ because of equation (5)) converge to high values and low INQ segments' $\hat{Q}$s converge to low values (see Figure 3(a)). Specifically, the $\hat{Q}$ val-ues of those INQ segments corresponding to the UPQs above the user's satisfaction threshold (0.75) converge proportionally to their corresponding UPQs. The higher the corresponding UPQ, the higher the $\hat{Q}_i$'s convergence value, because the recommenda-tions from a segment corresponding to higher UPQs receive more immediate reward than those corresponding to lower UPQs. The $\hat{Q}$ values of those segments that corre-spond to the UPQs below 0.75 converge to negative values, since they do not receive rewards if their recommendations are displayed. Moreover, the convergence is inde-pendent of the specific form of equation (5). Specifically, once there is a unique UPQ level corresponding to each INQ level (even high INQ corresponding to low UPQ), the $\hat{Q}$ value of an INQ segment corresponding to a high UPQ will always converge to a high level (since it induces high immediate rewards). However, with a poor method,

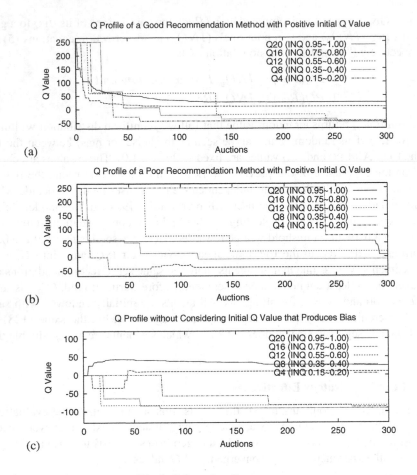

Fig. 3. Q-Learning Convergence

an agent's $\hat{Q}$ values cannot converge such that high INQ segments' $\hat{Q}$s converge to high values (see Figure 3(b)). This is because a specific INQ corresponds to very different UPQs (and very different immediate rewards) at different times because of equation (6).

To exemplify that our learning algorithm (4) overcomes the bias problem that may occur in (2), we organized another set of experiments with all agents taking zero initial $\hat{Q}_i$ values (all other settings remained unchanged (see Figure 3(c))). From Figure 3(c), we can see that $\hat{Q}_{12}$ is updated only once and with a very small value of -82 (this gives the corresponding action virtually no chance of being selected in future). $\hat{Q}_{16}$ also produces a bias in the beginning. In even worse cases, $\hat{Q}_{16}$ can never update itself like $\hat{Q}_{12}$ (although, it should actually have a positive expected revenue). However, with positive initial $\hat{Q}_i$ values, such biases do not occur (see Figure 3(a)).

Individual Rationality: The agents with good methods are able to know what recommendations better satisfy the user. Therefore, they can achieve more immediate rewards.

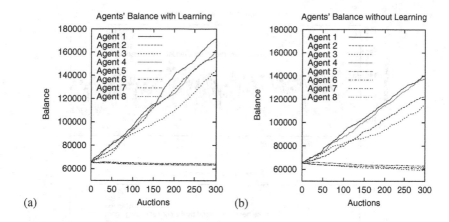

Fig. 4. Recommenders' Balance

Thus, good recommendations are raised more frequently by a learning agent than by a non-learning one. This, in turn, means learning agents can maximize their revenue by selecting good recommendations. In particular, Figure 4 shows that good recommendation methods with learning capability (the first four agents in Figure 4(a)) make, on average, significantly greater amounts (about 43%) of credit than those without (the first four agents in Figure 4(b)). With a poor method, the agents cannot relate their bids to the user's interest and therefore bid randomly. Thus, they cannot consistently achieve positive immediate rewards and their revenue is low (the last four agents in Figure 4 (a) and (b)).

Quick Market Convergence: We have shown that market convergence enables the agents to know what prices to bid for recommendations relating to certain UPQs so as to gain maximal revenue [3, 4]. Thus, quick market convergence lets agents reach this state quickly. To evaluate this, we organized two sets of experiments (using the same settings as the experiments assessing the convergence). The first one contains all learning agents and the other contains none. We find that a marketplace with learning agents always converges quicker than the one without. From Figure 5, we can see that a marketplace with learning agents (Figure 5(a)) converges after about 40 auctions, whereas one without (Figure 5(b)) converges after about 120 auctions. Indeed, as the learning agents' $\hat{Q}$ profiles converge, more high quality recommendations are consistently suggested (since their high $\hat{Q}$ values induce high probability for the agent to bid these items because of equation (3)) and low quality ones are deterred. This, in turn, accelerates effective price iterations to chase the market equilibrium. It takes approximately one third of the time for a market with learning agents to chase the equilibrium compared to one without.

Best Recommendation's Identification: To evaluate the learning strategy's ability to identify the best recommendation (from the viewpoint of the user, i.e. the top UPQ item) quickly and bid it consistently, we use the same set of experiments that were used to assess the market convergence. We then trace the top UPQ item highlighted by a randomly selected learning agent with a good recommendation method and a correspond-

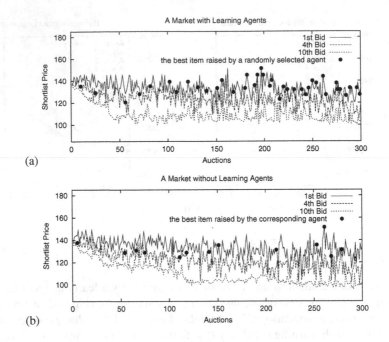

Fig. 5. Market Convergence

ing one from a non-learning agent in Figure 5 (a) and (b) respectively. We do this by plotting this top UPQ items' bidding prices with circle points in the figures. To clearly display the points of the trace and not to damage the quality of lines (representing the three displayed bids), we do not display the points when this item is raised by other agents. From Figure 5(a), we can see that this item's bidding price keeps increasing till it converges to the first bid price of the displayed items. This means that as long as the randomly selected agent chooses this particular item to bid in an auction (after the market converges), it is always displayed in the top position displayed to the user. However, in contrast, this phenomenon in a market without learning agents proceeds slowly (see Figure 5(b)). This means that a learning market can satisfy the user more quickly than a non-learning one. Additionally, a learning market raises the best recommendation more frequently (39 times by the selected learning agent, see Figure 5(a)) than a market without learning capability (13 times by the corresponding non-learning agent, see Figure 5(b)).

5   Related Work

The learning strategy presented in this paper significantly improves our previously reported market-based recommender system [3, 4] by speeding up the market's ability to make good recommendations. Previously, the strategy we developed for selecting which recommendations to bid was random (i.e. an agent randomly selects an item from any one of the G INQ segments in one auction round) [4]. While this strategy performed sufficiently to enable the viability of the market-based recommender to be evaluated, it sometimes presented poor recommendations for too long and learned the user's interests too slowly. In contrast, by learning the expected revenue of each INQ segment and consistently bidding on those items that have high expected revenue (since they satisfy the user), an agent quickly identifies the best recommendation and maximizes its revenue (making 43% more credits than our previous method). With all agents employing the learning strategy, the market converges quickly (in about one third of the time of the previous method) and satisfies the user more consistently (making high quality recommendations about three times as often as the previous method).

In terms of learning users' interests, most existing recommender systems use techniques that are based on two kinds of features of recommendations: objective features (such as textual content in content-based recommenders) and subjective features (such as user ratings in collaborative recommenders). For example, LIBRA is a book recommender system that extracts textual information from books that a user has previously indicated a liking for and learns his/her interests through the extracted contents [10]. GroupLens is a Usenet news recommender that predicts the INQ of a specific recommendation based on other users' ratings on it [8]. However, many researchers have shown that learning techniques based on either objective or subjective features of recommendations cannot successfully make high quality recommendations to users in all situations [11, 12, 2]. Thus, no one learning technique is universally best for all users in all situations. The fundamental reason for this is that these existing learning algorithms are built *inside* the recommenders and, thus, the recommendation features that they employ to predict the user's preferences are fixed and cannot be changed. Therefore, if a learning algorithm is computing its recommendations based on the features that are relevant to a user's context, the recommender is able to successfully predict the user's preferences (e.g. a customer wants to buy a "blue" cup online and the recommendation method's learning algorithm is just measuring the "colour" but not the "size" or the "price" of cups). Otherwise, if the user's context related features do not overlap any of those that the learning algorithm is computing on, the recommender will fail (e.g. the user considers "colour" and the learning algorithm measures "size").

To overcome this problem and successfully align the features that a learning technique measures with a user's context in all possible situations, we seek to integrate multiple recommendation methods (each with a different learning algorithm) into one single system and use an overarching marketplace to coordinate them. Essentially, our market-based system's learning technique encapsulates more learners and each learner computes its recommendations based on some specific features. Thus, our approach has a larger probability of relating its features to the user's context and so, correspondingly, has a larger opportunity to offer high quality recommendations.

In terms of general work on market-based recommendations, the most related work to our own is that of [9]. This work uses a market to competitively allocate consumers' attention space in the domain of retailing online products (such as PC peripherals). Here, the scarce resource is the consumer's ability to focus on a set of banners or products. However, both this work and our own use the market mechanisms in different ways to help recommendations. The market in [9] is used only to coordinate agents' bidding, whereas ours is used not only for this purpose, but also to correlate the INQ to the UPQ of recommendations (i.e. the quality classification and alignment).

6   Conclusions and Future Work

To be effective in a multi-agent recommender system (such as our market-based system), an individual agent needs to adapt its behaviour to reflect the user's interests. However, in general, an agent initially has no knowledge about these preferences and it needs to obtain such information, but, in so doing, it needs to ensure that it continues to maximize its revenue. To this end, we have developed a quality classification mechanism and a reinforcement learning strategy that achieve this balance. Essentially, our approach enables an agent to classify its recommendations into different categories (based on its own quality measure) and then direct the right categories of items to the right users (by learning their interests by bidding and by receiving rewards). Specifically, through empirical evaluation, we have shown that our strategy works effectively at this task. In particular, a good recommendation method equipped with our learning strategy is capable of rapidly producing a profile of the user's interests and maximizing its revenue. Moreover, a market in which all agents employ our learning strategy converges rapidly and identifies the best recommendations quickly. Finally, we showed that our Q-learning strategy with positive initial $\hat{Q}$ values avoids bias. For the future, however, we need to carry out more extensive field trials with real users to determine whether the theoretical properties of the strategy do actually hold in practice.

References

1. Resnick, P., Varian, H.R.: Recommender Systems. Communications of the ACM **40** (1997) 56–58
2. Herlocker, J., Konstan, J., Terveen, L., Riedl, J.: Evaluating collaborative filtering recommender systems. ACM Transactions on Information Systems **22** (2004) 5–53
3. Wei, Y.Z., Moreau, L., Jennings, N.R.: Recommender systems: A market-based design. In: Proceedings of International Conference on Autonomous Agents and Multi Agent Systems (AAMAS03), Melbourne (2003) 600–607
4. Wei, Y.Z., Moreau, L., Jennings, N.R.: Market-based recommendations: Design, simulation and evaluation. In: Proceedings of International Workshop on Agent-Oriented Information Systems (AOIS-2003), Melbourne (2003) 22–29
5. Mitchell, T.: Machine Learning. McGraw Hill (1997)
6. Kaelbling, L.P., Littman, M.L., Moore, A.W.: Reinforcement learning: A survey. Journal of Artificial Intelligence Research **4** (1996) 237–285
7. Thorndike, E.L.: Animal intelligence: An experimental study of the associative processes in animals. Psychological Monographs **2** (1898)
8. Konstan, J.A., Miller, B.N., Maltz, D., Herlocker, J.L., Gordon, L.R., Riedl, J.: Grouplens: Applying collaborative filtering to usenet news. Communications of the ACM **40** (1997) 77–87
9. Bohte, S., Gerding, E., Poutré, H.L.: Market-based recommendation: Agents that compete for consumer attention. ACM Transactions on Internet Technology **4** (2004) 420–448

10. Mooney, R.J., Roy, L.: Content-based book recommending using learning for text catego-
    rization. In: Proceedings of the 5th ACM Conference on Digital Libraries, TX, US (2000)
    195–204
11. Shardanand, U., Maes, P.: Social information filtering: algorithms for automating "word
    of mouth". In: Proceedings of Conference on human factors in computing systems. (1995)
    210–217
12. Montaner, M., Lopez, B., Dela, J.L.: A taxonomy of recommender agents on the internet.
    Artificial Intelligence Review **19** (2003) 285–330

SNet Reloaded: Roles, Monitoring and Agent Evolution

Günter Gans[1], Dominik Schmitz[1], Thomas Arzdorf[1], Matthias Jarke[1,2], and Gerhard Lakemeyer[1]

[1] RWTH Aachen, Informatik V, Ahornstr. 55, 52056 Aachen, Germany
[2] Fraunhofer FIT, Schloss Birlinghoven, 53754 Sankt Augustin, Germany
{gans, schmitz, jarke, lakemeyer}@cs.rwth-aachen.de

Abstract. In previous work, we proposed the prototype environment SNet for the representation and dynamic evaluation of agent-based designs for inter-organizational networks. A key feature of SNet is the automatic translation of extended i* models into the action language ConGolog. In order to run realistic simulations, the resulting agents are deliberative in that they can choose between different courses of action according to some utility measure. When applying SNet to modelling an existing entrepreneurship network, we discovered a number of deficiencies of our current proposal, in particular, the lack of a role concept, the ability to monitor the execution of plans that depend on other agents' contributions and the ability to model agents that evolve over time. In this paper we will sketch the example domain and discuss how these new features can be incorporated in the SNet framework.

1 Introduction

In previous work, we proposed the prototype environment SNet to model strategic inter-organizational networks, which are comprised of human, organizational, and technological actors [5]. A crucial aspect of these networks are the interdependencies among the various actors, which result, for example, from the need to delegate certain activities, which in turn requires a certain level of trust between the (human) members of the network. The agent-based graphical modelling language i* [19], which was developed for early requirements engineering, has proven to be particularly suitable as a modelling means in this context because it explicitly deals with dependency relations, besides other notions of actors, goals, resources and tasks. To capture the dynamic aspects of agent networks we [3] and Wang and Lespérance [18] independently proposed to amalgamate i* and the action formalism ConGolog [2]. To bridge the gap between the two formalisms we extended i* by features to describe task preconditions and effects. These extended i* diagrams are automatically translated into executable ConGolog programs, supported by the metadata manager ConceptBase [9]. Running simulations for different scenarios within a network is useful for analyzing its properties and can provide the foundation of a decision-support tool for network members.

P. Bresciani et al. (Eds.): AOIS 2004, LNAI 3508, pp. 68–84, 2005.
© Springer-Verlag Berlin Heidelberg 2005

In recent work [4] we introduced a decision-theoretic planning component for each network representative to run even more realistic simulations, but up to now we modelled only toy examples. Currently we are considering, for the first time, a real-world example taken from the entrepreneurship domain. modelling the MIT entrepreneurship network in SNet in detail – based on transcripts of interviews colleagues made on site – has revealed three major deficiencies of our current proposal.

- The original i* framework already supports agent abstraction mechanisms called *roles*. These are missing in the current version of SNet, which makes it very awkward to use when modelling large applications.
- When delegating tasks to other agents, it is often important for the delegator to *monitor* the progress of the delegatee's activities. So far, however, there is no support for this in SNet.
- As we will see, an important feature of the entrepreneurship domain is that agents evolve over time in systematic ways, and it would be helpful to explicitly represent these transitions within the model.

In this paper, we will introduce the entrepreneurship domain and discuss ongoing work on how roles, monitoring and agent evolution can be incorporated into the SNet framework.

The rest of the paper is organized as follows. In Section 2, we introduce our SNet simulation and modelling tool and the example from the entrepreneurship domain. After that, each of the three identified challenges is presented in its own section, i. e. the ideas concerning a role concept are discussed in Section 3, the monitoring mechanism in Section 4, and agent evolution in Section 5. We end the paper with a brief discussion.

2   The Modelling and Simulation Environment SNet

2.1   The Architecture of the SNet Tool

We base our modelling and simulation environment SNet for inter-organizational networks on a combination of two formalisms: i^* – a graphical modelling language originally intended for describing early requirements – for statically modelling the network and *ConGolog* – a logic-based high-level programming language – for simulations so that dynamic aspects such as trust can be analyzed. We take an agent-oriented view in that each actor of an inter-organizational network is represented by a deliberative agent. We will discuss the features of the two formalisms in more detail later on. First we give a short overview of their overall interplay. The SNet architecture is depicted in Figure 1.

We use *OME3* (Organization Modelling Environment) – a graphical model editor developed at the University of Toronto [11] – to build up static models of inter-organizational networks in the modelling language i* [19]. The semantics of i* are defined in the knowledge representation language Telos [15], which is also the formalism underlying *ConceptBase* [9], a deductive metadata repository.

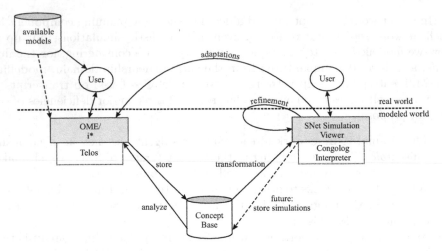

Fig. 1. SNet Architecture

The ConceptBase query language can be used for static analyses and especially for the transformation into ConGolog. The execution of the resulting ConGolog program is shown in a step-by-step view by the simulation viewer, which also provides access to control the simulation run, i.e. the user creates scenarios by simulating the proactivity of network members and investigates how this and resulting delegations affect relationships (especially trust). Conclusions derived by the user from such simulations might lead to modifications of the model or scenario conditions that provide the basis for new simulation runs.

2.2   The Entrepreneurship Domain

During a four-month-stay at MIT Sloan School Entrepreneurship Center, colleagues interviewed about 20 different kinds of people inside the entrepreneurship community. Based on this information we are currently building up an example of a strategic inter-organizational network.

Figure 2 gives a rough impression of the actors involved in the entrepreneurship network as well as their dependencies, represented as a strategic dependency model in the i* formalism. Roughly, the circles denote actors, and labelled directed connections between them denote dependencies (for the meaning of the different labels see the legend of Figure. 3). The entrepreneurship centre plays a central role and has a vitalizing effect on the whole network culture. By participating in networking events, all members can exchange information and it is quite easy for potential entrepreneurs to get in touch with possible investors and to communicate their business ideas. Such a network depends highly on trust relationships. Venture capitalists (VCs), e.g., who plan to support an entrepreneur financially, trust in the professional expertise of faculty members concerning business ideas.

The Technology Licensing Office (TLO) is responsible for handling intellectual property. At MIT, the TLO awards the intellectual property developed at

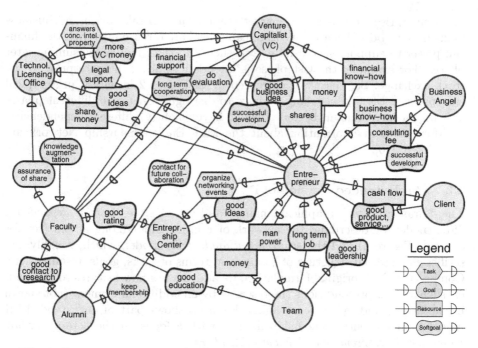

Fig. 2. Strategic Dependency (SD) Model of the MIT Entrepreneurship Network

MIT-laboratories in equal shares to the inventor (a potential entrepreneur), the faculty and MIT. In return, the TLO provides legal support to protect intellectual property.

An entrepreneur evolves in phases which correlate with financing rounds [16]. Financial support is typically provided by business angels and venture capitalists. In general, the former were successful entrepreneurs in the past with domain-specific knowledge who prevailingly invest in the so-called seed stage

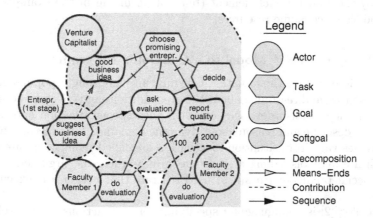

Fig. 3. Modelling in i*/SNet

of an enterprise. In this stage, market studies have to take place and business plans have to be elaborated. Venture capitalists are often banks with the financial power to support successful entrepreneurs in their money consuming later phases. For example, the last phase is intended to bring the enterprise to the stock exchange. So, the actor entrepreneur in Figure 2 is only a prototypical entrepreneur. Strictly speaking we have to distinguish between different phases of being an entrepreneur, because they all have (slightly) different dependencies.

More detailed information about the MIT Entrepreneurship Network are available in [10].

2.3   An Extended Version of i*

The i* framework is a graphical language and includes the *strategic dependency (SD)* model for describing the network of relationships among actors (see for example Figure 2) and the *strategic rationale (SR)* model, which, roughly, describes the internal structure of an agent in terms of tasks, goals, resources etc. Compared to Yu's original formulation, we added a few new features to SR models such as task preconditions (represented by an additional element (not shown in the figure) and by sequence links). Figure 3 shows part of an extended SR model from the entrepreneurship domain with a focus on the actors *Venture Capitalist, Entrepreneur* and *Faculty Members*.

The venture capitalist's task *choose_promising_entrepreneur* is decomposed into three subtasks, which are partially ordered using *sequence links* (an easy to use form of a task precondition). The task *suggest_business_idea* is delegated to the actor *Entrepreneur*. Goals like *ask_evaluation* provide a means of specifying alternatives from which the modelled agent (respectively represented network member) can choose at runtime. In this example, the venture capitalist can choose to ask *Faculty Member 1* or *Faculty Member 2* for evaluation. Softgoals are used to specify the criteria on which the deliberative component bases its decision, e. g. *report_quality*. Tasks can have preconditions and effects, represented by their own model element (but not occurring in the example above), and produce or consume resources.

2.4   Mapping the i* Model to a ConGolog Program

ConGolog is based on the situation calculus, an increasingly popular language for representing and reasoning about the preconditions and effects of actions [14]. It is a variant of first-order logic, enriched with special function and predicate symbols to describe and reason about dynamic domains. Relations and functions whose values vary from situation to situation are called *fluents*, and are denoted by predicate symbols taking a situation term as their last argument. There is also a special predicate $Poss(a, s)$ used to state that action a is executable in situation s.

ConGolog [2] is a language for specifying complex actions (high-level plans). For this purpose, constructs like sequence, procedure and *if-then-else*, but also non-deterministic (e. g. *ndet*) and concurrency (e. g. *conc*) constructs are provided. ConGolog comes equipped with an interpreter, which maps these plans into sequences of atomic actions assuming a description of the initial state of the world, action precondition axioms and successor state axioms for each fluent. For details see [2].

The mapping of the i* elements results in a possibly non-deterministic program. A complex task is transformed into a procedure whereby the body is derived from the sub-elements. The sequential relations between the sub-elements are reflected via the use of sequence and *conc*. There are primitive actions preceding and following the body, so that the preconditions to and effects of this element can be reflected in the program. Resources and softgoals are represented by fluents. Precondition/effect elements (and for consistency reasons also sequence links) are mapped to precondition axioms and effect axioms, respectively.

Here is an excerpt of the transformation into ConGolog of the *Venture Capitalist* modelled in Figure 3.

$$proc(choose\_promising\_entrepreneur(venture\_capitalist),$$
$$[\,pre\_choose\_promising\_entrepreneur(venture\_capitalist),$$
$$delegate(suggest\_business\_idea(entrepreneur)),$$
$$ask\_evaluation(venture\_capitalist),$$
$$decide(venture\_capitalist)$$
$$post\_choose\_promising\_entrepreneur(venture\_capitalist)])$$

The task *choose_promising_entrepreneur* is turned into a procedure. In general, while calling its sub-elements, concurrency is used whenever possible. Delegated subtasks are specially marked. (Sub-)Tasks which are not decomposed any further are turned into primitive actions such as *decide*, for which precondition axioms (*poss*) and effect axioms (see Sect. 3) need to be specified.

$$poss(decide(venture\_capitalist), s) \equiv$$
$$fulfilled(ask\_evaluation(venture\_capitalist), s)$$

The task *decide(venture_capitalist)* is executable in situations s *iff* the fluent *fulfilled(ask_evaluation(venture_capitalist), s)*, which denotes that the goal *ask_evaluation(venture_capitalist)* has been achieved, holds in situation s.

The transformation of goal elements and their fulfilling tasks is rather similar to the one of complex tasks, but the sub-elements are combined by the nondeterministic choice operator *ndet* to reflect the fact that one of these alternatives has to be chosen at runtime. We leave this out here for reasons of space.

To run simulations we provide an environment which equips each agent with a decision theoretic planning component to reason about which alternative to choose according to the specified criteria (softgoals). See [4] for details.

2.5   From Limits Towards New Challenges

In the following we concentrate on three challenges which result from the attempt to model the MIT entrepreneurship network in SNet.

Role concept. As can easily be seen from the example, real-world models can become very large (see for example Figure 2 which is on the SD modelling level only!). It is unrealistic to expect that, for such big networks modelling each agent instance individually in the SR model is feasible. Furthermore, a key feature of strategic networks is redundancy. Despite minor differences there are often several network members capable of doing the same task,[1] e. g., in the entrepreneurial environment there is not just one venture capitalist and not just one faculty member able to assess business ideas. To enforce explicit modelling of the same capability over and over again seems a waste of effort. Thus, the idea now is to use roles and positions, which are already present in the original i*, to specify capabilities more generally and provide the instantiation separately. The challenges concerning this will be discussed in Sect. 3.

Monitoring. In the current SNet implementation, the delegator is not in a position to observe, evaluate and influence any of the tasks she delegated until they are finished. Especially in the context of long term delegations, this seems unnatural. For instance, the venture capitalist wants to be aware of the entrepreneur's activities, after giving him $ 1,000,000. Monitoring progress during the execution of tasks is one means of estimating possible risks in order to be able to avert worst-case scenarios and emphasizes the important role of distrust in inter-organizational networks as proposed in [3]. More details are discussed in Sect. 4.

Agent evolution. Another aspect which becomes apparent from our real-world example is that network members evolve over time. As already mentioned, several financial stages through which an entrepreneur evolves can be identified (see [16]). During evolution, possibilities, capabilities and dependencies of a network member change. Since our goal is to provide decision support for members of real-world networks, the agent society representing the network under consideration must reflect what is happening in the real world. This means also that the development of agents in a simulation is not arbitrary. A specification of how an agent can evolve might be known in advance and a way to specify this should accordingly be provided. Ideas concerning this challenge are presented in Sect. 5.

3   Modelling Roles Instead of Individual Agents

In [20] Yu and Mylopoulos present a detailed description of the actor elements available in i*. They define a *role* to be an abstract actor with which dependencies should be associated if they apply, regardless of who plays the role. In contrast to this, an *agent* is a concrete manifestation of an actor and can have dependencies that apply regardless of what roles are played by this agent. Finally, a *position*

---

[1] This results from the insight that, to enforce flexibility, competition between network partners should occur.

is used as an intermediate abstraction in that it describes a set of roles that are typically assigned jointly to one agent. A position is said to cover roles and an agent is said to occupy a position. *Actor* is used as the unifying general concept with all the described sub types as specializations.

In the entrepreneurial environment only the Technology Licensing Office (TLO) and the entrepreneurship centre can be seen as individual agents, because only one instance exists. For all the other actors (e. g. venture capitalist) we implicitly see them as roles which have to be instantiated.

For a choice between redundant capabilities to make sense, their offerings must differ. Thus, elements of a role or a position must be identified that can be instantiated. A close look at our current modelling practice (see Section 2 or more detailed in [4]) reveals that at least the *duration of tasks* and the *contributions towards softgoals* should be parameters to a role and thus specified during instantiation. The range of these parameters is simply numerical.

For example, the two faculty members who were introduced in the example in Figure 3 differ in the way they do evaluations. Say *Faculty Member 1* needs only 1 week whereas *Faculty Member 2* needs 2 weeks but provides a more detailed analysis which manifests itself in a higher *report_quality*.

For the instantiation of roles, parameterized by duration and softgoal contributions (note that an agent is of course allowed to instantiate more than one role), we propose as a first realization a simple table-based approach which queries the prespecified parameters for each instance of a role. Since this information simply extends the abstract model, it is easy to allow for constructing different scenarios that can then be evaluated in simulations.

Although there is a big conceptual difference between our previous practice of explicit agent modelling and modelling roles that have to be instantiated, this so far does not have a great impact on the transformation procedure and the resulting ConGolog programs. We already use the identifier of an agent as a parameter to all primitive actions, procedures or fluents which result from its modelling. Thus, the different instantiations of a role can simply be "compiled" into ConGolog code. For instance, the different contributions to the softgoal *report_quality* by the two faculty members are reflected as follows:

$$report\_quality(do(a, s)) = rq \quad \equiv$$
$$(a = do\_evaluation(faculty\_member\_1) \land rq = report\_quality(s) + 100)$$
$$\lor\ (a = do\_evaluation(faculty\_member\_2) \land rq = report\_quality(s) + 2,000)$$
$$\lor\ (a \neq do\_evaluation(faculty\_member\_1)$$
$$\land\ a \neq do\_evaluation(faculty\_member\_2)\ \land\ rq = report\_quality(s))$$

Executing an action a in situation s leads to a new situation where the fluent *report_quality* gets a new value: rq. If a is *do_evaluation(faculty_member_1)* (*do_evaluation(faculty_member_2)*) then rq, the report quality in situation s, is increased by 100 (2, 000). Otherwise, the report quality stays the same.

One obvious advantage of this new feature is that alternatives for delegating a task need not be represented explicitly any more (see [4])). The transformation procedure expands a delegation to a wide non-deterministic choice between the instantiating agents upon which the delegator agent has to decide at runtime using its deliberative planning component.

In earlier papers (e. g. see [4]) we discussed more general differences between Wang and Lespérance's [18] and our approach to the combination of i* and Con-Golog. Concerning the transformation of roles and positions they map a role only into a procedure but similarly use a parameter to identify instances. In contrast to our proposal they do not provide any means to allow for differences between instances. Furthermore in SNet the execution of a role's activity is initiated on demand (i. e. results either from simulated pro-activity or a delegation request) and is not simply procedurally driven.

The means to instantiate a role presented here are still rather simplistic and presumably not sufficient. Instances of a role can differ in more than only parameters concerning duration and softgoal contributions, e. g., a third faculty member might be able to internally choose between alternatives to serve both types of evaluation requests – fast ones and extensive high-quality ones. While i* admits specialization links between actor elements a clear formalization is missing. But with ConGolog as a foundation it seems possible to provide a formalization of specializing behavior, an area we are currently investigating.

4   Monitoring in SNet

4.1   A General Monitoring Framework

We begin by sketching a general framework for monitoring within strategic inter-organizational networks. We concentrate on monitoring between two actors (delegator and delegatee) who have an ongoing delegation relationship. Figure 4 gives an overview of the framework. Conceptually we distinguish between a *rationale layer* and an *activity layer*. The former is used to specify the underlying agent-internal rationales. The latter details how an actor actually performs monitoring. We propose three phases namely initiating monitoring, gathering information, and drawing conclusions. This control cycle like structure may constitute monitoring in our context.

The *Rationale Layer* shows how, within an ongoing delegation relationship, the delegator decides on the *monitoring importance* on the basis of experiences made with the delegatee and the subjective *expectation* of the delegatee's progress. The monitoring importance together with the *costs* for the various possible monitoring activities serve as the input for the computation of the *monitoring utility*, which subsequently determines when, how and to which degree to monitor next.

Initiating Monitoring. At the activity layer, the *initiating monitoring* component's responsibility is to activate monitoring at the right time. If, for example, the delegator has had good experiences with the delegatee, the losses to be expected are low – maybe the importance of the task is low – or monitoring in this context is expensive, then the next monitoring time need not occur soon.

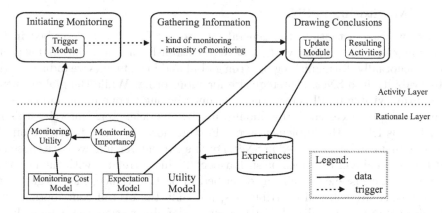

Fig. 4. A General Monitoring Framework

Gathering Information. Monitoring can be done at different levels, which often correlates with costs and the quality of information. For example, the venture capitalist gets information about the entrepreneur she gave a lot of money to by reading the newspaper, making phone calls, visiting the entrepreneur or even – more expensively – hiring a consultant with domain-specific knowledge.

Drawing Conclusions. The delegator's utilities and experiences with the partner have to be updated after information has been gathered. New information serves as a better estimation of the current risks and the expectations concerning the monitored task. Additionally, the extent of the discrepancy between the expected performance of the delegated task and the monitored performance has an influence on what further activities the delegator takes (increase future monitoring activities, reconsider situation by searching for better alternatives or even abort the cooperation directly to avoid wasting any more resources). In our example it might be a suitable decision for the VC to cancel her financial funding if the entrepreneur fails to meet her expectations.

In [6] De Giacomo, Reiter, and Soutchanski describe execution monitoring of high-level robot programs within the action language ConGolog. They introduce a logic-based mechanism for recovering from observed discrepancies between the real world and its internal representation. While they monitor an agent's own plan in execution, we propose to monitor tasks that are delegated to other agents. Consequently we do not have a direct influence but can only revise the cooperation. Monitoring is also done in financial risk management systems – as one representative see [17], which is based on intelligent agents. Here it is important that monitoring happens in real-time. The agents are purely reactive and are specialized, e. g., on the collection of data or to give an alert whenever predefined thresholds are exceeded. In other words, these agents are only a kind of "intelligent sensors" and do not represent human actors.

4.2   Monitoring in SNet

Before we can instantiate the general monitoring framework described in the preceding section for SNet we first have to establish some foundational aspects. By conceptually distinguishing between global and local fluents we induce partial observability into SNet, a prerequisite for monitoring. While the global fluents are always visible to all actors, the local ones belong to one actor and can only temporarily be accessed during monitoring by the delegator. Enforcing this restriction is left to the implementation. Furthermore, we have to decide on the aspects that can be monitored in SNet. For the current version, we have chosen to let the softgoal contributions be such aspects. This correlates with the fact that these are also instance-specific as described in Sect. 3. Hence, the delegator can see intermediate softgoal contributions, not only the overall contribution after the delegated task is finished. Further aspects of observation might be included in the future.

In the remaining monitoring section, we illustrate our first monitoring mechanism for SNet by referring again to the entrepreneurship example. We mainly focus on the rationale layer, which enables us to determine the next monitoring time and briefly sketch the other aspects. Figure 5 shows a long term delegation between a venture capitalist (VC) and an entrepreneur. The situation is as follows. The VC has agreed to the business plan proposed by the entrepreneur. A market study has taken place and as a result the whole project seems to have a realistic chance of big success. Additionally, an appropriate office has been found and the VC is willing to support the first three months financially in order to give the entrepreneur the chance to hire five employees, buy hardware and make a first prototypical implementation of the software to be developed.

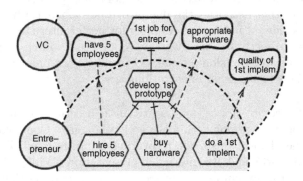

Fig. 5. A long term delegation

Thus, to instantiate the expectation model of the general framework the delegator must have an expected development of each softgoal contribution in her mind. These are represented by real-valued functions $\hat{e}(t)$, $\hat{h}(t)$, and $\hat{i}(t)$ over the time (defined in Figure 6).

A utility function combines these expected softgoal contribution functions to a function of the expected utility development over the time. To keep it simple

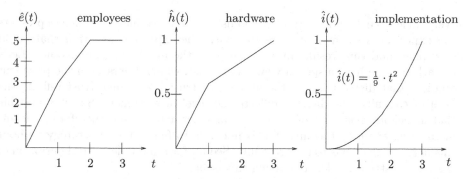

Fig. 6. Expected development of contributions

the utility-functions are user-defined linear combinations. Thus, the relevance of the different criteria can be controlled by their weights, i.e. a weight of zero is assigned if a criterion is irrelevant.

$$Util(t) = 4,000 \cdot e(t) + 20,000 \cdot h(t) + 60,000 \cdot i(t)$$
$$ExpUtil(t) = 4,000 \cdot \hat{e}(t) + 20,000 \cdot \hat{h}(t) + 60,000 \cdot \hat{i}(t)$$

While $ExpUtil(t)$ is the expected utility at time t, with $Util(t)$, we denote the utility based on the actual contributions – $e(t)$, $h(t)$, and $i(t)$ – which are the values of the corresponding (local) fluents visible for the delegator via the information gathering activity at the monitoring time t. So, for example, the overall expected utility of the whole delegation, i.e. after 3 months, is

$$ExpUtil(3) = 4,000 \cdot 5 + 20,000 \cdot 1 + 60,000 \cdot 1 = 20,000 + 20,000 + 60,000 = 100,000.$$

The trigger module uses this as one important input to derive the next monitoring time (we use a discrete time model, see [4] for details) by determining the smallest value nmt satisfying the following inequality:

$$ExpUtil(nmt) - ExpUtil(now) > \frac{\alpha}{Distrust} \cdot MonitoringCosts$$

where now is the current moment, $Distrust \in [0,1]^2$ and α a positive real constant. $1/\alpha$ denotes the maximum portion of the expected utility gain the delegator is willing to spend on monitoring. The $MonitoringCosts$ must be specified by the user because they are domain specific. Notice that monitoring importance and monitoring utility are not instantiated explicitly but encoded into the formula above. In our example, since normally the VC has the right to see the entrepreneur's performed tasks and can take a look into the books, the information gathering is quite easy and therefore the resulting monitoring costs are low.

As a very SNet-specific feature the above computation includes *distrust*. In SNet a delegator stores a distrust value – a real between zero and one – for

---

[2] For $Distrust = 0$ monitoring need not occur. Thus, nmt is set to ∞.

every delegatee as one part of a sophisticated trust model, which represents the experiences so far and correlates with the expected deviation that could take place and thus results in a measure for the monitoring importance. Let's remark that we have a special view on distrust, which differs from the prevalent opinion, that distrust is just the absence of trust [12]. While trust reflects the level of commitment, distrust reflects the level of awareness. So, it is possible that somebody has a lot of distrust in another actor – and therefore performs monitoring again and again – but is not able to find a better strategy without this actor. So, she has to act trustfully. See [3] for a more detailed description of the trust-distrust model supporting this issue.

Now intuitively the above inequality does the following. Let's suppose the distrust-value is maximal, i. e. 1. Monitoring is useful if the increment of the expected utility from now till the next monitoring point is higher than the multiple α of the monitoring costs. For instance α is chosen to be 10 and the *MonitoringCosts* are 2,000 then monitoring should happen when the expected utility has grown by 20,000. If distrust is halved the next threshold for monitoring would be doubled. Of course, the proposed formula is quite simple and – among others – does not mention monitoring results. Thus, it will presumably be elaborated in the future.

Beside the re-calculation of the distrust value, which thus indirectly influences the determination of the next monitoring time, the VC in our example might notice that the entrepreneur is not able to hire any employees, i. e. supporting the corresponding softgoal. Thus, as one way to draw conclusions she might decide to ask an agent who is specialized on hiring employees and willing to help. The specification of this could be incorporated into the i* model by means of an exception or fault handling mechanism similar to the one in BPEL4WS [1]. This is left for future work.

5   Meta Agent Development *(MAD)*

Using the term "Meta Agent Development" to describe this framework emphasizes that specifying the possibilities regarding how an agent might evolve concerns a different level than specifying the functioning of a role and the dependencies towards other roles. Agent evolution inevitably concerns time and taking history into account. It must be possible to refer to roles played earlier, to the time that has passed since, maybe also to some measure on how successful an agent was playing a role.

Furthermore, the introduction of the concept of agent development enforces a different transformation of the i* model in that we can no longer provide a hardwired representation of an agent's capabilities. Mathieu, Routier, and Secq [13] propose a model of agency that is able to represent agent development. They consider an agent to be built from an atomic agent by dynamic skill acquisition. In our context, this can be achieved by means of a relational fluent $roles(Agent, Role, s)$ and appropriate actions modifying this fluent. This enables the assignment to be dynamically accessed and modified from within simulations.

Returning to our example from the entrepreneurship domain, one could state that an entrepreneur e in Stage 1 is allowed to evolve to Stage 2 iff a faculty f certifies successful development, a venture capitalist vc decides to invest more money and the entrepreneur has been in the first stage for at least 3 months.[3]

$precondition$(entrepreneur2ndStage, e, s) $\equiv$
$\exists f$ ($roles(faculty, f, s) \wedge confirm\_successful\_development(f, e, s)$)
$\wedge$ $\exists vc$ ($roles(venture\_capitalist, vc, s) \wedge decision\_to\_invest(vc, e, s)$)
$\wedge$ $\exists s'$ ($time(s) = now \wedge time(s') = t \wedge (now - t) > 3\ months$ $\wedge$
$\forall s''(s \geq s'' \geq s' \supset roles(e, \text{entrepreneur1stStage}, s'')$)))

To eventually install the feature of agent development we need some new high-level mechanism (similar to the planning component) provided by the simulation environment which allows an agent to change (acquire, loose) roles according to the conditions specified. While for a first realization we assume that satisfied conditions enforce a role transition, for some domains it might be more realistic to allow an agent to deliberate about possible role transitions. In this case, some additional criteria on which to base the decision must be modelled. This is also the reason why we propose to avoid specifying transitions explicitly (e. g. via automata or procedural descriptions) but prefer to associate preconditions with each role. This provides more flexibility in that it allows for development (i. e. a series of roles) that the modeler possibly has not thought of – thus combining the ability to specify development with self-adaptability of the agents during a simulation.

Returning to our example, the above formula would then be associated with the role *Entrepreneur 2nd stage* as a precondition, e. g. as an attribute. Since currently we assume that satisfied conditions enforce role transitions, this can simply be realized by a primitive action *change_role* which changes the fluent *roles* appropriately via an effect axiom if the corresponding condition is fulfilled.[4]

$roles(Agent, Role, do(a, s))$ $\equiv$
$(a = change\ role \wedge precondition(Role, Agent, s))$ $\vee$ $\ldots$

The reader should note the difference between the role concept of Section 3 and agent evolution. While roles (contrasting individual agents) are used *statically* when instantiating the model, agent development as described in this section occurs at *runtime.*

Finally, we remark that Gross and Yu [7] are also concerned with a form of system evolution. However, they are mainly concerned with changing business goals, which are introduced into the model manually, that is, they do not envisage making the process of evolution part of the model itself, as in our case. One reason for this might be that in the RE context, in which i* normally is used, agent

---

[3] That a new role enforces losing a role played earlier, e. g. an entrepreneur that evolves can only be in one stage at a time, has to be modelled explicitly. Furthermore a Markovian version of this formula can easily be imagined by collecting information concerning roles played earlier in some agent specific fluent.

[4] Despite conceptual differences here a *precondition* somehow equals a *poss* axiom.

evolution is much less predictable. Hoogendoorn et al. [8] deal with the integration of change processes in a formal multiagent organizational model. Similar to our approach, they describe the structure of and the dynamics within organizations separately (of course we regard networks). Their underlying formalism for specifying the dynamic aspects (Temporal Trace Language) is comparable to the situation calculus we use. However, while in their approach the change process is driven by the organizational view, we focus on the development of the individuals.

6   Conclusion

In this paper we proposed extensions to our modelling and simulation environment SNet, which aim at coping with real-world examples taken from the entrepreneurship domain. We concentrated on three aspects: a role concept, monitoring and agent evolution. The introduction of the role concept improves the modelling facilities by segregating the more abstract model from the details of agent instances and thus alleviates the modelling of larger networks. The monitoring considerations relate to our model of trust especially the distrust component and respond to the demand to be able to cope with long-term delegations. Similarly, the extension concerning agent evolution also reflects a requirement of the real world where such knowledge is available and hence should also be regarded in the simulations.

For each aspect we see that further improvements can be achieved. In particular, a more sophisticated way to instantiate a role by specializing behavior can be formalized with the help of ConGolog. In the proposed monitoring concept especially the possibilities for specifying reactions to monitoring results are much more multifaceted than captured up to now. In our model of agent evolution the interactions between roles and their evolution can be elaborated. But most important is the evaluation of the whole approach, since it is now possible to model real-world examples.

Acknowledgment

This work was supported in part by the Deutsche Forschungsgemeinschaft in its Priority Program on Socionics, and its Graduate School 643 "Software for Mobile Communication Systems".

References

1. T. Andrews.   Business process execution language for web services, IBM, version 1.1, 2nd public draft release.   http://www.ibm.com/ developerworks/ webservices/library/ws-bpel, May 2003.
2. G. de Giacomo, Y. Lespérance, and H.J. Levesque. ConGolog, a concurrent programming language based on the situation calculus: language and implementation. *Artificial Intelligence*, 121(1-2):109–169, 2000.

3. G. Gans, M. Jarke, S. Kethers, and G. Lakemeyer. Continuous requirements management for organization networks: A (dis)trust-based approach. *Requirements Engineering Journal, Special Issue on selected papers from RE'01, Springer*, 8(1):4–22, Feb. 2003.

4. G. Gans, M. Jarke, G. Lakemeyer, and D. Schmitz. Deliberation in a modeling and simulation environment for inter-organizational networks. In *Proc. of the 15th Int. Conf. on Advanced Information Systems Engineering (CAiSE03)*, LNCS 2681, pages 242–257, Klagenfurt, Austria, June 2003.

5. G. Gans, M. Jarke, G. Lakemeyer, and T. Vits. SNet: A modeling and simulation environment for agent networks based on i* and ConGolog. In *Proc. of the 14th Int. Conf. on Advanced Information Systems Engineering (CAiSE02)*, LNCS 2348, pages 328–343, Toronto, Canada, May 2002.

6. G. De Giacomo, R. Reiter, and M. Soutchanski. Execution monitoring of high-level robot programs. In *Proc. of the 6th Int. Conf. on Principles of Knowledge Representation and Reasoning (KR'98)*, pages 453–465, 1998.

7. D. Gross and E. Yu. Evolving system architecture to meet changing business goals: an agent and goal-oriented approach. In *ICSE-2001 Workshop: From Software Requirements to Architectures (STRAW 2001)*, pages 13–21, Toronto, Canada, May 2001.

8. M. Hoogendoorn, C. Jonker, M. Schut, and J. Treur. Modeling the organisation of organisational change. In *Proc. of the 6th Int. Bi-Conf. Workshop on Agent-Oriented Information Systems (AOIS04)*, pages 29–46, 2004.

9. M. Jarke, S. Eherer, R. Gallersdörfer, M. A. Jeusfeld, and M. Staudt. Concept-Base - a deductive object base for meta data management. *Journal of Intelligent Information Systems, Special Issue on Advances in Deductive Object-Oriented Databases*, 4(2):167–192, 1995.

10. M. Jarke, R. Klamma, and J. Marock. *Zu den Wirkungen des regionalen Kontexts auf Unternehmensgründungen*, chapter Gründerausbildung und Gründernetze im Umfeld technischer Hochschulen: ein wirtschaftsinformatischer Versuch, pages 115–154. EUL-Verlag, 2003.

11. L. Liu and E. Yu. Organization Modeling Environment (OME). WWW, [Accessed March 1, 2005]. http://www.cs.toronto.edu/km/ome.

12. S. Marsh. *Formalising Trust as a Computational Concept*. PhD thesis, Dept. of Computer Science and Mathematics, University of Stirling, April 1994.

13. P. Mathieu, J.-C. Routier, and Y. Secq. Dynamic skills learning : a support to agent evolution. In *Proceedings of AISB'01*, pages 25–32, York, 2001.

14. J. McCarthy. Situations, actions and causal laws. Technical report, Stanford University, 1963. Reprinted 1968 in Minsky, M.(ed.): Semantic Information Processing, MIT Press.

15. J. Mylopoulos, A. Borgida, M. Jarke, and M. Koubarakis. Telos - representing knowledge about information systems. *ACM Transactions on Information Systems*, 8(4):325–362, October 1990.

16. K. Nathusius. *Grundlagen der Gründungsfinanzierung. Instrumente - Prozesse - Beispiele*. Gabler, Wiesbaden, 2001.

17. H. Wang, J. Mylopoulos, and S. Liao. Intelligent agents and financial risk monitoring systems. *Comm. of the ACM*, pages 83–88, March 2002.

18. X. Wang and Y. Lespérance. Agent-oriented requirements engineering using ConGolog and i*. In *Working Notes of the Agent-Oriented Information Systems (AOIS-2001) Workshop, Montreal, QC*, May 2001.

19. E. Yu. *Modelling Strategic Relationships for Process Reengineering.* PhD thesis, University of Toronto, 1995.
20. E. Yu and J. Mylopoulos. Understanding "why" in software process modelling, analysis and design. In *Proc. of the 16th Int. Conf. on Software Engineering (ICSE)*, pages 159–168, Sorrento, Italy, 1994.

Analyzing Multiparty Agreements with Commitments

Feng Wan and Munindar P. Singh

Department of Computer Science,
North Carolina State University,
Raleigh NC 27695, USA

Abstract. Multiparty agreements often arise in a multiagent system where autonomous agents interact with each other to achieve a global goal. Multiparty
agreements are traditionally represented by messaging protocols or event-
condition-action rule sets in which agents exchange messages in a predefined
sequence to ensure both global and local consistencies. However, these models
do not readily incorporate agents' autonomy and heterogeneity, which limits their
ability to help build a flexible open system. Commitments have been studied for
modelling various agent interactions. This paper introduces commitments as the
key elements in formulating multiparty agreements. Our model focuses on how
agents may negotiate with each other to build a mutual agreement based on their
individual constraints. The actual execution sequence is validated by checking the
compliance of commitment casual relations. Our approach is geared toward constructing business processes where agents are mutually constrained in a manner
that preserves their autonomy and heterogeneity.

1   Introduction

In a multiagent system, agents can autonomously decide on whether to perform or not
perform a particular action. When agents coordinate with each other to achieve a global
task, they need to first create a multiparty agreement, that would satisfy global goals as
well as the agents' individual constraints. Multiparty agreements in agent communities
are more subtle than in other software systems where agreements are represented by
fixed protocols and each party has to follow the same execution sequences. Agents are
able to perceive, reason and act so that they can more freely express themselves and
flexibly interact with each other.

Researchers have studied multiparty agreements from several perspectives, such as
developing FIPA standards [3] for heterogeneous agents to communicate with and understand each other; implementing domain-specific protocols such as the fish market
and auction protocols; approaches toward building software agents such as designing
AUML [7] and statecharts [5]; developing business processes using BPEL [1]. Existing
approaches define interaction frameworks that limit agents' choices.

An example scenario is when a buyer wants to buy some goods from a seller. The
buyer may require the seller to ship the goods before he would pay. The seller may
require the buyer to pay before he would ship. Various approaches exist to resolve such
a situation in the real world. For instance, the buyer can make an advance deposit; or
the buyer can give the seller his credit card but the seller will ship the goods before he

P. Bresciani et al. (Eds.): AOIS 2004, LNAI 3508, pp. 85–96, 2005.

charges the card; or the buyer and seller can use an escrow service to ensure successful execution of all the instructions. In the computer world, the different approaches lead to different protocols that each software agent must follow. This leads to two questions of interest. How can the agents derive different protocols to achieve agreement? What semantics must be incorporated into the agreements?

There is a rich literature on how agents form teams and negotiate on global execution plans, e.g., [10]. Here we present another idea which starts from the representation of multiparty agreements based on commitments. Commitments represent the obligations made between pairs of agents and are used to model interactions in a multiagent system. Commitments help agents express promises and monitor each other's compliance without regard to internal details. This paper uses commitments as the basic elements to form multiparty agreements. Next, it detects potential deadlocking constraint dependencies and resolves them by executing selected protocols that are proposed here.

The paper is organized as follows. Section 2 introduces the basic concepts of commitments and their causal relations. Section 3 shows how multiparty agreements can be represented by commitments. Section 4 describes how to detect and resolve commitment inconsistencies. Section 5 discusses our contributions.

2   Commitments and Causality

A commitment is an obligation from a debtor to a creditor about a particular condition. For debtor x, creditor y, and condition p, the relevant commitment is notated $C(x, y, p)$ and is read as "agent x commits to y to bring about p." There are two kinds of commitments, unconditional and conditional.

- *Unconditional commitment.* A commitment whose condition is a simple proposition, such as shipping goods or making payment.
- *Conditional commitment.* A commitment of the form $C(x, y, e \rightarrow p)$, where e could be a condition, an event or another commitment and p is a condition to be brought about (or an action to be performed). p is activated when e becomes true. An example of a conditional commitment is when a customer promises to pay for a trip only if his travel agent confirms one for him.

Commitments enable agents to express prospective actions while retaining flexibility about how to respond to unexpected circumstances. This substantially differentiates them from abstractions such as actions, whose occurrence are more definite and thus reduce the agents' flexibility. This paper shows how commitments help model flexible and sound agreements.

2.1   Commitment Operations

Commitments support several operations that combine to capture mutual and multiparty scenarios [9]. For the sake of simplicity, this paper is limited to four main operations. The four operations, *create*, *update*, *discharge*, and *cancel*, drive the lifecycle of commitments. A commitment is initially created when an agent makes a promise to another agent. If the commitment has been fulfilled, e.g., the actions involved have been performed or the conditions have become true, then the commitment is discharged. However, before the commitment is discharged, the agents involved can possibly update the

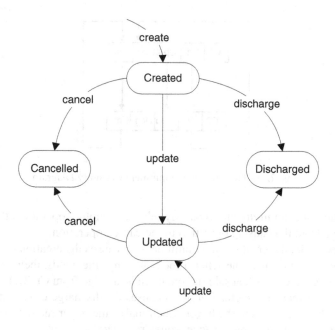

Fig. 1. Commitment life cycle

commitment. The update operation gives flexibility in manipulating agents' context to react to any potential requirement changes or exceptions. Agents can also cancel their commitments, e.g., to accommodate exceptions. However, to cancel a commitment, agents usually face penalties that compensate for whatever inconsistencies that they may have introduced. Figure 1 shows the state diagram of the commitment lifecycle.

2.2   Commitment Causality

In previous work [12], we showed that causal relations among commitments are crucial to understanding the chain of commitment operations because they drive an interaction along significant states where the real transactions of domain value occur. A *commitment causality diagram (CCD)* is a graph showing potential causality between each pair of commitment operations. A CCD highlights the important stages within the information flows and hides details of the interaction protocols that can vary depending on the actual implementation. From a designer's standpoint, a CCD reflects the high-level business logic that specifies what agreements should be achieved.

Figure 2 shows a CCD derived based on the following two commitments, in which a buyer commits to a seller that if the seller commits to ship the goods then the buyer will pay for it, and the seller commits to the buyer to ship the goods.

$$C_1 = C(buyer, seller, C(seller, buyer, ShipGoods) \rightarrow Pay)$$
$$C_2 = C(seller, buyer, ShipGoods)$$

Each node consists of five elements, namely, the commitment identifier and its associated four operations: *create* (Crt), *update* (Upd), *discharge* (Dcg) and *cancel* (Cnl).

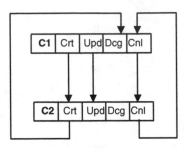

Fig. 2. An Example of Commitment Causality Diagram

If an operation of a commitment is causally related to another operation, then there is a directed edge from the causing operation to the caused operation.

In this example, the creation of commitment C_1 causes the creation of commitment C_2 since the buyer promises the seller if the latter ships the goods, then the former will pay for it. To represent this causal relation, there is an edge from $Crt(C_1)$ to $Crt(C_2)$.

For the same reason, the creation of C_2 causes the discharge of C_1 since the seller promises to ship the goods to the buyer which makes the buyer ready to pay the seller. This relation is represented by the edge from $Crt(C_2)$ to $Dcg(C_1)$.

The edge from $Upd(C_1)$ to $Upd(C_2)$ denotes that the buyer could change his original condition in C_1. For example, he may require that the buyer ship goods by a specific date. This change may still be acceptable to the seller because he definitely wants to sell the goods. Therefore the seller will update his commitment C_2 and thus keep the business activity valid.

If any exception arises, such as the buyer deciding to cancel the order or the seller finding that the goods are out of stock, then either commitment could be cancelled, which results in the cancellation of the other commitment.

A CCD helps us glue the operations under the same commitments together, which simplifies the business process modelling. Therefore, the primary goal of our current approach is to derive a CCD from a business agreement. This inevitably leads to the development of this paper, which describes how to represent multiparty agreements using commitments and how to validate the consistency of the agreements and produce a sound CCD.

3   Representing Multiparty Agreement Using Commitments

Let's first discuss the basic forms of commitments of relevance to agreements. A multiparty agreement is expressed by a set of the following four basic commitments. These commitments are differentiated by the preconditions that need to be satisfied for the debtor to make a commitment to its creditor.

F_1: Unconditional Commitment $C(x, y, q)$.
      Agent x commits to y to perform q unconditionally.
      For example, $C(seller, buyer, ShipGoods)$.

F_2: Action-Triggered Commitment $C(x, y, p \to q)$.

Agent x commits to y to perform q only if p happens.

For example, $C(seller, buyer, InStock \to ShipGoods)$.

F_3: Unconditional Commitment-Triggered Commitment $C(x, y, C(z, x, p) \to q)$.

Agent x commits to y to perform q only if agent z commits to x to perform p.

For example, $C(seller, buyer, C(buyer, seller, Pay) \to ShipGoods)$. Here $z = y$ $= buyer$.

F_4: Conditional Commitment-Triggered Commitment $C(x, y, C(z, x, p \to r) \to q)$.

Agent x commits to y to perform q only if agent z commits to x to perform r when p happens. For example,

$C(seller, buyer, C(buyer, seller, ShipGoods \to Pay) \to ShipGoods)$. Here $z = y = buyer$.

Based on the commitment definition described in section 2, we can see that form F_1 is an unconditional commitment and form F_2, F_3 and F_4 are conditional commitments. Classifying conditional commitments into the three forms enable us to study the subtleties of the causal dependencies. For example, the fulfilment of F_2 relies on a concrete action to be performed, but the fulfilment of F_3 relies only on a promise that is built upon the trustiness between the two agents. F_4 also relies on promises but is weaker than F_3 since the promise is conditional and may not be fulfilled if the condition does not hold.

Definition 1. *A multiparty agreement A is given by a set of commitments $\{C_1, C_2, \cdots, C_n\}$ where $C_i \epsilon \{F_1, F_2, F_3, F_4\}$*

Definition 2. *A multiparty agreement is satisfiable if and only if for any $C(x_i, y_i, q_i)$, q_i will eventually become true or is performed; or for any $C(x_i, y_i, p_i \to q_i)$, q_i will eventually become true or is performed if p_i becomes true.*

The intuition is that, if the CCD derived from a commitment set has cycles involving either *create* or *discharge* nodes, then the preconditions of the commitments on those cycles form deadlocking dependencies. This means that no condition would be brought about, so that the commitment set is not satisfiable. Therefore, we have the following theorem.

Theorem 1. *If the CCD derived from a multiparty agreement shows cycles on its* create *or* discharge *nodes, then the corresponding multiparty agreement is not satisfiable.*

3.1   Derivation Rules

Here we give a set of rules to reduce an agreement (or a commitment set) to a set of conditions that all the agents would eventually bring about. The purpose of the deductions is to show how the interactions progress given a commitment set. This will also give us a way to detect potentially deadlocking agreements. For simplicity, we do not consider the *cancel* and *update* operations, which usually digress from normal executions and do not help detecting deadlocks introduced by the original commitment set.

In the following rules, the notation $p \xrightarrow{t} q$ states that if p happens, then q must happen within a finite time t. If q does not happen, which means the agent does not make q true after p becomes true, then we call it a violation of the rule.

$E_1 : Discharge(\mathsf{C}(x, y, q)) \Rightarrow q$

$E_2 : Discharge(\mathsf{C}(x, y, p \rightarrow q)) \Rightarrow q$

$E_3 : Create(\mathsf{C}(x, y, p)) \Rightarrow Discharge(\mathsf{C}(x, y, p))$

$E_4 : p \wedge Create(\mathsf{C}(x, y, p \rightarrow q)) \Rightarrow Discharge(\mathsf{C}(x, y, p \rightarrow q))$

$E_5 : Create(\mathsf{C}(z, x, p)) \wedge Create(\mathsf{C}(x, y, \mathsf{C}(z, x, p) \rightarrow q))$

$\quad \Rightarrow Discharge(\mathsf{C}(x, y, \mathsf{C}(z, x, p) \rightarrow q)) \xrightarrow{t} Discharge(\mathsf{C}(z, x, p))$

$E_6 : Create(\mathsf{C}(z, x, p \rightarrow r)) \wedge Create(\mathsf{C}(x, y, \mathsf{C}(z, x, p \rightarrow r) \rightarrow q))$

$\quad \Rightarrow Discharge(\mathsf{C}(x, y, \mathsf{C}(z, x, p \rightarrow r) \rightarrow q)) \wedge (p \xrightarrow{t} Discharge(\mathsf{C}(z, x, p \rightarrow r)))$

E_1 and E_2 show that the results of the *discharge* of both unconditional and conditional commitments are the conditions or actions they bring about; E_3 states that an unconditional commitment will be eventually discharged after it is created. E_4 states that an action-triggered commitment will be discharged after the action occurs; E_5 states that an unconditional commitment-triggered commitment will be discharged after the unconditional commitment is created, and this discharge eventually trigger the discharge of the unconditional commitment; E_6 states that a conditional commitment-triggered commitment will be discharged after the conditional commitment is created, and the conditional commitment must be discharged if its condition is satisfied.

3.2   An Example Derivation

Now we can put the two commitments C_1 and C_2 in section 2.2 into one agreement $A = \{\mathsf{C}_1, \mathsf{C}_2\}$. Based on the above rules, we have the following derivation

$A \longrightarrow Create(\mathsf{C}(seller, buyer, ShipGoods)) \wedge$

$\qquad Create(\mathsf{C}(buyer, seller, \mathsf{C}(seller, buyer, ShipGoods) \rightarrow Pay))$

$\xrightarrow{E_5} Discharge(\mathsf{C}(buyer, seller, \mathsf{C}(seller, buyer, ShipGoods) \rightarrow Pay)) \xrightarrow{t}$

$\qquad Discharge(\mathsf{C}(seller, buyer, ShipGoods))$

$\xrightarrow{E_2} Pay \xrightarrow{t} Discharge(\mathsf{C}(seller, buyer, ShipGoods))$

$\xrightarrow{Pay} Discharge(\mathsf{C}(seller, buyer, ShipGoods))$

$\xrightarrow{E_1} ShipGoods$

By collecting all the actions or conditions on the derivation arrows, which is Pay in this example, and the results of the derivation, which is ShipGoods, we see that both actions in the two commitments have been performed, thus we say this agreement is satisfiable.

4   Building Satisfiable Agreements

In a multiagent system, each individual agent can have its local constraints. The agents' commitments not only specify their protocols, but also factor in their local constraints (which in essence limit what the agents can promise others). However, since the agents are autonomous, the constraints of different agents may form cyclic dependencies. Let us return to the example described in the introduction. A buyer wants the seller to ship the goods first before he makes the payment, but the seller may want the buyer to pay first before he ships the goods. The two commitments can be expressed as follows.

$$C_1 = C(buyer, seller, ShipGoods \rightarrow Pay)$$
$$C_2 = C(seller, buyer, Pay \rightarrow ShipGoods)$$

Apparently, neither party will proceed because of the deadlocking dependencies. Our goal is to detect these cyclic constraint dependencies and propose several protocols to resolve them and produce a satisfiable commitment set.

4.1   Detecting Unsatisfiable Agreements

Algorithm 1 detects whether an agreement is satisfiable or not. The symbol $*$ refers to a wildcard that matches any agent or condition. For the sake of simplicity, the condition p and q here are atomic predicates which only serve for specifying constraint dependencies. In the future, we will extend p and q to compound predicates and derive the subsumptive relations among these conditions so as to deal with more complicated business agreements.

By executing this algorithm on the above commitment set, we obtain the following graph (as shown in Figure 3). Apparently both the *create* and the *discharge* paths are cyclic, which means this commitment set is not satisfiable and cannot be enacted.

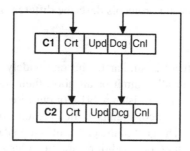

Fig. 3. A Deadlocking Agreement

4.2   Resolving Agreement Deadlocks

Deadlocking constraints imposed on a group of agents do not mean that these agents can not engage activities at all. Autonomous agents can negotiate to serve their interests. To break these deadlocking dependencies, all the agents may choose to commit what they promise to do for the others regardless of what constraints they impose on the others, or

---

1 Draw a node for each commitment with its identifier and two operations, Crt and Dcg;
2 **for** *each commitment* C_i **do**
   | **switch** C_i **do**

3 | | **case** $C(x, y, p)$ *or* $C(x, y, * \to p)$
   | | | For any commitment C_j where $C_j = C(y, *, p \to *)$ or
   | | | $C(y, *, C(x, y, p) \to *)$, add an edge from Dcg($C_i$) to Dcg($C_j$);

4 | | **case** $C(x, y, p \to *)$ *or* $C(x, y, C(*, x, p) \to *)$
   | | | For any commitment C_j where $C_j = C(*, x, p)$ or $C(*, x, * \to p)$, add an
   | | | edge from Crt(C_i) to Crt(C_j);

5 | | **case** $C(x, y, C(*, x, * \to r) \to q)$
   | | | For any commitment C_j where $C_j = C(*, x, * \to r)$, add an edge from
   | | | Crt(C_i) to Crt(C_j);

6 In the resulting graph, if there exists at least one cycle in one of the *create* or *discharge*
   paths, then the commitment set is not satisfiable; otherwise, it is.

Algorithm 1. Detecting Unsatisfiable Agreements

some of the agents may concede to satisfy the others first before their own constraints are satisfied. All these approaches lead to a variety of protocols for forming satisfiable multiparty agreements.

For the sake of simplicity, this paper only introduce the protocols that resolve the constraint conflicts created from the action-triggered commitments (F_2). For generality, we choose a three commitment scenario shown below,

$$C(x, y, p \to q), C(y, z, q \to r), C(z, x, r \to p)$$

By applying algorithm 1, we can tell the *create* and *discharge* path are cyclic and there exist deadlocks. The following protocols describe different approaches to resolve this inconsistency.

2PC Protocol. This protocol is similar to the one widely used in database systems where task executors either all commit or all abort their transactions to achieve task atomicity and preserve system consistency [4]. For our research, we apply this protocol to agents that have deadlocking constraints, which prevents them from discharging any commitment to each other. The goal of the protocol is to make sure that all the involved agents commit first before their preconditions are met. Our 2PC protocol only resolves the cyclic *discharge* path since, in this scenario, the discharge of one commitment will satisfy the precondition of another commitment and we can let all the discharges unconditionally happen so that all commitments will be fulfilled. Algorithm 2 shows the steps of the 2PC protocol.

By executing the 2PC protocol, q, r, and p will be unconditionally performed by x, y, and z, respectively. Once these conditions become true, they also satisfy each precondition in the above commitments. In terms of this aspect, the 2PC protocols essentially convert all the conditional commitments to their corresponding unconditional

1 A coordinator tells all the agents that are involved in a cyclic *discharge* path that a 2PC protocol is started;

2 Each agent will send yes or no to indicate whether they want to unconditionally discharge their commitments or not;

3 If all the answers are yes, then the coordinator sends yes to each agent and then each agent will replace its conditional commitment with a corresponding unconditional commitment by removing the preconditions;

4 If at least one answer is no, then the coordinator sends no to each agent and an alternative protocol will be pursued.

Algorithm 2. 2PC Protocol

commitments under all agents' willingness. Therefore, the above three commitments become

$$C(x, y, q), C(y, z, r), C(z, x, p)$$

An assumption of the 2PC protocol is that, for any commitment $C(x, y, p \rightarrow q)$, p is not required to happen before q, but must happen eventually. However, some commitments may require that p happens before q can happen. In this case, when not all the agents are willing to commit unconditionally, we need to seek other protocols to resolve the conflicts.

Unconditional Yield. If one agent is willing to convert its conditional commitment to an unconditional commitment, we say that this agent yields unconditionally. In the above example, agent x may promise y to perform q without being satisfied by p first. This usually happens when the debtor of p, which is z in this example, has developed enough credit with x that makes the latter believe that p will be eventually performed by z, even after x's unilateral concession. Here we construct a protocol to convey x's intention and propagate it to other agents to make corresponding commitment changes.

1 A coordinator notifies all the agents that are involved in a cyclic *discharge* path and a Unconditional Yield protocol is started;

2 Each agent will send yes or no to indicate whether they want to unconditionally discharge their commitments or not;

3 If at least one agent answers yes, then the coordinator picks the first agent (say agent x) who answers yes and notify the results to all the agents;

4 The agent x convert its action-triggered commitment (F_2) to an unconditional one (F_1) and all other agents will keep their commitments (F_2) unchanged.

Algorithm 3. Unconditional Yield Protocol

By executing the protocol on the above example, the 3 commitments are changed to

$$C(x, y, q), \ C(y, z, q \rightarrow r), \ C(z, x, r \rightarrow p)$$

Agent x will commit q unconditionally to y based on its belief that agent z will eventually commit p to it if r happens.

Conditional Yield. Conditional yield is similar to unconditional yield, but differs in that the agent willing to make an unconditional commitment does not have enough trust in any other agents. It must conditionally rely upon other agents' promises to it before it can perform its action. In such a case, the agent will replace its action-triggered commitment with a conditional commitment-triggered commitment. The protocol is described as Algorithm 4.

---

1 A coordinator notifies all the agents that are involved in a cyclic *discharge* path and a Conditional Yield protocol is started;

2 Each agent will send yes or no to indicate whether they want to conditionally discharge their commitments or not;

3 If at least one agent answers yes, then the coordinator picks the first agent (say, agent x) who answers yes and notify the results to all the agents;

4 The agent x converts its action-triggered commitment (F_2) to a conditional commitment (F_4) and all other agents will keep their commitments (F_2) unchanged.

Algorithm 4. Conditional Yield Protocol

By executing the protocol on the above example, the 3 commitments are changed to

$$\mathsf{C}(x, y, \mathsf{C}(z, x, r \rightarrow p) \rightarrow q), \ \mathsf{C}(y, z, q \rightarrow r), \ \mathsf{C}(z, x, r \rightarrow p)$$

Looking back the two conflicting commitments shown in section 4, the Conditional Yield protocol will produce the following outcome.

$$\mathsf{C}_1 = \mathsf{C}(buyer, seller, \mathsf{C}(seller, buyer, Pay \rightarrow ShipGoods) \rightarrow Pay)$$
$$\mathsf{C}_2 = \mathsf{C}(seller, buyer, Pay \rightarrow ShipGoods)$$

This result shows that the buyer yields to the seller to pay first by taking the promise from the seller saying if the buyer pays then the seller ships the goods.

To improve efficiencies, in the future work, we will study decentralized protocols which allow agents to relax their constraints without a centralized coordinator and the voting processes. In such decentralized settings, we need to consider protocol safeties to prevent agents who do not have global views of constraints from discharging their commitments prematurely which may lead to inconsistencies.

5 Discussion

A recent development in teamwork theory [8] presents an idea on forming teams among heterogeneous agents who have no coordination capabilities in a manner that ensures robust execution of the teamwork. The authors use a proxy called Teamcore to wrap those stand-alone agents with teamwork capabilities so that any type of agents can join a team and collaborate with others to achieve a global goal. This research differs from ours in that it searches for passive agents with special capabilities and convert them to team members, whereas ours is based on active agents who seek services from or do business with other agents. It is these active agents who decide how to perform a team task instead of a team organizer who picks agents and imposes behaviours on them.

The research of constraint satisfaction problems (CSP) in distributed systems, e.g., [6], has shown much promise. The models behind CSP are computational since the entire multiagent environment and individual agents are represented by variables, formulae, and constraints, which are made ready to compute based on mathematical rules. However, these models in most cases require homogeneous agents who sense and act in exactly the same manner, so they are not suitable for a real business-to-business world where parties are heterogeneous and loosely coupled. Our approach trades off complexity in the agent models with flexibility of the agents' behaviors. The outcome of our problem-solving is a set of satisfiable commitments.

Commitments are widely recognized as the key elements to capture the interactions among pairs of agents [2]. The essence of the commitments is to create a structure to specify the obligations that each agent makes to others. By tracking the lifecycles of these commitments, we are able to monitor agents' external behaviors and detect any violation and system inconsistency without knowing the agents' internal structure [11]. Most researchers emphasize how commitments are fulfilled or whether they are violated after they have been created, but few have studied whether the commitment can coexist at the very beginning. This is the aspect studied in this paper. In other words, we develop a means to detect deadlocking commitments and resolve them to ensure the progress of agent interactions.

Business-to-business applications are the main motivation for our ideas. By looking at the existing approaches that model business processes, such as Agent UML (AUML) [7], Business Process Execution Language (BPEL) [1], or state charts [5], we can observe that they all impose inflexible protocols in which things must happen in the predefined order in order for a successful business execution. Agents have no chance to express whether they want to perform tasks differently or not. Commitments enable agents to tell each other what they are going to do and what conditions that have to be satisfied to make it happen. All these communications could keep going until a sound agreement to be made before a single domain-level task is performed. This not only enables autonomous agents to perform their tasks based on their self interest but also avoids potential deadlocking system interactions caused by improper assumptions made by each agent. The goal of our approach is to incorporate commitment concepts into the above protocol standards and enable an open and flexible environment for various parties doing business.

This paper introduced commitments as the key elements to formulate a multiparty agreement by which we derive agent interactions, detect potential commitment deadlocks and resolve these deadlocks. The approach is a natural extension of our recent work on commitment casual relations where the interaction among business agents can be modeled by commitments and their causal relations while agent autonomy and heterogeneity are still preserved.

Key future directions include several aspects. One, we will study a decentralized protocols to resolve commitment deadlocks which eliminates an extra point of failure caused by the centralized coordinator. Two, during the execution of a multiparty agreement, new unsatisfiable commitments could be created, so we need an algorithm to detect them during runtime. Three, we will develop a XML specification for the commitment based model and incorporate it into the existing BPEL4WS specifications which enable the agent technology into real B2B applications so as to reveal its concrete usability.

References

1. BPEL. Business process execution language for web services, version 1.1, May 2003. www-106.ibm.com/developerworks/webservices/library/ws-bpel.
2. Cristiano Castelfranchi. Commitments: From individual intentions to groups and organizations. In *Proceedings of the International Conference on Multiagent Systems*, pages 41–48, 1995.
3. FIPA. FIPA interaction protocol specifications, 2003. FIPA: The Foundation for Intelligent Physical Agents, http://www.fipa.org/repository/ips.html.
4. Jim Gray and Andreas Reuter. *Transaction Processing: Concepts and Techniques*. Morgan Kaufmann, San Mateo, 1993.
5. David Harel, Amir Pnueli, Jeanette P. Schmidt, and Rivi Sherman. On the formal semantics of statecharts. In *IEEE Symposium on Logic in Computer Science*, pages 54–64. IEEE Computer Society Press, 1987.
6. Jiming Liu, Han Jing, and Y.Y. Tang. Multi-agent oriented constraint satisfaction. *Artificial Intelligence*, 136:101–144, 2002.
7. James Odell, H. Van Dyke Parunak, and Bernhard Bauer. Extending UML for agents. In *Proceedings of the Agent Oriented Information Systems Workshop at the 17th National Conference on Artificial Intelligence (AAAI)*, 2000.
8. David V. Pynadath and Milind Tambe. An automated teamwork infrastructure for heterogeneous software agents and humans. *Journal of Autonomous Agents and Multi-Agent Systems*, 7:71–100, 2003.
9. Munindar P. Singh. An ontology for commitments in multiagent systems: Toward a unification of normative concepts. *Artificial Intelligence and Law*, 7:97–113, 1999.
10. Milind Tambe. Agent architectures for flexible, practical teamwork. In *Proceedings of the National Conference on Artificial Intelligence*, pages 22–28, 1997.
11. Mahadevan Venkatraman and Munindar P. Singh. Verifying compliance with commitment protocols: Enabling open Web-based multiagent systems. *Autonomous Agents and Multi-Agent Systems*, 2(3):217–236, September 1999.
12. Feng Wan and Munindar P. Singh. Commitments and causality for multiagent design. In *Proceedings of the 2nd International Joint Conference on Autonomous Agents and MultiAgent Systems (AAMAS)*, pages 749–756. ACM Press, July 2003.

Fact-Orientation Meets Agent-Orientation

Terry Halpin

Northface University, Salt Lake City, USA
`terry.halpin@northface.edu`

Abstract. The pragmatic value of any information system, whether agent-oriented or not, depends critically on its fidelity in modelling the relevant aspects of the underlying business domain. Fact-oriented approaches to information modelling facilitate high fidelity models by lifting the specification of business facts and rules to a truly conceptual level where they can be easily validated with non-technical domain experts. Incorporating aspects of fact-orientation into agent-oriented approaches may well offer similar benefits. This paper reviews the principal concepts behind fact-orientation, and then discusses some lessons learned from early attempts to combine fact-orientation with two agent-oriented approaches.

1 Introduction

In developing an information system to model a practical business domain, one often encounters business facts that are most easily expressed in terms of n-ary or nested relationships, as well as business rules that that go beyond simple rules like multiplicity constraints. Adding agent behaviour to an information system extends the range of business semantics that must be carefully captured. Although business facts and rules may be implemented in many ways, they should first be specified at the conceptual level, using concepts and language easily understood by the business domain experts who are best qualified to validate the rules. These subject matter experts understand the business domain even if they are unfamiliar with technical notations used by professional analysts.

Fact-oriented approaches to information modelling facilitate high fidelity models by specifying business facts and rules in simplified natural language, using an attribute-free approach that enables all fact structures to be conveniently populated with sample populations, thus enabling meaningful validation by non-technical domain experts. Incorporating aspects of fact-orientation into agent-oriented approaches may well offer similar benefits. This paper reviews the principal concepts behind fact-orientation, and then discusses some lessons learned from early attempts to combine fact-orientation with two agent-oriented methods.

Section 2 briefly overviews basic terminology and language criteria for specifying business facts and rules. Section 3 illustrates the main concepts and advantages of fact-orientation for information modelling of non-agent based systems, focusing on *Object-Role Modelling* (ORM), currently the most popular fact-oriented approach used in industry. Section 4 summarizes the main additional modelling tasks addressed

P. Bresciani et al. (Eds.): AOIS 2004, LNAI 3508, pp. 97 – 109, 2005.

by agent-orientation. Section 5 explores some potential benefits of using ORM in concert with the Design and Engineering Methodology for Organizations (DEMO). Section 6 investigates some synergies between ORM and the Agent-Object-Relationship (AOR) modelling approach. Section 7 reviews the main contributions and suggests areas for future research.

2 Business Facts and Rules

Underlying any business domain are the *facts* that the business users communicate to one another about their business. A *fact instance* is a proposition taken to be true, and is expressed by a declarative sentence (e.g. "The Language named 'Japanese' is spoken in the Country named 'Japan'."), consisting of a *predicate* symbol (e.g. ... is spoken in ...) applied to a sequence of one or more object terms (e.g. "The Language named 'Japanese'", "The Country named 'Japan'"). An *object type* is a kind of object, e.g. Language, Country. A *fact type* includes predicate and object type(s) but not instances, e.g. Language is spoken in Country. A *fact-role* is a part played by an object in a predicate. In the context of a predicate, a fact-role is simply called a *role*. The number of roles in a predicate is called its *arity*.

Table 1 shows some fact types with arities from 1 to 4. Each role corresponds to an object placeholder (depicted here as an ellipsis "...") in the predicate. Here predicates are displayed in *mixfix* notation, allowing object terms to be placed in a sentence at any position.

Table 1. Sample fact types with their predicates expressed in mixfix notation

Fact Type	Predicate	Arity
Person smokes	... smokes	1 (Unary)
Person was born in Country	... was born in ...	2 (Binary)
Person played Sport for Country	... played ... for ...	3 (Ternary)
Person matched Person to Person on Date	... matched ... to ... on ...	4 (Quaternary)

Business rules come in many varieties and may be specified using graphical and/or textual languages. A *static business rule* is a constraint or derivation rule that applies to each individual state of the business, taken one state at a time. For example, Each Person was born on at most one Date is a *static constraint*. A derivation rule may define a *derived fact type* (e.g. Person₁ is an uncle of Person₂ **iff** Person₁ is a brother of Person₃ **who** is a parent of Person₂), or a *derived object type* (e.g. **Each** MalePerson **is a** Person **who** is of Gender 'M'). A *dynamic business rule* is a transition constraint that restricts how the business may change to new states (e.g. MaritalStatus **may change from** 'married' **only to** 'divorced' **or** 'widowed'). One kind of dynamic constraint common in agent-based systems is a *reaction rule*, which determines how the business reacts to an event in the presence of some condition—we discuss reaction rules fin more detail later.

Regardless of their kind, all business rules ultimately depend on business facts and are best applied to a *fact model* that identifies the fact types of interest to the business. Ideally, fact and rule analysis is a joint activity between the domain expert, who best understands the business domain, and the modeller, whose main task is to elicit and formalize the domain expert's informal knowledge. To optimize communication between the modeller and the domain expert, the facts and rules should be *verbalized* in an unambiguous version of the domain expert's natural language and backed up with sample fact populations (for static rules) and sample transitions (for dynamic rules).

In designing a textual language to express business rules, we adopted the following criteria: expressibility, clarity, flexibility, localizability and formality [8, 11]. Supporting predicates of any arity allows domain experts to verbalize the rules directly in terms of the way they think. This makes it much easier for them to understand and validate the rules. There is no excuse for imposing on the domain experts a binary straightjacket that forces them to recast a fact type they would normally verbalize as a quaternary in terms of a binarized equivalent. Similarly, we should not force domain experts to recast unary facts such as Country 'US' is large in terms of Boolean attribute assignments (e.g. US : Country.isLarge = True).

Once we accept that predicates of any arity must be supported, using natural verbalizations, it follows that mixfix notation must be supported. In Table 1, the ternary and quaternary predicates require mixfix because they have more than two object placeholders. Although prefix or postfix notation could be used, such as PlayedFor(X, Y, Z), this would be unnatural for non-technical people. Localizability also requires mixfix notation since, even for binary predicates, the verb-phrase need not occur in the infix position. For example, verbs are usually placed last in Japanese.

Since rules build on facts, mixfix notation is also desirable for business rules (e.g. **It is forbidden that the same** Room at **the same** HourSlot is booked for **more than one** Activity). Like most business rules, this example is *deontic* in its modality. A typical business model also includes some *alethic* rules (e.g. **It is impossible that some** Person is a parent of **itself**).

A decade ago, we specified a verbalizer component that is currently implemented in a database modelling tool [12]. The verbalizer automatically translates ORM graphical constraints into English, as well as Japanese, German and French in the localized versions. In later work [2], we co-designed a conceptual query language called ConQuer, that allows any first order rule to be expressed naturally in terms of an ORM schema, with automatic transformation to SQL. Currently, we are extending these language efforts to provide a unified language that is suitable for very high level specification of business models and business queries at the conceptual level.

Based on our industrial modelling experience, we found the following *dimensions* to be pragmatically useful in characterizing ways in which business rules may be textually formulated for validation with domain experts: *form* (positive, negative, default); *modality* (alethic, deontic), *style* (relational, attribute, mixed); *context* (local, global); *formality* (informal, semi-formal, formal). For a detailed discussion, see [11].

An informal verbalization of business rules may be useful, if it is unambiguous to the domain expert who has to validate the rules. The RuleSpeak sentence templates [19] provide one way to do this. To exploit the benefits of model-driven development however, business rules should be expressed in a *formal* language, so that they can be automatically transformed into executable code. The Object Constraint Language (OCL 2) provides a formal rule language, but its syntax is far too mathematical in nature for non-technical users [17, 23].

A few commercial tools allow querying directly in unrestricted English, and then translate the queries into database languages such SQL or MDX (e.g. Microsoft

English Query and English Language Frontend (ELF)). However, such tools typically require extensive, technical set up of access paths (e.g. pre-joins) for any non-trivial access (e.g. joins that are not based on FK to PK relationships).

The Object-oriented Systems Analysis (OSA) model [4, 5] supports high level, informal rules as well as formal rules in a predicate calculus notation. Our ORM-based approach instead uses a single language that is both formal and conceptual, so that it can serve for communication and validation with domain experts, as well as being executable. In its English version, our textual rule language bears many similarities in both design goals and scope to Sowa's current work on Common Logic Controlled English [21], though we believe our syntax is easier for non-technical people to master and understand (e.g. support for pronouns, natural definite description schemes and a wide variety of pre-defined constraint types).

Regardless of which syntax is finally chosen, industrial experience with the use of very high level rule specification for validating fact-oriented business models with domain experts strongly suggests that any effort made to raise the level of agent-based rules to the same level will be amply rewarded by higher fidelity rules.

3 Object-Role Modelling

Unlike the Entity Relationship (ER) and Unified Modeling Language (UML) [16, 18, 22] approaches, *fact-oriented approaches* depict all facts as relationships over one or more objects, rather than wrapping some facts up as attributes of other objects. This *attribute-free* approach enables facts, fact types and rules to be verbalized naturally, and enables all fact structures to be easily populated with concrete examples to assist validation. This attribute-free nature also dramatically improves the *semantic stability* of both the information model and queries based on it, since typical changes that add fact types or modify rules have no impact on the semantics of existing paths through the schema [2], as illustrated by an example at the end of this section. While avoiding attributes leads to less compact models, this apparent disadvantage is immediately removed by allowing attribute-based views as derived models, together with the use of role names to allow attribute-style specification of rules when desired.

Object-Role Modelling (ORM) is currently the main exemplar of the fact-oriented approach to information modelling. Other fact-oriented approaches exist, including Natural-language Information Analysis Method (NIAM) [24], Fully-Communication-Oriented Information Modelling (FCO-IM) [1], the Predicator Set Model (PSM) [15] and OSA, but their current industrial adoption lags behind ORM. For such reasons, we now focus our treatment of fact-orientation on ORM. This section provides a brief overview of some of the main concepts and notations underlying the use of ORM for non-agent based approaches. Other sources on ORM provide a detailed summary [7], a thorough treatment [8] and a comparison with ER and UML [9, 10].

ORM includes both a graphical and a textual language for specifying information models, a set of modelling procedures for using these languages to construct models, a suite of transformations for reshaping schemas into equivalent or implied schemas, a set of algorithms and heuristics for mapping ORM schemas to/from low level schemas (e.g. relational database schemas, UML schemas, XML schemas), and a textual language for specifying queries directly on ORM models and mapping these to SQL.

ORM's graphical language for static constraints is far more expressive than that of industrial ER or UML, and is formally grounded in first order logic plus arithmetic and set and bag comprehension. A sample ORM schema and sample fact population is shown in Figure 1.

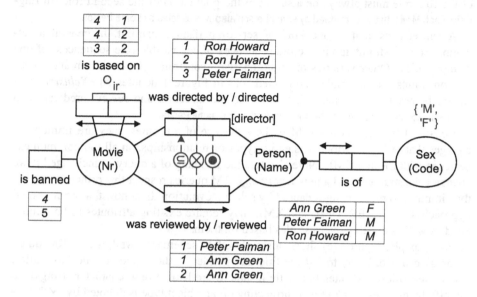

Fig. 1. Sample ORM schema plus fact population

The ORM model in Figure 1 includes three object types (Movie, Person and Sex) and five fact types: Movie is banned; Movie is based on Movie; Movie was directed by Person; Movie was reviewed by Person; Person is of Sex. Inverse readings are supplied for two associations: Person directed Movie; Person reviewed Movie. One role is named ("director"). Simple identification schemes may be abbreviated in parentheses. For example, Movie(Nr) abbreviates the injective (1:1 into) association Movie has MovieNr. For simplicity, persons in this domain are identified by name. In this example, all fact types are unary or binary. We could add Movie was released in Country in Year as a ternary fact type.

ORM classifies business rules into constraints and derivation rules. The ORM model in Figure 1 includes constraints but no derivations. The *value constraint* { 'M', 'F'} indicates the possible sex codes. Arrow-tipped lines across one or more roles denote *uniqueness constraints*, indicating that instantiations of that role sequence must be unique. For example, the uniqueness constraint on the first role of Person is of Sex indicates that entries in the fact column for that role must be unique. The English version of ORM's formal textual language verbalizes this constraint as: **Each** Person is of **at most one** Sex.

A solid dot (possibly circled) connected to a set of one or more roles denotes a *mandatory constraint* over that role set. For example, the mandatory dot connected to the first role of Person is of Sex indicates that **Each** Person is of **some** Sex. The mandatory dot connected to the other two roles played by Person depicts an *inclusive-or constraint*: **Each** Person directed **some** Movie **or** reviewed **some** Movie (possibly both).

The ^{O}ir symbol connected to the roles of the fact type Movie is based on Movie denotes the irreflexive *ring constraint*: **no** Movie is based on **itself**. The circled subset symbol "⊆" connected by an arrow from the first role of Movie was reviewed by Person to the first role of Movie was directed by Person denotes a *subset constraint*, indicating that the population of the first role must always be a subset of the population of the second role. In English: **Each** Movie **that** was reviewed by **some** Person **also** was directed by **some** Person.

A subset constraint is one kind of set-comparison constraint. In general a set-comparison constraint applies across sequences of compatible role sequences (of one or more roles). Other varieties of set-comparison constraints are exclusion and equality constraints. For example, the circled "X" in Figure 1 denotes an *eXclusion constraint* between the role-pairs that comprise the direction and review predicates. In English: **No** Movie was directed by **and** reviewed by **the same** Person.

Because base models in ORM eschew the use of attributes, they are immune to changes that reshape attributes as entity types or relationships, an all too common experience with ER and UML. Note also that the meaning of a query is unchanged if we change a constraint or add a new fact type. ORM queries respect this principle and are thus immune to most changes caused by schema evolution. In contrast, attribute-based approaches such as ER, UML and XML may require existing attributes to be remodelled as well as existing queries/rules based on them.

For example, Figure 2(a) shows a simple ORM schema, as well as an ORM query (expressed in ConQuer) to list the title and gender of those people who have titles. The dotted ellipse indicates that Title instances are lexical (e.g. character strings), so identify themselves. In ConQuer, projecting on an object type is denoted by "✓". Figure 2(b) shows an equivalent schema in UML (minus the constraint that social security numbers are unique, since UML has no official graphic notation for unique attributes), together with the query expressed in an attribute-based language (in this case, SQL). The SQL query is harder for a non-technical person to understand, but at least it works.

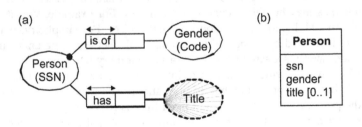

List titled people and their gender.

```
✓Person
  ├─has ✓Title
  └─is of ✓Gender
```

```
select ssn, gender
from Person
where title is not null
```

Fig. 2. Original schema and query in (a) ORM and ConQuer, and (b) UML and SQL

Now suppose that we modify the business domain to allow more than one title to be recorded for the same person and, moreover, the order in which these titles are listed is significant. For example, Prof. Dr. Zweistein may demand to be called that instead of "Dr. Prof. Zweistein". The modified schemas and queries to deal with these changes are shown in Figure 3.

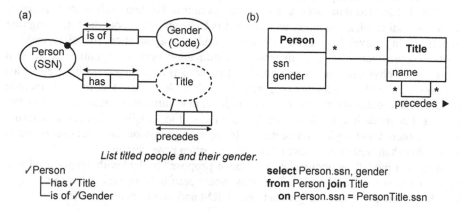

List titled people and their gender.

```
✓Person                                    select Person.ssn, gender
 ├─has ✓Title                              from Person join Title
 └─is of ✓Gender                           on Person.ssn = PersonTitle.ssn
```

Fig. 3. Modified schemas and queries in (a) ORM and ConQuer, and (b) UML and SQL

First note that the change to the ORM schema is trivial. The semantics of the original path connecting Person to gender and title is unchanged (only a constraint is changed). In contrast, the UML schema had to be drastically modified, because we can't record facts about a title if a title is a merely an attribute. More importantly, the ORM query still works without change, since the meaning of the query is unchanged. Unfortunately, the SQL query also had to be drastically modified since the relational database now contains three tables instead of one, with the relevant information spread over two tables, thus requiring either a join or subquery. The current ORM tool implementing ConQuer automatically generates the new SQL without the user having to change the original ORM query. The benefit of greater semantic stability conferred by the attribute-free approach of fact-orientation should now be apparent.

ORM provides additional advantages over ER and UML such as full orthogonality, cleaner semantics and richer coverage of predefined constraints [9, 10, 13]. Unlike UML however, ORM currently has no pre-defined support for agent-based aspects, since ORM's focus is on information modelling rather than behavioural modelling. The next section briefly reviews some of the additional modelling tasks required for agent-based systems.

4 What Does Agent-Orientation Add to the Modelling Task?

Following Ferber [6], we define an *agent* to be a physical or virtual entity with capacities such as the following. An agent is capable of acting (and reacting) in an environment, communicating with other agents, exhibiting goal-directed behaviour (survival or satisfaction), has resources of its own, has limited perception of its environment and can offer services. A multi-agent system includes an environment containing passive objects as well as active objects (agents), where objects may bear relationships to one another and agents may perform operations to perceive, produce, consume, manipulate or transform objects, in conformity to certain rules.

Many of these features seem to be found in modelling approaches (data flow diagrams, process modelling etc.) that have been used for decades to deal with building distributed/federated databases and real-time systems. To deal with such features at the conceptual level, a minimum requirement is to be able to model the following two aspects at a high level: inter-agent interaction; and intra-agent states (of relevance).

Inter-agent interaction may include communication between agents (information flow) and/or physical acts on one another (material flow), subject to business rules that constrain such interactions (e.g. reaction rules). *Intra-agent states* may include obligation and commitment stores accrued from communication acts, as well as belief-sets. For modelling the latter, we favour classical logic with belief revision rather than non-monotonic logic, and prefer a stronger emphasis on the intended propositions rather than sentences whose utterances are often time-deictic.

Dozens of modelling approaches have been proposed to deal with agent-based features. The next two sections briefly review some results from preliminary investigations to explore possible synergies between ORM and two such approaches.

5 ORM and DEMO

The *Design and Engineering Methodology for Organizations (DEMO)* was largely developed by Jan Dietz [3]. It adds *performatives* (e.g. request, promise, question, assertion) to propositions to model communication acts, and uses four models to capture essential business processes. The *state model* is similar to a simplified version of ORM, covering object types, fact types and associated business rules. The *operation model* considers action and decision rules for actor roles. The *process model* considers coordination steps as well as causal relationships. The *construction model* focuses on actor roles, transactions and information sources.

Figure 4 depicts part of a state model in DEMO for a simple library. The additional DEMO models needed to complete the business specification may be found in [3]. While DEMO's state model is similar to an ORM model in many ways, there are differences in both notational style and semantic coverage. For example, DEMO sometimes uses diamonds to depict predicates. More importantly, DEMO attempts to ignore all information aspects relating to how individual entity types may be identified, since decisions about identification schemes are considered to be irrelevant to the essential business processes underlying the business domain. For example, how a book or a library loan is referred to in actual discourse is not captured at all.

In contrast, ORM requires modelling of at least one way by which humans may linguistically identify objects in the business domain. In practice, this requirement often avoids many modelling errors, while still allowing final decisions about identification schemes to be delayed until the business wants to make recommendations in this regard. A partial ORM model for the same library domain is shown in Figure 5. Prepending "<<" to a predicate reverses its reading direction (the default is left-right, top-down). Business rules are specified using ORM's graphical and textual languages.

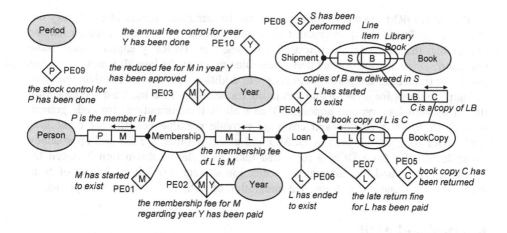

Fig. 4. Part of a state model for a library domain, expressed in DEMO

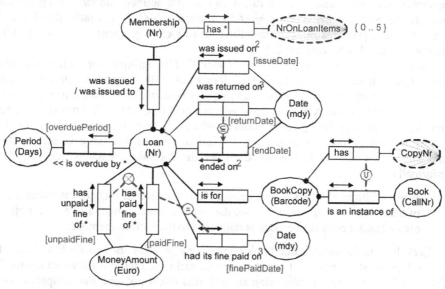

[2] **For each** Loan, endDate >= issueDate
[3] **For each** Loan, finePaidDate >= returnDate

* Membership.nrOnLoanItems =**count each** Loan **that** was issued to Membership
                                and was returned on **no** Date
* Loan is overdue by Period **iff** Loan ended on **no** Date
                    and Period = **today** - Loan.issueDate - Loan.issueDate.year.normalLoanPerioc
                    and Period > 0
* Loan.unpaidFine = Loan.overduePeriod **nrUnits** * Loan.issueDate.year.dailyLateFee
* Loan.paidFine = (Loan.returnDate - Loan.issueDate - Loan.returnDate.year.normalLoanPeriod **nrUnits**
                * Loan.returnDate.year.dailyLateFee

Fig. 5. Part of an ORM model for the library domain

The other ORM models to fully specify the information content of the library domain may be found in [3]. In contrast to DEMO models, ORM models are formal and executable, they include identification schemes, they typically capture many more constraints, they support formal derivation rules and they declare all temporal aspects explicitly (including temporal granularity). In addition, ORM provides detailed modelling procedures for creating and validating models (e.g. data use case seeding, validation by verbalization and population), as well as transformations for code generation. Such added precision and coverage provide possible benefits for combining ORM with an approach such as DEMO and possibly other agent-based approaches. Possible benefits from DEMO for ORM include a clearer distinction between the business system and the automated information system, explicit modelling of communication acts and transactions, and integration of static and dynamic viewpoints.

6 ORM and AOR

As indicated earlier, ORM has little support for modelling reactive behaviour (e.g. dynamic constraints and reaction rules) and no pre-defined support for agent-based aspects. In contrast, the *Agent-Object-Relationship (AOR)* approach, developed by Gerd Wagner, provides built-in modelling primitives (e.g. *agent* and *event* types) to deal with agent-based aspects [22].

An interaction process type in AOR is specified by defining, for each participating agent (type), a set of inter-related behaviour rules, called *reaction rules*. A reaction rule has four parts: event; condition; action; and postcondition. To explore the impact of such features, some AOR concepts were adapted to ORM [14]. For example, entities were partitioned into *passive entities* and *agents*, and *interaction diagrams* were added to display ordered collections of *lexical actions* (message communication) and *non-lexical actions* (physical). Consider the following reaction rule, expressed informally.

> When a library receives a book request from a member, it checks whether a copy of that book is available and, if so, the request is confirmed, a new loan object is created and a copy of the book is delivered to the faculty member.

Each loan is for exactly one book copy. The rule does not specify time limits for the actions to take place, so it is not an operational rule. Figure 6 shows an interaction diagram for this reaction rule, using an extended ORM notation that adapts concepts from AOR. Member$_1$ and BookCopy$_1$ are individual *object variables*, and theLibrary is an *external unit type* (there is exactly one library that exists external to the information model itself). Member is an agent type, whereas BookCopy is a passive entity type. RequestBook is a message type performed by Member$_1$ and perceived by theLibrary. ConfirmRequest is a message type performed by the Library and perceived by Member$_1$. These lexical actions are named inside dashed arrow heads. Physical actions are named inside solid arrowheads. TheLibrary performs the DeliverBookCopy action, as perceived by Member$_1$, with BookCopy$_1$ passively involved. Member$_1$ performs the ReturnBookCopy action, as perceived by theLibrary, with BookCopy$_1$ passively involved. The order of these actions is indicated by numbered circles.

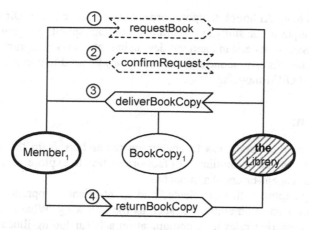

Fig. 6. An interaction sequence diagram in ORM-AOR notation for library loans

The graphical part of the ORM schema for the underlying library domain is shown in Figure 7. For simplicity, all textual constraints and derivation rules are omitted.

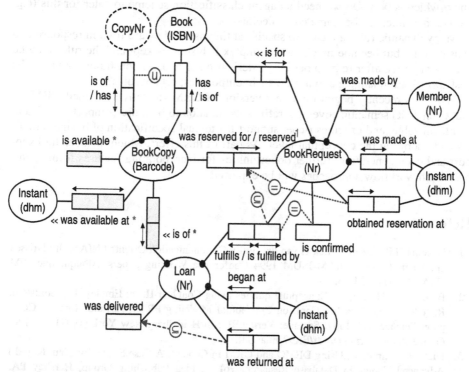

Fig. 7. Graphical part of the ORM schema for the library domain underlying the reaction rule

The temporal order inherent in the interaction model (Figure 6) and reaction rule is captured by subset constraints in either explicit (circled "⊆") or implicit form (e.g. implied by mandatory constraint). For example, a book request is confirmed only if it is fulfilled by a loan. Although temporal order may be modelled in ORM using mandatory, subset, equality or subtype constraints, the corresponding dynamic processes are typically easier to understand and validate using interaction diagrams and reaction rule verbalizations. Such dynamic specifications may be used in conjunction with data use cases to seed ORM models.

7   Conclusion

The main aim of this paper was to encourage researchers from the agent-oriented community who may be unfamiliar with fact-orientation to explore possible synergies between fact- and agent-oriented approaches.

To optimally exploit both fact-oriented and agent-oriented approaches, several research questions need to be addressed, such as the following. What is an appropriate metamodel for capturing relevant communication acts (including illocutionary forces over propositions)? To what extent can corresponding features of dynamic and static models be automatically transformed into one another? What formal logics are best for capturing the dynamic and language-act semantics of social interactions? Business processes may be manual, automated or semi-automated, and initially we might not know which is best. Do we need an agent classification scheme to cater for this (e.g. human, machine, semi-automated, undecided?).

Many dynamic rules are easy to specify at the instant they are fired in response to a causal event, but become much more complex if history is kept and the rules may be fired at any time after (e.g. to perform a derivation or apply a constraint). What is the best specification language to handle such temporal aspects of rules?

Work has recently begun on a new version of ORM (tentatively named ORM 2), that extends its semantic coverage, refines its notation to be more compact, consistent and localizable, and provides richer support for textual specification of business models and queries at the conceptual level. As part of this effort, which includes tool support and code generation, further opportunities for incorporating features from agent-based and workflow approaches will be explored.

References

1. Bakema G.P., Zwart J., Lek H van der: Fully Communication Oriented NIAM. In: Nijssen G., Sharp J (eds.): NIAM-ISDM 1994 Conference Working papers, Albuquerque, NM USA, (1994) pp L1-35.
2. Bloesch, A; Halpin, T.: Conceptual queries using ConQuer-II. In: Embley, D.; Goldstein, R. (eds.): Proc. 16th Int. Conf. on Conceptual Modeling ER'97. Lecture Notes in Computer Science, vol. 1331. Springer-Verlag, Berlin Heidelberg New York (1997) 113-126. Online at www.orm.net/pdf/ER97-final.pdf.
3. Dietz, J., Halpin, T.:.Using DEMO and ORM in Concert: A Case Study. In: Siau, K. (ed.) Advanced Topics in Database Research, vol. 3, Idea Publishing Group, Hershey PA, (2004) 218-236.
4. Embley, D.; Kurtz, B.; Woodfield, S.: Object-Oriented Systems Analysis: A Model-Driven Approach. Prentice Hall, Englewood Cliffs, NJ (1992).
5. Embley, D.: Object Database Management. Addison-Wesley, Reading, MA (1998).
6. Ferber, J.: Multi-Agent Systems. Addison-Wesley, Edinburgh Gate (1999).

7. Halpin, T.: Object-Role Modeling (ORM/NIAM). In: Bernus, P., Mertins, K, Schmidt, G. (eds.) Handbook on Architectures of Information Systems. Springer, Heidelberg (1998) 81-102.

8. Halpin, T.: Information Modeling and Relational Databases. Morgan Kaufmann, San Francisco (2001).

9. Halpin, T.: Information Analysis in UML and ORM: a Comparison. In: Siau, K (ed.): Advanced Topics in Database Research, vol. 1, Idea Publishing Group, Hershey PA (2002) 307-323.

10. Halpin, T.: Metaschemas for ER, ORM and UML Data Models: A Comparison. In: Siau, K (ed.): Journal of Database Management, vol. 13, no. 2 (2002) 20-29, Idea Publishing Group.

11. Halpin, T.: Business Rule Verbalization. In: Doroshenko, A., Halpin, T., Liddle, S., Mayr, H. (eds.): Information Systems Technology and its Applications. Lecture Notes in Informatics, vol. P-48. Gesellschaft für Informatik, Bonn (2004) 39-52.

12. Halpin, T.; Evans, K.; Hallock, P.; MacLean, W.: Database Modeling with Microsoft® Visio for Enterprise Architects. Morgan Kaufmann, San Francisco (2003).

13. Halpin, T.: Constraints on Conceptual Join Paths. In: Krogstie, J.; Halpin, T.; Siau, K. (eds.): Information Modeling Methods and Methodologies, Idea Publishing Group, Hershey (2004) 258-277.

14. Halpin, T.; Wagner, G.: Modeling Reactive Behavior in ORM. In: Conceptual Modeling – ER2003, Proc. 22nd ER Conference, Chicago, Springer LNCS (2003).

15. Hofstede, A. ter, Proper H., Weide th P. van der: Formal definition of a conceptual language for the description and manipulation of information models. Information Systems 18:7 (1993) 489-523.

16. Object Management Group: UML 2.0 Infrastructure Specification. Online at: www.omg.org/uml (2003).

17. Object Management Group: UML 2.0 Object Constraint Language. Online at: www.omg.org/uml (2003).

18. Object Management Group: UML 2.0 Superstructure Specification. Online at: www.omg.org/uml (2003).

19. Ross, R.; Lam, G.: RuleSpeak Sentence Templates: Developing Rules Statements Using Sentence Patterns. Business Rule Solutions. Online at www.BRCommunity.com (2001).

20. Rumbaugh, J.; Jacobson, I.; Booch, G.: The Unified Modeling Language Reference Manual. Addison-Wesley (1999).

21. Sowa, J. Common Logic Controlled English. Draft paper online at http://www.jfsowa.com/clce/specs.htm (2004).

22. G. Wagner: The Agent-Object-Relationship Meta-Model: Towards a Unified View of State and Behavior. *Information Systems* 28:5 (2003) 475-504.

23. Warmer, J.; Kleppe, A.: The Object Constraint Language: Getting Your Models Ready for MDA, Second Edition. Addison-Wesley (2003).

24. Wintraecken, J.: The NIAM Information Analysis Method: Theory and Practice. Kluwer, Deventer (1990).

Towards Ontological Foundations for Agent Modelling Concepts Using the Unified Fundational Ontology (UFO)

Giancarlo Guizzardi[1] and Gerd Wagner[2]

[1] Centre for Telematics and Information Technology, Univ. of Twente,
Enschede, The Netherlands
guizzard@cs.utwente.nl
[2] Brandenburg Univ. of Technology at Cottbus, Computer Science Department,
Cottbus, Germany
G.Wagner@tu-cottbus.de

Abstract. Foundational ontologies provide the basic concepts upon which any domain-specific ontology is built. This paper presents a new foundational ontology, UFO, and shows how it can be used as a foundation of agent concepts and for evaluating agent-oriented modelling methods. UFO is derived from a synthesis of two other foundational ontologies, GFO/GOL and OntoClean/DOLCE. While their main areas of application are the natural sciences and linguistics/cognitive engineering, respectively, the main purpose of UFO is to provide a foundation for conceptual modelling, including agent-oriented modelling.

1 Introduction

A foundational ontology, sometimes also called an'upper level ontology', defines a range of top-level domain-independent ontological categories, which form a general foundation for more elaborated domain-specific ontologies. A well-known example of a foundational ontology is the Bunge-Wand-Weber (BWW) ontology proposed by Wand and Weber in a series of articles (e.g., [28,29,30]) on the basis of the original metaphysical theory developed by Bunge [1,2].

As has been shown in a number of recent works (e.g., [31,8,5,10,11,20]), foundational ontologies can be used to evaluate conceptual modelling languages and to develop guidelines for their use. Agent-based conceptual modelling can be viewed as an extension of more traditional conceptual modelling approaches by the explicit consideration of intentional entities. The position defended here is that agent modelling languages should also be based in a foundational ontology that accounts for both the concepts underlying basic conceptual modelling constructs, and their extension in terms of intentional entities.

A unified foundational ontology represents a synthesis of a selection of foundational ontologies. Our main goal in making such a synthesis is to obtain a foundational ontology that is tailored towards applications in conceptual modelling. For this purpose we have to capture the ontological categories underlying natural language and human cognition, which are also reflected in conceptual modelling

P. Bresciani et al. (Eds.): AOIS 2004, LNAI 3508, pp. 110–124, 2005.

languages such as ER diagrams or UML class diagrams. In [6], this approach is called a 'descriptive ontology' as opposed to 'prescriptive ontology', which claims to be 'realistic' and robust against the state of the art in scientific knowledge.

For UFO 0.2, the second[1] (still experimental) version of our Unified Foundational Ontology (UFO), we combine the following two ontologies:

1. the General Formal Ontology (GFO), which is underlying the General Ontological Language (GOL) developed by the OntoMed research group at the University of Leipzig, Germany; see www.ontomed.de and [4];
2. the OntoClean ontology [32] and the Descriptive Ontology for Linguistic and Cognitive Engineering (DOLCE) developed by the ISTC-CNR-LOA research group in Trento, Italy, as part of WonderWeb Project; see http://wonderweb.semanticweb.org/.

Our choice is based on personal familiarity and preferences and not on an evaluation of all alternatives. Nonetheless, in previous attempts, GFO has been proven insightful in providing a principled foundation for analyzing and extending conceptual modelling and ontology representation languages and constructs [10,11,19].

We have obtained our synthesis by:

1. selecting categories from the union of both category sets,
2. renaming certain terms in order to create a more 'natural' language, and
3. adding some additional categories and corresponding theories,

based on relevance for conceptual modelling according to our experience.

Using the acronyms "BWW", "owl", "UML", "ISO", and "BSBR", we also make references to BWW, the Web ontology language OWL[2], the Unified Modelling Language (UML), the terminology standard ISO1087-1:2000 [17], and to the Business Rules Team submission to the OMG Business Semantics for Business Rules RFP [3]. For making a distinction between terms used differently in different vocabularies, we use the XML namespace prefix syntax and write, e.g., "BWW:thing" and "owl:Thing" for distinguishing between the concepts termed "thing" in BWW and in OWL.

We present UFO 0.2 both as a MOF/UML model [21] and as a vocabulary in semi-structured English, similar to the BSBR Structured English of [3]. MOF/UML is a fragment of the UML class modelling language that is recommended by the OMG as a language for defining modelling languages; in other words, MOF/UML is used as a meta-modelling language. There are two reasons for using MOF/UML for defining a foundational ontology: first, it allows expressing it graphically in the form of a UML class diagram; second, it facilitates the communication of the foundational ontology by making it accessible to the large (and still growing) language community of people familiar with the UML.

---

[1] UFO 0.2 differs from UFO 0.1, which has been presented at the AOIS Workshop at CAiSE'04, by adding the categories of datatype, process and business process.

[2] http://www.w3.org/TR/owl-semantics/.

An alternative, and more flexible, mode of expression for defining a modelling language such as UFO consists of using semi-structured English to specify the vocabulary of the modelling language. Our UFO vocabulary has three kinds of entries marked up with different font styles:

- <u>term</u> : a term in this font style denotes being of a type and is used to refer to things of that type; e.g., the term <u>individual</u> in the phrase "<u>individual</u> that is wholly present whenever it is present" stands for a thing of type "individual" (i.e. it stands for an individual);
- <u>*name*</u> : a name of an individual or a type; when <u>abc</u> is a type term referring to things of that type, <u>*abc*</u> is a name referring to the type itself;
- <u>term1</u> relationship predicate <u>term2</u> : an expression that denotes being of a relationship type and that is used to refer to relationships of that type.

A vocabulary entry may contain, additionally,

- 'Corresponding terms' (or 'corresponding relationship type expressions'): terms (or relationship type expressions) that are roughly equivalent;
- Examples; and
- Constraints: logical statements that have to hold in any given ontology based on UFO 0.2.

When there is a primary source for a definition, we append it in brackets, like [based on GFO].

UFO is divided into three incrementally layered *compliance sets*:

1. UFO-A defines the core of UFO, excluding terms related to perdurants and terms related to the spheres of intentional and social things;
2. UFO-B defines, as an increment to UFO-A, terms related to perdurants; and
3. UFO-C defines, as an increment to UFO-B, terms related to the spheres of intentional and social things, including linguistic things.

This division reflects a certain stratification of our "world". It also reflects different degrees of scientific consensus: there is more consensus about the ontology of endurants than about the ontology of perdurants, and there is more consensus about the ontology of perdurants than about the ontology of intentional and social things.

We hope that this division into different compliance sets will facilitate both the further evolution of UFO and the adoption of UFO in conceptual modelling and ontology engineering. In the next section we present UFO-A 0.2, while UFO-B 0.2 and UFO-C 0.2 are presented in sections 3 and 4, respectively.

2   UFO-A 0.1 – The Core of a Unified Foundational Ontology

2.1   Things, Sets, Entities, Individuals and Types

We first present the upper part of UFO-A 0.2 as a MOF/UML model in Fig. 1. Notice the fundamental distinction made between *sets* and *entities* as things that are not sets (called 'urelements' in GFO).

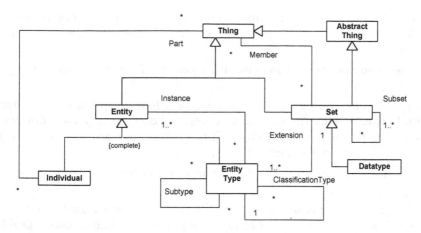

Fig. 1. The upper part of UFO 0.2 as a MOF/UML model

In structured English, the upper part of UFO 0.2 can be introduced as follows.

thing: anything perceivable or conceivable [ISO:object]. *Corresponding terms*: GFO:entity; DOLCE:entity, owl:Thing; BSBR:thing

set   :   thing that has other things as members (in the sense of set theory)

thing is member of set :   name of a formal relationship type that is irreflexive, asymmetric and intransitive

member :   role name that refers to the first argument of the *thing is member of set* relationship type

set is subset of set :   name of a formal relationship type that is reflexive, asymmetric and transitive. *Constraint*: For all t:thing; s_1, s_2 : set – if t is member of s_1 and s_1 is subset of s_2, then t is member of s_2

entity: thing that is not a set; neither the set-theoretic membership relation nor the subset relation can unfold the internal structure of an entity [GFO:urelement]

entity type :   entity that has an extension (being a set of entitys that are instances of it) and an intension, which includes an applicability criterion[3] for determining if an entity is an instance of it; and which is captured by means of an axiomatic specification, i.e., a set of axioms that may involve a number of other entity types representing its essential features. An entity type is a space-time independent pattern of features, which can be realized in a number of different individuals. [based on GFO:universal]. *Corresponding terms*: UML:class; DOLCE:universal; owl:Class; BSBR:'generic thing'

entity is instance of entity type :   name of a formal relationship type (called *classification*)

instance :   role name that refers to the first argument of the *entity is instance of entity type* relationship type

---

[3] The notion of applicability criterion (or principle of application) and its role in conceptual modelling are discussed comprehensively in (Guizzardi et al, 2004).

set is extension of entity type : name of a formal relationship type. *Constraint:* For all *e*:entity, *t*:entity type, *s*:set – if *e* is instance of *t* and *s* is extension of *t*, then *e* is member of *s*.

extension : role name that refers to the first argument of the *set is extension of entity type* relationship type

entity type is subtype of entity type : name of a formal relationship type that is irreflexive, asymmetric and transitive (also called *generalization*). *Constraint:* For all t_1, t_2 : entity type; s_1, s_2 : set – if t_1 is subtype of t_2 and s_1 is extension of t_1 and s_2 is extension of t_2, then s_1 is subset of s_2.

subtype : role name that refers to the first argument of the *entity type is subtype of entity type* relationship type

individual : entity that is not an entity type. An entity type that classifies individuals is called individual type. *Corresponding terms*: GFO:individual; DOLCE: particular.

thing is part of individual : name of a formal relationship type that is reflexive, asymmetric and transitive (also called *aggregation*). For a fuller treatment of part-whole relations in which we consider both modality and context-sensitivity, one should refer to [11].

part : role name that refers to the first argument of the *thing is part of individual* relationship type

entity type is classification type of entity type : name of a formal relationship type where the first argument is a higher-order entity type whose instances form a subtype partition of the second argument (also called *higher-order classification*). *Examples*: BiologicalSpecies is classification type of Animal; PassengerAircraftType is classification type of PassengerAircraft. *Constraint*: For all t_1, t_2, t_3: entity type – if t_3 is classification type of t_1 and t_2 is instance of t_3, then t_2 is subtype of t_1.

classification type : role name that refers to the first argument of the *entity type is classification type of entity type* relationship type. *Corresponding names*: GFO:"higher-order universal"; BSBR:"categorization type"; UML:powertype.

entity type is classified by entity type : name of a formal relationship type that is the inverse of the *entity type is classification type of entity type* relationship type. *Corresponding relationship type expressions*: BSBR:"type has categorization-scheme".

2.2 Different Kinds of Types

In UFO, we make a fundamental distinction between *datatypes*, which are sets, and *entity types*, which are not sets, but whose extensions are sets. Based on [33,18,15,16], we distinguish between several different kinds of entity types, as shown in Figure 2. These distinctions are elaborated in [14], in which we present a philosophically and psychologically well-founded theory of types for conceptual modelling. In [13], this theory is used to propose: (i) a profile for UML whose elements represent finer-grained distinctions between different kinds of types; (ii) a set of constraints defining the admissible relations between these elements. One should refer to [13,14] for: (a) an in-depth discussion of the theory underlying these categories as well as the constraints on their relations; (b) a formal characterization of the profile; (c) the application of the profile to propose an ontological design pattern that addresses a recurrent problem in the practice of conceptual modelling.

In structured English, the different kinds of types are defined as follows.

datatype : set whose members are data values. In UFO, a datatype is a set-theoretic representation of a conceptual space and the constraints imposed by its geometrical structure (see [13]). *Examples*: *Colour* domain composed of *hue*, *saturation* and *brightness* subdomains; *Weight* and *Mass* domains as linear orders homomorphic to the half-line of non-negative numbers .

sortal type : entity type that carries a criterion for determining the individuation, persistence and identity[4] of its instances. An identity criterion supports the judgment whether two instances are the same. Every instance in a conceptual model must have an identity and, hence, must be an instance of **sortal type**.

base type : sortal type that is rigid (all its instances are necessarily its instances) and that supplies an identity criterion for its instances [OntoClean:type]. *Examples*: Mountain; Person. *Corresponding terms*: BWW:"natural kind".

phase type : sortal type that is anti-rigid (its instances could possibly also not be instances of it without losing their identity) and that is an element of a subtype partition of a base type [OntoClean:"phased sortal"]. *Examples*: Town and Metropolis are phase subtypes of City; Baby, Teenager and Adult are phase subtypes of Person.

role type : sortal type that is anti-rigid and for which there is a relationship type such that it is the subtype of a base type formed by all instances participating in the relationship type [OntoClean:role]. *Examples*: DestinationCity as role subtype of City; Student as role subtype of Person.

mixin type : entity type that is not a sortal type and can be partitioned into disjoint subtypes which are sortal types (typically role types) with different identity criteria. Since a mixin is a non-sortal it cannot have direct instances [OntoClean:non-sortal]. *Examples*: Object; Part; Customer; Product

relationship type : type whose instances are (material or formal) relationships

Notice that role types and phase types cannot supply an identity criterion for their instances. For this reason, they must be derived from a suitable base type from which they inherit their identity criterion.

The theory of types which is part of UFO-A provides a foundation for a number of modelling primitives that, albeit often used, are commonly defined in an ad hoc manner in the practice of conceptual modelling (e.g. kind, phase or state, role, mixin).

---

[4] For a deeper discussion on the notion of individuation, persistence and identity criteria and its role in conceptual modelling one should refer to (Guizzardi et al, 2004).

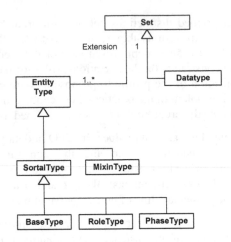

Fig. 2. Different kinds of types in UFO-A 0.2

In particular, this theory can be considered as an elaboration in the way types are accounted for in the BWW approach. In one of the BWW papers [5], it is proposed that a UML class should be used to represent a BWW-natural kind (it should be equivalent to functional schema of a BWW-natural kind). A natural kind is in the same ontological footing as what is named here a Base type, i.e., it is a rigid type that provides an identity criterion for its instances. As demonstrated in several works in the literature [32,15,33,18,13], this kind of type construct constitutes only one of the sorts that are necessary to represent the phenomena available in cognition and language. In other words, a conceptual modelling construct representing a base type is only one of a set of modelling constructs which should be available to the conceptual modeler.

2.3 Different Kinds of Individuals

We distinguish a number of different kinds of individuals, as shown in Figure 3.

In structured English, these different kinds of individuals are explained as follows.

<u>endurant</u>   : <u>individual</u> that is wholly present whenever it is present, i.e. it does not have temporal parts. An endurant is something which persists in time while keeping its identity. Examples are a house, a person, the moon, a hole, the redness of an apple and an amount of sand. [DOLCE]

Corresponding terms: GFO:3D-individual

<u>perdurant</u> : <u>individual</u> that is composed of temporal parts; whenever a perdurant is present, it is not the case that all its temporal parts are present. The distinction between endurants and perdurants can be understood in terms of the intuitive distinction between "objects" (things, entities) and "processes" (events). Examples of perdurants are a race, a conversation, the Second World War and a business process [DOLCE]

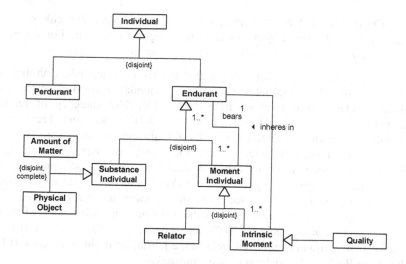

Fig. 3. Different kinds of individuals in UFO-A 0.2

substance individual :   endurant that consists of matter (i.e., is 'tangible' or concrete), possesses spatio-temporal properties and can exist by itself; that is, it does not existentially depend on other endurants, except possibly on some of its parts) [based on GFO:substance]. Examples: a house; a person; the moon; an amount of sand.

   Corresponding terms: BWW:thing

moment individual :   endurant that cannot exist by itself; that is, it depends on other endurants, which are not among its parts [based on GFO:moment]. *Examples*: the redness of a certain apple; a belief of Noam Chomsky; a flight connection between two cities.

endurant bears **moment individual** :   designated relationship [based on GFO: "substance bears moment"]

physical object :   substance individual that satisfies a condition of unity and for which certain parts can change without affecting its identity. *Examples*: a house; a person; the moon.

amount of matter :   substance individual that does not satisfy a condition of unity; typically referred to by means of mass nouns. Amounts of matter are, in general, mereologically invariant, i.e., they cannot change any of their parts without changing their identity [DOLCE]. *Examples*: a liter of water; a piece of gold; a pile of sand.

intrinsic moment :   moment individual that is existentially dependent on one single individual

intrinsic moment inheres in **endurant** :   designated relationship [GFO]

quality :   intrinsic moment that inheres in exactly one endurant and can be mapped to a value (quale) in a quality dimension [13]. *Corresponding terms*: GFO:quality;

DOLCE:quality; BWW: "intrinsic property". *Examples*: the colour (height, weight) of a physical object; an electric charge. *Constraint*: For all e_1, e_2 : endurant; q:quality — if q inheres in e_1 and q inheres in e_2, then e_1 is equal to e_2.

relational moment: moment individual that is existentially dependent on more than one individual. Relational moments provide a foundation for the construction of material relationships between individuals [13]. The category of relational moments in UFO is based on the concept of a [GFO:Relator]. The notion of relators is supported in several works in the philosophical literature [23,24] and, the position advocated here is that, they play an important role in: (i) distinguishing material relations such as *'being married to'* and *'studies at'* from their formal counterparts (e.g. 5 *is greater than* 3, this day is *part-of* this month); (ii) answering questions of the sort: what does it mean say that John is married to Mary? Why is it true to say that Bill works for Company X but not for Company Y? *Corresponding terms*: BWW:"mutual property". *Examples*: a particular employment (Susan is employed by IBM); a particular flight connection (LH403 flies from Berlin to Munich); a kiss; a handshake.

Putting all UFO-A terms and relationship type expressions together in one UML/MOF diagram results in figure 8 in APPENDIX A.

2.4   An Application of UFO-A 0.2 to Agent-Oriented Modelling

2.4.1 Modelling Agent Roles
In figure 4, the role type *Customer* is defined as a supertype of *Person* and *Corporation*. This model is deemed ontologically incorrect for two reasons: first, not all persons are customers, i.e. it is not the case that the extension of *Person* is necessarily included in the extension of *Customer*. Moreover, an instance of *Person* is not necessarily a *Customer*. Both arguments are also valid for *Organization*. In a series of papers [25,26], Steimann discusses the difficulties in specifying supertypes for Roles that can be filled by instances of disjoint types[5]. As a conclusion, he claims that the solution to this problem lies in the separation of role type and base type (named natural type in the article) hierarchies; a solution which would strongly impact the metamodel of all major conceptual modelling language. By using the theory of types underlying UFO-A, we can show that this claim is not warranted and we are able to propose a *design pattern* that can be used as an ontologically correct solution to this recurrent problem [14].

In this example, Customer has in its extension individuals that obey different identity criteria, i.e., it is not the case that there is a single identity criterion that applies both for Persons and Corporations. Customer is hence a mixin type (a non-sortal) and, by definition, cannot supply an identity criterion for its instances. Since every instance in the model must have an identity, every instance of Customer must be an instance of one of its subtypes (forming a partition) that carries an identity criterion. For example, we can define the sortals PrivateCustomer and Corporate-

---

[5] This problem is also mentioned in (van Belle, 1999): *"how would one model the customer entity conceptually? The Customer as a supertype of Organisation and Person? The Customer as a subtype of Organisation and Person? The Customer as a relationship between or Organisation and (Organization or Person)?."*

Customer as subtypes of Customer (Figure 5). These sortals, in turn, carry the (incompatible) identity criteria supplied by the base types Person and Corporation, respectively.

In summary, in many modelling problems, we have to model agent types that are role mixin types, which implies that

1. there is a disjoint partition into subtypes, and
2. these subtypes are role types, that is they are subtypes of appropriate base types.

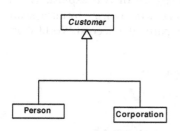

Fig. 4. An ontologically incorrect model of roles

Fig. 5. An ontologically correct version of (Figure 4) according to UFO 0.2

3 UFO-B 0.2 – Perdurants

A complete treatment of an ontology of perdurants requires a an ontology of *temporal entities* (GFO:chronoids) [4]. In this section, instead, we restrict our attention to the most basic perdurant categories for defining UFO-B 0.2 as a foundation for defining some intentional and social entities in section 4. In the sequel we discuss the following basic kinds of perdurants shown in Figure 6: (atomic and complex) events and states.

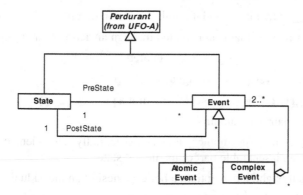

Fig. 6. The perdurant categories of UFO-B 0.2

state : perdurant that is homeomeric (each temporal part of it is again a state) [based on DOLCE]

event : perdurant that is related to exactly two states (its pre-state and its post-state). An event is related to the states before and after it has happened.

atomic event : event that happens instantaneously, i.e. an event without duration, relative to an underlying time granularity [based on BWW:event and GFO:change]. *Examples*: an explosion; a message reception.

complex event : event that is composed of other events by means of event composition operators. *Examples*: a parallel occurrence of two explosions; an absence of a message reception (within some time window); a storm; a heart attack; a football game; a conversation; a birthday party; the Second World War; a Web shop purchase.

state **is pre-state of** *event* : name of a formal relationship type

state **is post-state of** *event* : name of a formal relationship type

4   UFO-C 0.2 – Intentional, Social and Linguistic Things

The 'objective' perdurant categories *event*, *process* and *state* defined in UFO-B are essential concepts for process modelling, but they are not sufficient for *business process* modelling, where intentional and social concepts such as *action*, *activity* and *communication* are needed. The following account of intentional and social things is at an early stage of development and therefore rather incomplete. Nevertheless, we think that it gives an impression of the range of ontological categories that is needed to explain business process modelling.

physical agent : physical object that creates action events affecting other physical objects, that perceives events, possibly created by other physical agents, and to which we can ascribe a mental state

   Examples: a dog; a human; a robot

action event : event that is created through the action of a physical agent

non-action event : event that is not created through an action of a physical agent

physical agent creates action event: designated relationship

physical agent perceives event: designated relationship

non-agentive object : physical object that is not a physical agent

   Examples: a chair; a mountain

mental moment : intrinsic moment that is existentially dependent on a particular agent, being an inseparable part of its mental state

   Examples: a thought; a perception; a belief; a desire; an individual goal

   Constraint: For all *mm* : mental moment; *e*:endurant — if *mm* inheres in *e* then *e* is physical agent

communicating physical agent :   physical agent that communicates with other communicating physical agents

   Examples: a dog; a human; a communication-enabled robot

institutional agent : institutional fact [22] that is an aggregate consisting of communicating agents (its *internal agents*), which share a collective mental state, and that acts, perceives and communicates through them

   Examples: a business unit; a voluntary association

agent : endurant that is either a physical agent or an institutional agent

communicating agent :   agent that communicates with other communicating agents

social moment :   relational individual that is existentially dependent on more than one communicating agent

   Examples: a commitment; a joint intention

The above categories are also defined in the MOF/UML model of figure 7.

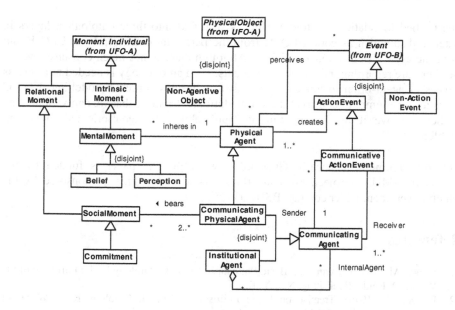

Fig. 7. The categories of the UFO-C 0.2 agent ontology

Agents may interact with their inanimate environment, or they may interact with each other involving some form of communication; in the latter case we speak of *social interaction*.

We consider a business process as a special kind of a social interaction process. Unlike physical or chemical processes, social interaction processes are based on communication acts that may create commitments and are governed by norms. We distinguish between an interaction process type and an interaction process individual, while in the literature the term business process is used ambiguously both at the type and at the instance level.

interaction process : process that includes at least one perception event and one action event perceived and performed by agents that participate in it. *Examples*: someone turning on the light in the office when it becomes dark outside; a football game; a conversation; a birthday party; the Second World War; a Web shop purchase.

social interaction process : interaction process that includes at least one communicative action event. *Examples*: a football game; a conversation; a birthday party; the Second World War; a Web shop purchase.

business process : social interaction process that occurs in the context of a business system and serves a purpose of that system. *Examples*: a football game; a Web shop purchase.

6 Conclusions

The unified foundational ontology UFO is stratified into three ontological layers in order to distinguish its core, UFO-A, from the perdurant extension layer UFO-B and from the agent extension layer UFO-C. Although there is not much consensus yet in the literature regarding the ontology of agents, such an ontology is needed not only as a basis of agent-oriented modelling but also of business process modelling. UFO-C 0.2 is a first attempt to construct these foundations. We hope that we can validate and further improve it by investigating its applicability to agent-oriented modelling problems.

Acknowledgement. Giancarlo Guizzardi's work on this paper is funded by the Freeband A-MUSE project. Freeband (http://www.freeband.nl) is sponsored by the Dutch government under contract BSIK 03025.

References

1. Bunge, M. (1977). Treatise on Basic Philosophy. Vol. 3. Ontology I. The Furniture of the World. D. Reidel Publishing, New York.
2. Bunge, M. (1979). Treatise on Basic Philosophy. Vol. 4. Ontology II. A World of Systems. D. Reidel Publishing, New York.
3. Chapin et al (2004). Business Semantics of Business Rules (BSBR). Initial Submission to OMG BEI RFP br/2003-06-03, 12 January 2004. Available from http://www.omg.org/cgi-bin/doc?bei/04-01-04.
4. Degen, W., Heller, B., Herre, H. & Smith, B. (2001). GOL: Towards an axiomatized upper level ontology. In Smith, B. & Guarino, N. (eds.), Proceedings of FOIS'01, Ogunquit, Maine, USA, October 2001. ACM Press.
5. Evermann, J. & Wand Y. (2001). Towards ontologically based semantics for UML constructs. In Kunii, H.S., Jajodia, S. & Solvberg, A. (eds.), Proceedings of ER 2001, pages 354–367, Springer-Verlag.

6. Gangemi, A., Guarino N., Masolo C., Oltramari, A. & Schneider L. (2002). Sweetening Ontologies with DOLCE. Proceedings of EKAW 2002, Siguenza, Spain.
7. Gärdenfors, P. Conceptual Spaces (2000): the Geometry of Thought. MIT Press, USA, 2000.
8. Green, P.F. & Rosemann, M. (2000). Integrated Process Modelling: An Ontological Evaluation. Information Systems 25 (2), 73-87.
9. Green, P.F. & Rosemann, M. (2002). Usefulness of the BWW Ontological Models as a "Core" Theory of Information Systems. In Proceedings Information Systems Foundations: Building the Theoretical Base, Canberra, 2002, 147-164.
10. Guizzardi, G., Herre, H. & Wagner G. (2002a). On the General Ontological Foundations of Conceptual Modelling. In Proceedings of 21th International Conference on Conceptual Modelling (ER 2002). Springer-Verlag, Berlin, Lecture Notes in Computer Science.
11. Guizzardi, G., Herre, H., Wagner G. (2002b): Towards Ontological Foundations for UML Conceptual Models. In Proceedings of 1st International Conference on Ontologies Databases and Applications of Semantics (ODBASE 2002), Springer-Verlag, Berlin, Lecture Notes in Computer Science.
12. Guizzardi, G., Wagner G., Guarino, N.; van Sinderen, M. (2004): An Ontologically well-Founded Profile for UML Conceptual Models, In Proceedings of the 16th International Conference on Advanced Information Systems Engineering (CaiSE). Springer-Verlag, Berlin, Lecture Notes in Computer Science.
13. Guizzardi, G., Wagner G., Herre, H. (2004): On the Foundations of UML as an Ontology Representation Language. In Proceedings of 14th International Conference on Knowledge Engineering and Knowledge Management (EKAW), Springer-Verlag , Berlin, Lecture Notes in Computer Science.
14. Guizzardi, G., Wagner G., van Sinderen, M. (2004): A Formal Theory of Conceptual Modelling Universals, In Proceedings of the International Workshop on Philosophy and Informatics (WSPI), Germany.
15. Gupta, A. (1980). The Logic of Common Nouns: an investigation in quantified modal logic, Yale University Press, New Haven.
16. Hirsch, E. (1982). The Concept of Identity. Oxford University Press, New York, Oxford.
17. ISO (2000). ISO 1087-1 Terminology work - Vocabulary - Part 1: Theory and application. Copies of all ISO standards can be purchased from ANSI, 25 West 43rd Street, New York, NY 10036, (212) 642-4980, info@ansi.org, or http:webstore.ansi.org".
18. Leeuwen, J. van (1991). Individuals and sortal concepts: an essay in logical descriptive metaphysics, PhD Thesis, University of Amsterdam.
19. Loebe, F. (2003): An Analysis of Roles: Towards Ontology-Based Modelling, Diploma Thesis, Institute for Medical Informatics, Statistics and Epidemiology (IMISE), University of Leipzig.
20. Opdahl, A.L. & Henderson-Sellers, B. (2002). Ontological evaluation of the UML using the Bunge-Wand-Weber Model. Software and Systems Journal 1 (1), 43-67.
21. OMG, Object Management Group (2003). Meta Object Facility (MOF) 2.0 Core Specification, version 2.0, http://www.omg.org/docs/ptc/03-10-04.pdf
22. Searle, J.R. (1995). *The Construction of Social Reality*. Free Press, New York.
23. Smith, B.; Mulligan, K. (1983): Framework for Formal Ontology, Topoi (3), 73-85.
24. Smith, B.; Mulligan, K. (1986): A Relational Theory of the Act, Topoi (5/2), 115-30.
25. Steimann, F. (2000a): On the representation of roles in object-oriented and conceptual modelling, Data & Knowledge Engineering 35:1, 83–106.
26. Steimann, F. (2000b): A radical revision of UML's role concept, in: A Evans, S Kent, B Selic (eds) UML 2000 Proceedings of the 3rd International Conference (Springer, 2000) 194–209.

27. van Belle, J.P. (1999). Moving Towards Generic Enterprise Information Models: From Pacioli to CyC. Proceedings of the 10th Australasian Conference on Information Systems, Wellington.
28. Wand, Y. & Weber, R. (1989). An ontological evaluation of systems analysis and design methods. In Falkenberg, E.D. & Lindgreen, P. (eds.), *Information System Concepts: An In-depth Analysis*, North-Holland.
29. Wand, Y. & Weber, R. (1990). Mario Bunge's Ontology as a formal foundation for information systems concepts. In Weingartner, P. & Dorn, G.J.W. (eds.), *Studies on Mario Bunge's Treatise*, Rodopi, Atlanta.
30. Wand, Y. & Weber, R. (1995). On the deep structure of information systems. Information Systems Journal 5, 203-223.
31. Wand, Y., Storey, V.C. & Weber, R. (1999). An ontological analysis of the relationship construct in conceptual modelling. ACM Transactions on Database Systems, 24(4):494–528.
32. Welty, C. & Guarino, N (2001). Supporting Ontological Analysis of Taxonomic Relationships. *Data and Knowledge Engineering*, 39(1), 51-74.
33. Wiggins, D. (2001). Sameness and Substance Renewed, Cambridge University Press.

APPENDIX A

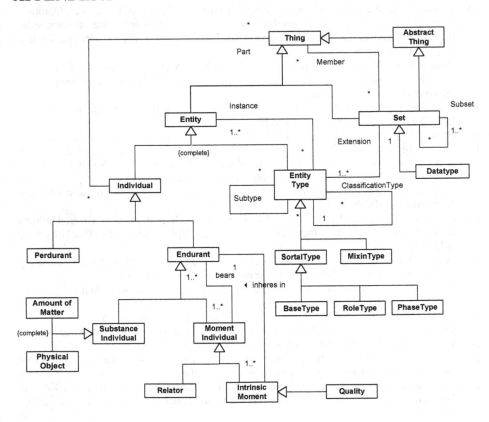

Fig. 8. UFO-A 0.2 as a MOF/UML model

AgentZ: Extending Object-Z for Multi-agent Systems Specification

Anarosa A.F. Brandão[1], Paulo Alencar[2], and Carlos J.P. de Lucena[1]

[1] PUC-Rio, Computer Science Department, SoC+Agent Group,
Rua Marques de São Vicente, 225 - 22453-900, Rio de Janeiro, RJ, Brazil
{anarosa, lucena}@inf.puc-rio.br
[2] University of Waterloo, Computer Science Department, Computer Systems Group,
Waterloo, Ontario, N2L 3G1 Canada
palencar@csg.uwaterloo.ca

Abstract. Agent-orientation has gained increased importance in recent years with the emergence and growth of the World Wide Web, both as an area of study in itself and as a component of other disciplines such as software engineering. As a result, this has led to an increased amount of research developing new informal and formal software engineering techniques to support agent-oriented system specification, design, validation and development. In this paper, we present a formal notation called AgentZ that combines the model concepts and structure proposed by TAO (Taming Agents and Objects), a conceptual framework that provides conceptual foundations for agents and objects, with the well known Z and Object-Z formal representation languages. AgentZ was built to provide a formal notation that allows the verification of design models, a key issue within the emerging agent-oriented software engineering research and, as a result, it can help to improve the quality of MAS.

1 Introduction

Nowadays, the use of software systems in business organizations is rapidly increasing and globalization is one of the trends behind the transformation of many of those systems into distributed information systems (DIS). Agent-orientation is emerging as a new paradigm in software engineering that seems to be well-suited for developing DIS using a multi-agent system (MAS) approach. In addition, the distribution of information and associated technologies indicate that open and distributed architectures are becoming essential for the development of software systems [14]. The complexity associated with these systems is growing fast and, in order to deal with this problem, the research community is developing new methodologies based on agent concepts. Several research results address the analysis and design development phases, and some modelling languages and methodologies such as MAS-ML[13], AUML [1], Gaia[19], MaSE [18], and AORML [17] have been proposed in the literature.

Software engineering of MAS is at its early stage of development and many related concepts and abstractions are still under development and formalization. Our research

P. Bresciani et al. (Eds.): AOIS 2004, LNAI 3508, pp. 125 – 139, 2005.
© Springer-Verlag Berlin Heidelberg 2005

group[1] is working to provide a better understanding of the interplay between the notions of agents and objects in the development of MAS from a software engineering perspective. Following this path, we have first developed TAO [14], a conceptual framework that provides an approach to agent and object-based software engineering, while defining an ontology that establishes the essential concepts or abstractions that can be used to develop an MAS. Thereafter, one of our colleagues developed MAS-ML. MAS-ML is a multi-agent system modelling language that extends UML (Unified Modelling Language) [16], based on the structural and dynamic properties presented in TAO. In this work we present a first version of a formal notation called AgentZ that combines the structure proposed in TAO for agents and objects with the well-known formal notation Z [15] and Object-Z[3,4].

The combination of agent and object-orientation structure with Z took advantage of the idea adopted by Object-Z of encapsulating state and operations in a single structure. AgentZ extends Object-Z with new constructs to enhance structuring and to accommodate new agent-oriented entities such as agents, organizations, roles and environments.

AgentZ is a formal notation that allows the verification of design models, a key issue within the emerging research area of agent-oriented software engineering. By design verification we mean the process of checking that a design conforms to its specification. We believe that AgentZ can help produce better system design models and, as a result, will help pave the way for the development of MASs using MDA approach [10].

The structure of this work is as follows. In Section 2 we describe the TAO conceptual framework, the MAS-ML modelling language and the Object-Z formal notation. In Section 3 we describe the abstract syntax of AgentZ and some of its semantics. In Section 4 we illustrate our approach by an example and in Section 5 we describe some related work. Finally, in Section 6 we present our conclusions and future work.

2 Background

The main reason for developing AgentZ is that agents and objects are conceptually different in essence. Actually, the state and behaviour of agents and objects differ in a way that prevents the general use of object-orientation extension mechanisms. The state of an object is composed of stored information about itself, about the environment and about other objects, and does not have any predefined structure as well. On the other hand, the agent state is composed of its goals, beliefs, plans and actions, and does have some predefined structure. Object behaviour is defined by the operations an object can perform, and agent behaviour is guided by the agency properties such as autonomy, interaction and adaptation.

Our research group has developed TAO, and, as a spin-off from this investigation, one of our colleagues developed MAS-ML by augmenting the UML metamodel with some new metaclasses that represent agent abstractions. Based on the idea that MAS-ML extends the UML metamodel, we have decided to extend the Object-Z

---

[1] www.teccomm.les.inf.puc-rio.br/socagents.

metamodel in a similar way to define AgentZ. Therefore, it will be possible to define a formal mapping between MAS-ML models and AgentZ specifications, since such a mapping can be defined between UML models and ObjectZ specifications [8]. Having such a mapping between MAS-ML models and AgentZ specifications will give a precise semantics to the MAS-ML models which entitle us to verify them. In the following we introduce the TAO conceptual framework and briefly describe MAS-ML and Object-Z.

The TAO Conceptual Framework

TAO (Taming Agents and Objects) is a conceptual framework developed by our research group for two main purposes. The first was to better understand the interplay between the notions of agents and objects, and the second was to provide a systematic approach to agent and object-based software engineering. This framework defines an ontology with the essential abstractions that can be used to develop an MAS.

In TAO, an MAS comprises classes and instances of agents, objects and organizations. TAO entities are agents, objects, organizations, roles (agent and object roles), environments and events. Agents, organizations and objects inhabit environments [7, 9]. While objects represent passive elements, such as resources, agents represent autonomous elements that manipulate objects. Agents have beliefs and goals, they know how to execute some actions and plans, and they are always playing a role in an organization. An organization describes a set of roles [2] that may limit the behaviour of its agents, objects and sub-organizations [20]. Furthermore, organizations have axioms that guide the behaviour of their agents based on the roles they play. Agents and objects can be members of different organizations and play different roles in each of them [11]. Agents may interact with each other and cooperate either to achieve a common goal, or to achieve their own goals [22]. Agent interactions with elements that are not agents are based on relationships. Interactions between agents occur when messages described in a specific communication language are exchanged. An agent can interact with agents from the same organization or with agents from a different one. The relationships defined on TAO are *Inhabit, Play, Ownership, Control, Dependency, Association* and *Aggregation*.

The MAS-ML Modelling Language

MAS-ML is an MAS modelling language that extends UML in a conservative way and is based on TAO metamodel [13]. MAS-ML adds new metaclasses to the UML metamodel in order to include TAO concepts that are not object-oriented. In the following, we describe the MAS-ML metamodel.

The MAS-ML metamodel extends (part of) the UML metamodel by adding new metaclasses to the metamodel and by creating new stereotypes to support agent-orientation. The new metaclasses *AgentClass, OrganizationClass, ObjectRoleClass* and *AgentRoleClass* extend the UML metaclass *Classifier,* and they refer to agent, organization, object role and agent role TAO abstractions, respectively. In addition, the new metaclasses *PlanClass, ActionAgent* and *ProtocolClass* extend the UML metaclass *Behavioural Feature* and they refer to plans, actions and protocols that an agent can perform.

The metaclass *AgentClass* has the structural features *Belief* and *Goal*. These features are defined by using stereotypes based on the *Attribute* metaclass, which is a specialization of the *StructuralFeature* UML metaclass. Moreover, an *AgentClass* is also associated with the new metaclasses *ActionAgent, PlanClass*, and *ProtocolClass*.

In our formal notation, we describe these new metaclasses as new constructs using a Z-like style following the Object-Z [3] idea. Furthermore, the new stereotypes define new or given sets. In this work we will focus on the *AgentClass*, the *AgentRoleClass* and the *OrganizationClass* constructs.

Object-Z

Object-Z is an extension of the formal specification language Z to accommodate object-oriented concepts. This extension introduces a *class* structure to Z structures that encapsulates a single state schema with the operations that may affect that state [4]. Instances of *class* structures are called *objects*. Also, Object-Z uses the same pattern of class instantiation in object-orientation, through the definition of *object containment*, which stores the object *id* every time a class is instantiated. In addition, Object-Z supports (multiple) inheritance, which means that complex classes can be specified in terms of simpler ones. One of the main benefits of Object-Z is to improve the clarity of large specifications through enhanced structuring [4].

3 AgentZ

Our formal notation is called AgentZ, which is obtained by adding some new constructs to Object-Z. As in the case of the Object-Z definition, we are also using the Z notation from [15]. In the following, we present the formal notation that will be illustrated in Section 4 through an example related to the supermarket domain.

Basic Concepts

The metamodel of AgentZ is based on the TAO conceptual framework. Moreover, as it shares the same basis as the MAS-ML metamodel, they present several similarities. The AgentZ metamodel is shown in Figure . As in MAS-ML the Class metaclass is borrowed from the UML metamodel, the (object) class in AgentZ is the *Class* schema borrowed from Object-Z. According to TAO, agents, objects, organizations, roles and environments are elements. Elements are entities that have properties and relationships, and agents are elements that extend objects by redefining their state and behavioural properties. In this sense, both agents and objects are element extensions that redefine the element state and behavioural properties. The structural properties of an agent are expressed by its beliefs and goals. The agent behavioural properties are expressed by its plans and actions and the roles it plays.

The AgentZ metamodel defines Agent, Organization, AgentRole, Environment, and Object as extensions of Element. As agents are always playing at least one role in an organization, they depend on agent roles. Organizations extend agents in the sense that organizations have the same structural (goals and beliefs) and behavioural (plans and actions) properties that agents have with additional capabilities. Environments extend Element since they have structural (and possibly behavioural) properties that characterize them, and they have relationships to other elements (such as *Inhabit* and *Association*, among others).

The main reason for extending Object-Z by adding structures to Object-Z instead of simply extending the *Class* schema of Object-Z is that the state of an agent is a mental state that, in contrast with the state of an object, includes structural (goals and beliefs) and behavioural (actions and plans) properties.

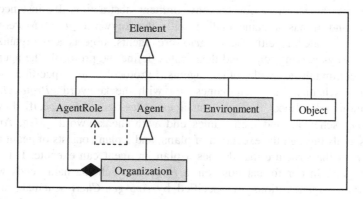

Fig. 1. The AgentZ metamodel

We adopt d'Inverno and Luck's [6] definition for Attribute: an attribute is every *perceivable feature*, and the set of all attributes is defined as [*Attribute*]. Beliefs and goals are perceivable features that can be defined as subsets of *Attribute*. The set of relationships defined in TAO is shown in Figure 2. The main AgentZ extension is the new *AgentClass* construct. We note that in principle agents cannot be simply defined as a stereotype of objects since they are object extensions that redefine the object state and behaviour, and we cannot use the *Class* construct of Object-Z to represent them.

Relationship := *Inhabit* | *Play* | *Specialization* | *Control* | *Dependency* | *Association* | *Aggregation* | *Ownership*

Belief == P*Attribute* and *Goal* == P*Attribute*

Fig. 2. Initial sets

In order to define some relationships described in Fig. 2., we define sets of names for each new construct of our formal notation. Each name is of type *String*, and this makes it possible to perform operations involving names. All the names are elements of the given set [*Names*]. The relationships are binary relations whose signatures are specified in Figure 3.

An *AgentClass* is the structure for the agent abstraction. Each *AgentClass* instance is an agent and it has a name ending with the keyword *_Agent*. Agents are related to agent roles, to organizations, to objects and to environments. An *AgentRoleClass* is the structure for the agent role abstraction. Each *AgentRoleClass* instance is an agent role and it has a name ending with the keyword *_AgRole*. Agent roles are related to agents, objects and organizations. An *OrganizationClass* is the structure for the organization abstraction. Each *OrganizationClass* instance is an organization that has a name ending with the keyword *_Org* and that is related to all TAO elements. *Elements* are agents, objects, organizations, agent roles and environments. An *Environment* is the structure for the environment abstraction. Its instance is an environment and it has a name ending with the keyword *_Env*. Moreover, an environment is related to citizens. *Citizens* are agents, objects and organizations. Agents are always playing roles, and these roles define the protocols the agent must follow to communicate with other agents. Protocols are specified via the *ProtocolClass* schemata and their names end with the keyword *_Protocol*. Agent communication is defined through messages. Messages are specified via the *MessageAgent* schemata and their names end with the keyword *_Msg*. An agent achieves its goals through the execution of plans, and a plan consists of agent actions. A *PlanClass* is the structure that defines a plan an agent can execute. It is always related to a goal. In our formal notation, a *PlanClass* schema name ends with the keyword *_Plan*. Agent actions are specified by *ActAgentClass* schemata and their names end with the keyword *_ActAgent*. Agents' beliefs and goals can be described as logical expressions. Organizations have axioms that describe the laws that guide the behaviour of their agents.

$$Inhabit : Citizen\_Name \times Env\_Name$$
$$Play : Citizen \_ Name \times Role \_ Name$$
$$Dependency : Roles\_Name \times Roles\_Name$$
$$Association : Element\_Name \times Element\_Name$$
$$Control : AgRole \_ Name \times AgRole \_ Name$$
$$Aggregation : Aggregated \_ Name \times Aggregated \_ Name$$
$$Specialization : Abstraction \_ Name \times Abstraction \_ Name$$
$$Ownership : Org \_ Name \times Roles \_ Name$$

Fig. 3. Signature of the relationships

The relationships defined in TAO are *Inhabit, Play, Dependency, Association, Control, Aggregation, Specialization/Inheritance* and *Ownership*. They are binary relations between elements. Elements encompass agents, objects, organizations, agent roles and environments. The *Inhabit* relationship relates each citizen to the environment in which it is registered. The *Play* relationship relates each citizen to the role it plays. *Dependency* is a relationship between agent roles. It establishes that a change in a role that supplies another role affects the supplied one. *Association* is a relationship between elements. *Control* is a relationship between agent roles, meaning that an agent that plays a role controlled by other agent role must do everything the controller asks it to do. *Aggregation* is a relationship between objects, between object roles, between agent roles and between organizations. It has the same meaning in object orientation, *e.g,*. the aggregated element is part of the aggregator element. *Specialization* is a relationship that relates a sub-element to a super-element in a sense that the sub-element can redefine the properties and relationships inherited from the super-element. *Ownership* is a relationship that relates an organization to the roles that are defined in it.

Our formal notation begins with the definition of an *Element* schema in the same way it is defined in TAO. An element is an entity that has properties and relationships but we have omitted its definition for brevity.

According to TAO, an *Environment* is an element that is the habitat for agents, objects and organizations, which define the set of citizens. The main characteristic of a citizen has to be registered in a specific environment.

Agent and Agent Role Structures

Syntactically, an *AgentClass* is a named box (Figure 4) that extends an *Element* and includes a list of inherited *AgentClass* schema names, a list of included *ActAgentClass* schemata, a list of included *PlanClass* schemata and two sets of *AgentRoleClass* names. The inherited *AgentClass* schemata provide support multiple inheritance. The included *ActAgentClass* and *PlanClass* schemata represent the actions and plans that can be performed by the agent, independently of the role it is playing. The sets of roles indicate the roles the agent can play during its lifecycle (*roles*) and the roles that it must play when the *AgentClass* is instantiated (*init_roles*). Following the way Object-Z was defined, there is an *Init* box inside the *AgentClass* structure, which enforces that when an *AgentClass* is instantiated the agent must be registered in an *Environment* and it must be associated with an initial role. This role must be one of the roles in the set *init_roles*, which means that the set *roles* contains *init_roles*.

An *AgentClass* also has an "axiom part". Separated from the descriptions previously described by a horizontal line, there is a specification of the *Element* extension and a restriction related to the sets of *AgentRoleClass* names. The *Element* extension is specified by the set of properties description as the union of the sets *Belief* and *Goal*, which represent the structural agent properties. In addition, the description of the relationships set is composed of the relationships *Inhabit, Play, Association* and *Specialization*. The restriction about the sets of roles specifies that the initial roles must be in the set of roles the agent can play during its lifecycle.

As can be seen, the *AgentClass* structure is quite complex, including in its description other new structures such as *ActAgentClass*, *PlanClass* and *AgentRoleClass*. We will describe these new structures in the following paragraphs and then illustrate them using an example from the market domain.

In order to describe the *AgentClass* construct in more detail we define constructs used in its definition. The *PlanClass* schema is a named box whose name finishes with the keyword *_Plan*, and it includes the set of goals that the plan can achieve and the associated actions. Separated from them by a horizontal line, it includes an axiom part consisting of the sequence of actions that need to be executed in order to achieve the goal(s). Plans are not necessarily defined as ordered sequences of actions. An agent must have at least one plan and, in the case of planner agents, a plan can consist of building a plan to achieve its goals. An example of a *PlanClass* can be found in Section 4.

The *ActAgentClass* schema differs from the *Operation* schema of Object-Z in a significant way: it does not contain a list of affected states, but includes a list of pre-conditions and the result the action must produce. The action result can be a goal achievement, the satisfaction of another action pre-condition or even the maintenance of the initial pre-condition (e.g., in this case the action is not executed successfully). An example of this schema can be found in Section 4.

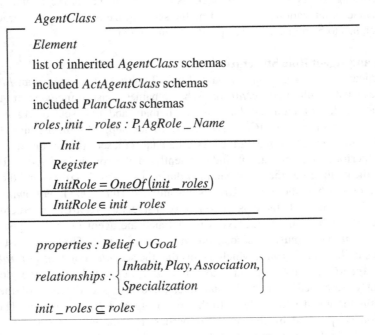

Fig. 4. AgentClass structure in AgentZ

According to TAO, an agent is always playing a role, which affects the agent behaviour by defining the protocols the agent must follow in order to interact with other agents, the actions it can execute and the actions it must execute to achieve its goals. We define an *AgentRoleClass* schema as a named box (Figure 4) and its name ends with the keyword *_AgRole*. Following this idea and the MAS-ML metamodel, an *AgentRoleClass* extends an *Element* and includes a list of *ProtocolClass* schemata, a set of *PlanClass* schema names (*plans*), and sets of action names (*duties* and *rights*). The set *duties* contains the actions the agent that play this role must perform and the set *rights* contains the actions the agent can perform. Following the same pattern used in the definition of the *AgentClass* schema, the extension of *Element* is specified by describing the *properties* as the union of the sets *Belief* and *Goal*, and by describing the relationships set as composed of *Control, Dependency, Association, Aggregation* and *Specialization*. The restriction about the sets *duties* and *rights* is that the former set is contained in the latter.

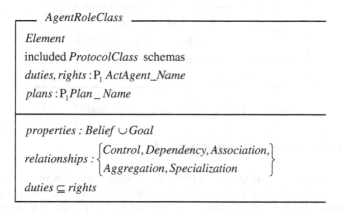

Fig. 5. AgentRoleClass structure in AgentZ

We note that in the *AgentRoleClass* schema there are some protocol schemata. In MAS-ML, protocols define the set of interactions that an agent must perform in order to communicate with other agents. Actually, these interactions are sequences of messages exchanged by agents while playing roles that can be defined as a relation between two sets of *Msg_Name*. The *ProtocolClass* structure definition includes a set of *Msg_Name* and a set of interactions.

Agent Organizations

The *OrganizationClass* schema is a named box (Figure 6) whose name ends with the keyword *_Org*. As an organization extends the properties an agent has, its schema includes agent properties and relationships. The extension is obtained via the specification of the organization relationships, a declaration stating that the set of initial roles to be played by an organization is empty, as well as a declaration stating that the content of the set *roles* is composed of the roles that can be played by this organization within the context of another. In addition, the *OrganizationClass* schema includes a list of *AgentClass* names. This list specifies the agents that are related to the organizations created from this schema. The *Ownership* relationship and the projection function *second* [15] define the set *roles*. The initial state of an organization is defined by its register in an environment. Moreover, an *OrganizationClass* schema has a set of axioms that contains the laws that guide the behaviour of the agents in the organization.

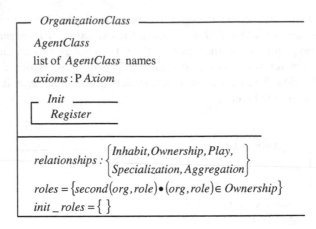

Fig. 6. OrganizationClass structure in AgentZ

4 Working Example: A Supermarket

The example we are considering, which involves a supermarket, is the same example as that used in [13]. We consider a market where buyers and sellers negotiate products. Sellers advertise their desire to sell products, publishing offers in the market. Buyers access the market in order to buy products. They look for offers that fulfil their needs. Buyers can buy wholesale or retail items. Usually, wholesale items have a lower price per unit. However, sometimes the buyer does not need all the units packaged as one item. Therefore, buyers can form groups to find other buyers interested in the same item. The group of buyers buys the item and distributes the units among the buyers.

Figure 7 shows an example of the *AgentClass* schema. It is part of the system model that represents the user agent. The user agent of the example can be initialized as a buyer or a seller. The user agent beliefs are *Item, RetailOffer, WholeSaleOffer, Proposal* and *CounterProposal*. The goal of this agent is to deal with items.

An example of the *AgentRoleClass* schema can be seen in Figure 8, where the role buyer, which can be played by the *User_Agent*, is described. The goal of this role is to buy an item and his duty is to look for items. The *rights* that the *User_Agent* has while playing the *Buyer_AgRole* include that one from *duties* added to the rights of accepting or rejecting an offer, receiving the item and of joining a group to participate in a wholesale. It uses the FIPA Propose protocol and the Deal protocol to interact with the other *User_Agent* playing the roles *Seller_AgRole* or *Mediator_AgRole*, in order to achieve its goal. The definition of which agent role it will interact with is given by the defined relationships. The roles *Mediator_AgRole* and *Member_AgRole* are the ones the agent must choose to participate in a wholesale.

The agent role *Buyer_AgRole* is owned by an organization called *Supermarket_Org*. This organization can be modelled as described in Figure 9. There are two agents that may play roles inside it (*User_Agent* and *System_Agent*). It is registered in the *Supermarket_Env*, the environment where the organization inhabits. *Supermarket_Org* owns the roles *Seller_AgRole, Buyer_AgRole, Member_AgRole, Mediator_AgRole*, and *Verifier_AgRole*. Moreover, the organization is associated with some objects such as *Item, Offer* and *Proposal*.

```
┌─ User_Agent ─────────────────────────────────────────────────────
│ beliefs : Belief
│ goals : Goal
│ relationships : Relationship
│ roles,init_roles : P AgRoles_Name
│ lookForItem_ActAgent; accept_ActAgent;
│ reject_ActAgent; receiveItem_ActAgent;
│ joinGroup_ActAgent
│ buyRetail_Plan; buyWholesale_Plan
│ ┌─ Init ──────────────────────────────────────────────────
│ │ Register(self, Supermarket_Env )
│ │ InitRole ∈ init_roles• (InitRole = Buyer_AgRole)∨ (InitRole = Seller_AgRole)
│ └──────────────────────────────────────────────────────────
│
│ beliefs = {Item, RetailOffer, WholeSaleOffer, Proposal, CounterProposal}
│ goals = {deal_With_Items}
│ init_roles = {Buyer_AgRole, Seller_AgRole}
│ roles = init_roles∪ {Mediator_AgRole, Member_AgRole}
│ relationships = {Inhabit, Play, Association}
│ (self, Supermarket_Env )∈ Inhabit
│ {(self, Buyer_AgRole)(self, Seller_AgRole)(self, Mediator_AgRole)(self, Member_AgRole)}⊂ Play
└──────────────────────────────────────────────────────────────────
```

Fig. 7. AgentClass structure example

```
┌─ Buyer_AgRole ───────────────────────────────────────────────────
│
│  beliefs : Belief
│  goals : Goal
│  duties, rights : P ActAgent_Name
│  plans : PPlan _Name
│  ProposeFIPA_Protocol; DealWith_Protocol
│ ─────────────────────────────────────────────────────────────────
│
│  beliefs = {Item, RetailOffer, WholeSaleOffer, Proposal, CounterProposal}
│  goals = {buyItem}
│  duties = {lookForItem_ActAgent}
│                  ⎧ accept_ActAgent, reject_ActAgent,        ⎫
│  rights = duties ∪⎨                                          ⎬
│                  ⎩ receiveItem_ActAgent, joinGroup_ActAgent ⎭
│  plans = {buyRetail_Plan; buyWholesale_Plan}
│  (self, Seller_AgRole)∈ Association
│  (self, Mediator_AgRole), (self, Member_AgRole)∈ Aggregation
└──────────────────────────────────────────────────────────────────
```

Fig. 8. AgentRoleClass structure example

$$
\begin{array}{|l}
\hline
\quad\text{Supermarket\_Org} \underline{\hspace{6cm}} \\
\text{User\_Agent} \\
\text{System\_Agent} \\
\quad\boxed{\begin{array}{l} \text{Init} \underline{\hspace{3cm}} \\ \text{Register}(self, Supermarket\_Env) \end{array}} \\
\hline
relationships = \{Inhabit, Ownership, Association\} \\
roles = \left\{ \begin{array}{l} Seller\_AgRole, Buyer\_AgRole, Member\_AgRole, \\ Mediator\_AgRole, Verifier\_AgRole \end{array} \right\} \\
(self, Supermarket\_Env) \in Inhabit; \\
\left. \begin{array}{l} (self, Seller\_AgRole)(self, Buyer\_AgRole)(self, Member\_AgRole) \\ (self, Mediator\_AgRole)(self, Verifier\_AgRole) \end{array} \right\} \subset Ownership \\
\left. \begin{array}{l} (self, Item)(self, RetailOffer)(self, WholesaleOffer) \\ (self, Proposal)(self, CounterProposal) \end{array} \right\} \subset Association \\
\hline
\end{array}
$$

Fig. 9. OrganizationClass structure example

$$
\begin{array}{|l}
\hline
\quad\text{buyRetail\_Plan} \underline{\hspace{6cm}} \\
goals : PGoal \\
actions : P\ ActAgent \\
\hline
goals = \{buyItem\} \\
seq\ actions = \left\langle \begin{array}{l} lookForItem\_ActAgent, accept\_ActAgent, \\ payFor\_ActAgent, receive\_ActAgent \end{array} \right\rangle \\
\hline
\end{array}
$$

Fig. 10. Example of PlanClass structure

$$
\begin{array}{|l}
\hline
\quad\text{lookForItem\_ActAgent} \underline{\hspace{4cm}} \\
item\ ? : Item \\
\hline
pre \equiv \neg find(item\ ?) \\
result \equiv find(item\ ?) \vee tryagain \\
\hline
\end{array}
$$

Fig. 11. Example of ActAgent Class structure

We note that in the *User_Agent* class schema, the user agent has some plans and associated actions. In the following, we describe the *buyRetail_Plan* (Fig.), a plan that agents can use to achieve the goal of buying an item being sold through a retail sale. This plan is composed of a sequence of actions and has *lookForItem_ActAgent* as its initial action (Figure 11).

As our focus is not on how the actions are implemented but on its pre-conditions and results, the *lookForItem_ActAgent* (Figure 11) just specifies that in order to find an item, this item must not have been already found. After the action is executed there are two possible results: either the item was found or the *tryagain* expression was obtained, which means that the pre-condition can still be true after the execution of the action.

5 Related Work

There are several research results related to the formal specification of MASs and most of them target specific system features such as agent communication and agent behaviour.

Hilaire *et al.* [5] combine Object-Z and statecharts to specify an MAS since they understand that each of them, when considered in isolation, lack the expressiveness to specify the complex features associated with MASs. In this sense, we agree that Object-Z does not have enough expressiveness to specify MAS. For instance, instead of combining Object-Z with another existing formalism we have decided to extend it by augmenting it with new structures in order to support the specification of agent-related abstractions.

d'Inverno and Luck [6] defined a formal framework for MAS specification using Z. Their work is general and the formal specification that uses their framework is *ad hoc*. In contrast, our work provides a basis for the formalization of MAS-ML models.

Perini et al, [12] combine formal and informal specification to model agent systems using the Tropos methodology and the Formal Tropos specification. A Formal Tropos specification extends a Tropos specification by adding annotations and constraints that characterize valid behaviours of the model. Their work is concerned with the specification of functional requirements of the model and ours is concerned with a specification that allows the verification of the design structure and properties.

AgentZ is a formal notation that addresses the systematic design of MAS using the specific set of modelling constructs defined in MAS-ML and, for this reason, it can be also used as a rigorous starting point for validation and implementation efforts.

6 Conclusions and Future Work

In this work we have presented the first version of AgentZ, a formal notation that combines the agent and object-oriented structures proposed in TAO with the formal notations Z and Object-Z. By defining AgentZ, we have intended to increase the expressiveness of Z and Object-Z by allowing the encapsulation of the complexity associated with both agent and object abstractions. Therefore, by using a notation such as AgentZ, specifications may be shorter and more understandable, and formally characterize design models.

AgentZ was developed to provide a formal notation that allows the verification of MASs design models. In principle, it can be used to validate design properties such as the ones related to the structure of MAS static diagrams, which includes the relationships and the entity types involved in a specific MAS static diagram (e.g. a class diagram, an organization diagram or a role diagram described in MAS-ML). In this sense, we believe it should help to improve the quality of the multi-agent system designs.

While a first version of AgentZ was described in this paper, there are many areas that need to be explored to improve this initial version. The semantics of AgentZ must be examined, which includes the definition of the new introduced types. The definition of a formal mapping between AgentZ models and MAS-ML models, which was one of the reasons that motivated us to begin the development of AgentZ, will also be part of our future activities. Finally, there is a need of tools for AgentZ support.

Acknowledgements. This work is partially supported by CNPq/Brazil under the project "ESSMA", number 5520681/2002-0 Anarosa A. F. Brandão and Carlos J. P. de Lucena and by grant No 140179/95-0 from CNPq/Brazil for Anarosa A. F. Brandão. Paulo Alencar research was supported by the Natural Sciences and Engineering Research Council of Canada (NSERC), Human Resources Development Canada (HRDC) and IBM Canada.

References

1. Bauer, B. Müller, J.P. and Odell, J. *Agent UML: A Formalism for Specifying Multiagent Software Systems* In: Ciancarini and Wooldridge (Eds) Agent-Oriented Software Engineering, Springer-Verlag, LNCS vol 1957, 2001.
2. Biddle, J; Thomas, E. *Role Theory: Concepts and Research*. John Wiley and Sons, New York, 1966
3. Carrington, D. and Smith, G. *Extending Z for Object-Oriented Specifications*, 5th Australian Software Engineering Conference, Sydney, May 1990.
4. Duke, R., King, P., Rose, G., Smith, G. *The Object-Z Specification Language: version 1*, Software Verification Research Centre, The University of Queensland, Technical Report 91-01, April 1991.
5. Hilaire, v., Koukam, A., Gruer, P and Müller, J-P. *Formal Specification and Prototyping of MAS*, In: Omicini, A et al (Eds) ESAW 2000, LNAI 1972, Springer-Verlag, pp 114-127, 2000.
6. d'Inverno, M. and Luck, M.: *Understanding Agent Systems*, Springer Verlag, 2001.
7. Jennings, N. *Agent-Oriented Software Engineering*. In: Proceedings of the 20th Intl. Conf. on Industrial and Engineering Applications of Artificial Intelligence, pp 4-10, 1999.
8. Kim, S-K. and Carrington, D. *A Formal Mapping Between UML Models and Object-Z Specifications*, In. Bowen,J.P. et al (Eds): ZB 2000, LNCS 1878, pp 2-21, Springer Verlag, 2000
9. Lind, J. *MASSIVE: Software Engineering for Multiagent Systems*, PhD Thesis, university of Saarland, 2000.
10. *MDA – Model Driven Architecture*, http://www.omg.org/mda/
11. Parunak, H. and Odell, J. *Representing Social Structures in UML*. In: Proceedings of Agent Oriented Software Engineering, pp 1-16, 2001.

12. Perini, A., Pistore, M., Roveri, M. and Susi, A . *Agent-oriented modelling by interleaving formal and informal specification*, in P. Giorgini, J. Muler and J. Odell (Eds) Modelling Agents and Multi-Agent-Systems, LNCS 2935, pp 36-52, Springer-Verlag, 2003.

13. Silva, V. and Lucena, C. *From a Conceptual Framework for Agents and Objects to a Multi-Agent System Modelling Language*, In: Sycara, K., Wooldridge, M. (Eds.), Journal of Autonomous Agents and Multi-Agent Systems, Kluwer Academic Publishers, Vol. 9, issue 1-2, pp.145-189, 2004.

14. Silva, V. , Garcia, A., Brandão, A., Chavez, C., Lucena, C., Alencar, P. *Taming Agents and Objects in Software Engineering*, Lecture Notes in Computer Science, vol 2603, 2003.

15. Spivey, J.M. *The Z Notation: a Reference Manual*, Prentice Hall, 2nd edition, 1992. (on-line version at http://spivey.oriel.ox.ac.uk/~mike/zrm/ - 14/05/2003)

16. *UML – The Unified Modelling Language*, http://www.omg.org/uml/

17. Wagner, G. *The Agent-Object-Relationship Metamodel: Towards a Unified View of State and Behaviour*, Information Systems, Vol 28, 5, 475 – 504, 2003

18. Wood, M.F. and DeLoach, S.A. *An Overview of the Multiagent Systems Engineering Methodology*, In: Ciancarini and Wooldridge (Eds) Agent-Oriented Software Engineering, Springer-Verlag, LNCS vol 1957, 2001.

19. Wooldridge, M., Jennings, N. and Kinny, David *The Gaia methodology for Agent-Oriented Analysis and Design*, Journal of Autonomous Agents and Multi-Agent Systems, vol 3, pp 285-312, 2000.

20. Wooldridge, M. and Ciancarini, P. *Agent-Oriented Software Engineering: The State of the Art*, In: Ciancarini and Wooldridge (Eds) Agent-Oriented Software Engineering, Springer-Verlag, LNCS vol 1957, 2001.

21. Wooldridge, M. and Ciancarini, P. *Agent-Oriented Software Engineering*, Handbook of Software Engineering & Knowledge Engineering Fundamentals, Chang, S. K. (ed), vol. 1, 2001.

22. Zambonelli, F., Jennings, N. and Wooldridge, M. *Organizational Abstractions for the Analysis and Design of Multi-Agent Systems*, In: Ciancarini and Wooldridge (Eds) Agent-Oriented Software Engineering, Springer-Verlag, LNCS vol 1957, 2001.

Incorporating Elements from the Prometheus Agent-Oriented Methodology in the OPEN Process Framework

Brian Henderson-Sellers, Quynh-Nhu N. Tran, and John Debenham

Faculty of Information Technology,
University of Technology, Sydney,
PO Box 123, Broadway,
NSW 2007, Australia
numitran@yahoo.com
{brian, debenham}@it.uts.edu.au

Abstract. As part of an extensive research programme to combine the benefits of method engineering and existing object-oriented frameworks (notably the OPEN Process Framework or OPF) to create a highly supportive methodological environment for the construction of agent-oriented information systems, we have analysed here contributions to the OPF repository of method fragments from the Prometheus agent-oriented methodology. We have identified three new Tasks, together with two new subtasks for a pre-existing Task and one additional Technique. Prometheus has also supplied the OPF with four new Work Products but no additional Roles or Stages.

1 Introduction

The increasing interest in agents and agent-oriented methodologies requires the construction of high quality software methodologies. There are an increasing number of stand-alone methodologies but none of these supports all methodology elements across the full lifecycle, instead focussing solely on agent-specific issues such as social interaction, autonomy and reasoning processes. There is also debate as to whether an agent-oriented methodology should be seen as a new mindset requiring a brand new approach or whether it can be considered as extending the object-oriented paradigm and methodology. While the former view has been advocated by e.g. Tropos [1], we have already shown [2,3] that this view can be accommodated within an object-oriented framework approach and it is this view that is taken in this paper.

Object-oriented (OO) methodologies do not take into account agency concepts. Recently, there has been interest in identifying how an object-oriented methodology might be extended or enhanced to support these newer ideas. Several proposals have been made. For instance, Gaia [4] takes as its basis the Fusion methodology [5]; ADELFE [6] starts with RUP [7] (although the citation is actually to the Unified Software Development Process [8]). Such methodologies have a specific and restricted focus, for instance to a particular lifecycle stage e.g. Tropos [1] has a strong

P. Bresciani et al. (Eds.): AOIS 2004, LNAI 3508, pp. 140–156, 2005.
© Springer-Verlag Berlin Heidelberg 2005

emphasis on early requirements engineering. Outside their stated scope, however, they have little or no application. Here, we focus on a *comprehensive* software development approach and seek a methodological environment that has the capacity to be flexible enough to support new ideas as they appear and become accepted as well as the old, well-established ones [9]. Merging of methodologies has been addressed from an informal viewpoint [10]; however, a more rigorous and highly promising approach to offer such support is that of method engineering [11,12,13].

This paper reports on part of an extensive research programme to combine the benefits of method engineering and existing object-oriented frameworks (notably the OPEN Process Framework or OPF [14,15]) to create a highly supportive environment for the construction of agent-oriented information systems. By starting with a repository of OO method fragments (sometimes called method chunks [16] or process components[1][15]), the research questions relate to the identification of new (or extended) method fragments necessary to support various flavours of agent-oriented applications development. To do this, we are examining each of the extant AO methodologies in turn to see what must be added to the OPF repository so that that particular AO methodology can be (re)created from the elements in the extended OPF. In this paper, we focus on the Prometheus AO methodology [17,18,19] to complement our previous analysis of, *inter alia*, Tropos [3], Gaia [20] and MaSE [21].

In Section 2, we outline the ideas of method engineering (ME) followed by a brief summary in Section 3 of our selected OO situational method engineering approach – that based on the OPF [15]. In Section 4, we describe the basics of Prometheus and then in Section 5 describe the elements of Prometheus not currently supported in the OPF and which we therefore propose for addition to the OPF repository.

2 Method Engineering

Method engineering [11,12] is a rational approach to the construction, either fully or partially, of methods (a.k.a. methodologies) from method fragments typically stored in a repository. The method itself is constructed by selection of appropriate method fragments followed by their configuration in such a way as to satisfy the requirements for the method [22] and create a meaningful overall method [23]. A method that is targetted at a particular project or environment is known as a situated or situational method and the means of its derivation known as situational method engineering (SME) [13].

Ideally, a method engineering approach to process/method construction will utilize a process metamodel from which current and future method fragments can be generated by the instantiation rule. These generated fragments will be consistent with the rules of the metamodel, a rule for instance that might state that a producer (usually a person) can utilize a work unit (such as a task) in order to product some kind of work product (e.g. documentation, code). Such rules also automatically impose some granularity constraints as noted in [23]. A second set of rules and guidelines is needed to assist in process/method construction [24], an approach that can also potentially be

---

[1] A methodology is a combination of a process and a set of products. We focus on the process portion. Thus, the words "method", "methodology", "process" are taken here effectively as synonyms.

automated [25,26]. Here, we call a combination of metamodel and generated method fragments (stored in a repository) a process framework.

3 The OPEN Process Framework

The OPEN (Object-oriented Process, Environment, and Notation) Process Framework (OPF) [15] combines a process metamodel and a repository of method fragments (Figure 1). Elements from the repository are selected and put together to form a specific situational method. Method elements are related to other method elements with a possibility value known as a deontic value [14]. Deontic matrices can be defined for (1) Process/Activity, (2) Activity/Task, (3) Task/Technique, (4) Producer/Task, (5) Task/Work Product, (6) Producer/Work Product and (7) Work Product/Language. Deontic values have one of five values ranging from mandatory through optional to forbidden. This gives a high degree of flexibility to the method engineer who can allocate different deontic values for any specific pair of method fragments depending upon the context i.e. the specific project, skills set of the development team etc. Allocating these deontic values is the responsibility of the method engineer, perhaps assisted by an automated tool along the lines recently proposed [25]. This deontic approach to method construction is one of OPEN's strengths that make it suitable for a wide range of project types.

When used on a specific project, this is known as a method(ology) instance. A company-customized OPEN version is then "owned" by the organization – it is their own internal standard, yet retains compatibility with the global OPEN user community.

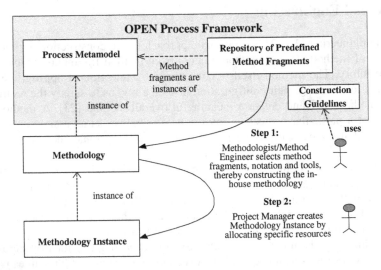

Fig. 1. The OPF defines a framework consisting of a metamodel and a repository of method fragments. Construction guidelines are used to create a site-specific or project-specific methodology, which can then be enacted (as a "methodology instance") on a specific project (modified from [27])

3.1 The OPF Metamodel

The OPF metamodel defines five main high level classes of method fragments:

Work Product: "is anything of value that is produced during the development process" [15]. Work Products are the result of producers (people) executing Work Units and are used either as input to other Work Units or delivered to a client. Pragmatically, they also include externally-supplied (e.g. by user) pre-existing artifacts used as inputs to Work Units.

Producer: "is responsible for creating, evaluating, iterating and maintaining Work Products" [15], one of its subtypes, important for agent-oriented methodologies, being Role.

Work Unit: a functionally cohesive operation that is performed by a Producer. There are three major classes of Work Unit: Activity, Task and Technique.

Language: a medium for documenting a Work Product.

Stage: an identified and managed duration within the process or a point in time at which some achievement is recognized.

Each of these metaclasses has many subclasses in the detailed metamodel (see Appendix G of [15]). From each of these subclasses one or more method fragments are generated by instantiation and stored in the OPF repository (Figure 1)

3.2 Method Fragments in the Repository

Initially, the OPF repository contained about 30 predefined instances of Activity, 160 instances of Task and 200 instances of Techniques (the three main kinds of Work Unit) as well as multiple instances of Role, Stage, Language etc. Some of these are orthogonal to all others in their group and some overlap. Consequently, during process/method construction both association and integration strategies [22] are needed. For example, there are several Techniques in the repository for finding objects e.g. textual analysis, use case simulations, CRC card techniques.

The Work Units in the OPF are perhaps the most obvious during the initial stages of process/method construction. At the highest abstraction level are Activities, which describe what needs to be undertaken. The overall software development process is often configured using half a dozen or so of these Activities so they are often (but not always) the first to be identified. Tasks are then added, which give more detail but still focus on "what" needs to be done rather than "how" it is do be done. Tasks can be readily tracked and project managed. They are typically allocated to a small team over a period of a few days. Scheduling comes from the planning Activities and Tasks combined with the project management elements embodied in the appropriate Tasks. Accomplishment of Tasks is by the use of appropriate Techniques. This set of method fragments is diverse since there are often parallel Techniques for any given Task.

Work Products, including models, documentation and metrics, are also important in any software development process – although a methodology that is driven by the desire to produce documentation often fails because it delivers the Work Products for their own sake. Care must therefore be taken in selection of appropriate method fragments for Work Products.

Producers bring in the human element (although some producers may be other software or indeed hardware). Producers play various roles within the methodology.

It is important to identify these roles rather than the people playing them. A large number of these are described in the OPF repository although it is a volatile set in comparison with, say, the instances of the WorkUnit class.

Since its first publication in 1997, several additions have been made to the OPF repository to enhance its support for

- Web development [28,29]
- Component-based development [30]
- Organizational transition [31,32]
- Usage-Centered Design [27]

As well as some initial work on agent extensions [3,33].

In Section 5 of this paper, we extend the OPF repository even further, to offer additional support for agent orientation (AO) by extracting new method fragments from the Prometheus AO methodology [17,18,19].

4 Major Elements of Prometheus

Prometheus is an agent-oriented methodology with three design phases ending in an implementation phase. First is the systems specification phase in which the basic functionality of the system is identified, using percepts (inputs), actions (outputs) and any necessary shared data storage. This is followed by the architectural design stage, which uses as input the outputs of the previous phase. Here, the agents and their interactions are identified. Finally, there is the detailed design phase in which the internal details of each agent are addressed.

Prometheus reuses as much as possible from object technology. In particular, it uses UML sequence diagrams (as Prometheus's interaction diagrams) and UML use cases form the basis for the Prometheus variant named scenario.

Within each of these three major Prometheus phases, we have identified a number of tasks, together with advice on appropriate techniques and work products generated or consumed. These are detailed in the following subsections, together with a brief comment on the stages (Prometheus phases) and languages recommended for use with the Prometheus approach to building agent-oriented software applications.

4.1 Tasks Characterizing Prometheus

- *'Identifying Percepts and Actions'*: "Percepts" are raw data obtained from the environment, while "actions" are agents' mechanisms for affecting the environment. This task determines how agents interact with their environment.
- *'Identifying System Goals and Functionality'*: This task aims to determine what the target system should do in a broad sense. Each goal is associated with a (set of) functionality. Each functionality is described in terms of various attributes (see Functionality Descriptor Work Product in Section 4.3 for more details).
- *'Specifying Use Case Scenarios'*: This task aims to give a more holistic view of the system processing (as compared to Functionality Specification which focusses on particular aspects of the system). This task also helps to identify further functionality which may otherwise be missed.

- *'Identifying Agent Types and Instances'*: Agent types are identified from functionality (by grouping closely-related functionality into one agent type). For each agent type, the designer needs to determine the number of agent instances, the lifetime of each instance, agent initialisation, agent demise, data used/produced and the events with which the agent will deal.
- *'Identifying Events'*: Events are derived from percepts. These events are things that the agent will notice, which will cause it to react in some way.
- *'Identifying and Specifying Shared Data Objects'*: If multiple agents write to the same shared data objects, this will require significant additional care for synchronization. At this step, the designer should also decide the appropriate data-sharing mechanism (e.g. having one agent managing the shared data object or having each agent storing its own version of the information). This step also helps to evaluate design, as a good design will minimize shared data objects.
- *'Specifying Agent Interaction'*: This task involves developing Interaction Diagrams to show the major sequences of interactions between agent types and, secondly, Interaction Protocols to elaborate each interaction (as shown in Interaction Diagrams) to show all potential variations.
- *'Designing Agent Internal Structure'*: This task involves a progressive refinement process in order to define the structure of each agent type by defining and then elaborating agent *capabilities*. These are refined in turn until all capabilities have been defined. At the bottom level, capabilities are defined in terms of plans, internal events and data.

4.2 Techniques Recommended by Prometheus

- *For 'Identifying Percepts and Actions'*: no specific techniques for identifying Percepts and Actions are identified in the Prometheus documentation.
- *For 'Identifying System Goals and Functionality'*: Functionality should be kept as narrow as possible, dealing with a single aspect or sub-goal of the system. If functionalities are too broad, they are likely to be less adequately specified leading to potential misunderstanding. Each functionality should be linked to some System Goal, while each goal should result in one or more functionality, although there may not be a one-to-one mapping. The identification of functionality can be performed in conjunction with Use Case Scenarios specification: typically some functionalities are defined, these being used to specify use case scenarios, which in turn identify more functionalities.
- *For 'Specifying Use Case Scenarios'*: The central part of a use case scenario is a sequence of steps describing the scenario. Each step should be annotated with the name of the functionality responsible and data read/written. These annotations allow for cross checking with the functionality description. The final set of use cases should provide a good overview of how the system will work.
- *For 'Identifying Agent Types and Instances'*: Functionalities are assigned to agents based on the criteria of *strong coherence* and *loose coupling*. Specifically, they are grouped to a single agent if they are related, use the same data and interact frequently with each other. Reasons against groupings include when functionalities are unrelated, exist on different hardware platforms or

when there exist security, privacy and modifiability issues. A simple heuristics test of whether a suitable name for an agent type can be found is useful for evaluating coherence. A coherent agent should be able to be described by a single term without any conjunctions. Data Coupling Diagrams and Agent Acquaintance Diagrams can be used to determine and evaluate the potential agent groupings. A design with an Acquaintance Diagram where each agent is linked to every other agent is undesirable.

- *For 'Identifying Events'*: Events should be generated as a result of percepts from the environment, either directly or after processing. The designer should look for changes between the current and previous percepts, or between believed states of world and percepts. Events can be externally generated (from percepts) or internally generated (from messages sent from one agent to another).

- *For 'Identifying and Specifying Shared Data Objects'*: Often what at first appears to be a shared data object can be reconceptualised to be a data source managed by a single agent, with information provided to other agents when needed. Alternatively, each agent may have its own version of the information, without there being any need for a single centralized data object. Data objects can be specified using traditional OO techniques or database design techniques.

- *For 'Specifying Agent Interaction'*: Interaction Diagrams and Interaction Protocols need to be developed. Interaction diagrams are borrowed directly from OO design, showing interaction between agents rather than objects. Designers can directly use the use case scenarios developed earlier to build corresponding Interaction Diagrams. Wherever there is a step in the use case that involves functionality from a new agent, there must be some interaction from a previously involved agent to the newly participating agent. Also, each major environmental event should have an associated Interaction Diagram. Interaction Protocols are generalizations of Interaction Diagrams. They define precisely which interaction sequences are valid within the system. Since protocols must show all variations, they are often larger than the corresponding Interaction Diagram.

- *For 'Designing Agent Internal Structure'*: Functionality (identified from the task 'Identifying System Goals and Functionality') provides a good initial set of capabilities. Sometimes functionality is required in multiple places - akin to library routines. Such functionality should also be extracted into a capability which can then be included in other capabilities or agents. Each capability is composed of input/output events, data read/written, plans and sub-capabilities.

4.3   Work Products Advocated by Prometheus

- *Functionality Descriptor*: This is a textual template that describes each functionality in terms of name, description, percepts, actions, data used/produced and a brief discussion of interactions with other functionality.

- *Use Case Descriptor*: This is a textual template that describes the sequence of steps involved in each use case scenario. Each step is either an incoming event/percept, message, action or activity (activity is anything *within* the functionality, e.g. some kind of computation). All of these elements can be derived from Functionality Descriptors.

- **Agent Class Descriptor**: This is a textual template that describes each agent in terms of functionality included, data used/produced, incoming events, actions, lifetime, initialisation, demise and other agents with which it interacts.
- **Agent Acquaintance Diagram**: This diagram type (Figure 2) shows undirected communication links between agent types. It is developed during the 'Identifying Agent Types and Instances' task to assist 'Agent Type Identification'.

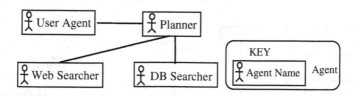

Fig. 2. Example of an Agent Acquaintance Diagram

- **System Overview Diagram**: This diagram provides a general understanding of how the system functions as whole. It shows agents, events, shared data objects and interactions between agents (Figure 3).

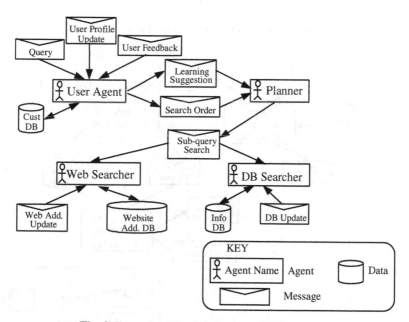

Fig. 3. Example of System Overview Diagram

- **Agent Interaction Model**: including Interaction Diagrams and Interaction Protocols - both diagrams expressed with AUML Sequence Diagrams (Figure 4).
- **Agent Overview Diagram**: This diagram provides the top level view of the agent internals. It shows the top level capabilities of the agent, events or task flows

between these capabilities, as well as data internal to the agent (Figure 5). Further levels of details will be provided by Capability Diagrams.

- **Capability Diagram**: Each Capability Diagram describes an agent's capability in details. At the bottom level, this diagram contains plans, internal events (which connect plans) and data used/produced by plans. Capability Diagrams are similar in style to System Overview (Figure 3) and Agent Overview Diagram (Figure 5), although plans are constrained to have a single incoming event.

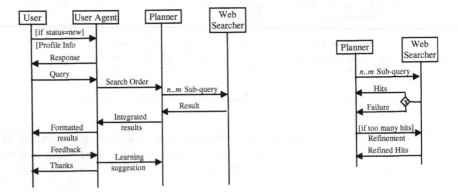

Fig. 4. Example of Interaction and Protocol Diagrams

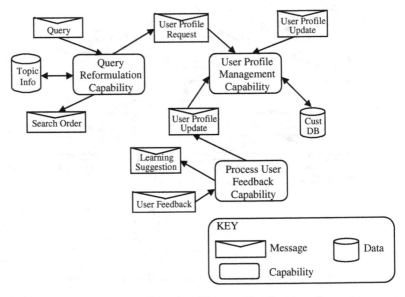

Fig. 5. Example of Agent Overview Diagram (for User Agent)

- **Plan, Event, Data Descriptor**: Each Plan Descriptor defines a plan in terms of triggering events, messages, actions and plan steps. Each Event Descriptor defines an event in terms of the event's purpose, together with data that the event carries. Each Data Descriptor defines a data object in terms of its fields and methods. All three descriptors are expressed as textual templates.

4.4 Stages Used in Prometheus

Cycle: Prometheus uses an iterative process over software engineering phases, thus fitting the *"Iterative, Incremental, Parallel Life Cycle"* model of OPEN.

Phases: Prometheus covers System Specification, Architectural Design and Detailed Design. Outputs of these phases can be directly fed into implementation and testing. In the context of OPEN, Prometheus supports *"Initiation"* and *"Construction"*.

4.5 Languages

For modelling, Prometheus proposes its own set of notation except for the Interaction Model, which employs the AUML Sequence Diagram [34]. For an implementation language, it is noted that Prometheus models can be implemented in any programming language although exemplar implementations have been undertaken using the JACK Development Platform [35].

5 Adding Support to the OPF Derived from Prometheus

In this section, we outline the various Tasks, Techniques and Work Products that are proposed in this paper as additions and modifications to the OPEN repository in order to incorporate agency concerns as identified in Prometheus. These new method fragments are identified from the literature and proposed here for inclusion into the OPF method fragment repository.

In total, three new Tasks are identified, together with two new subtasks for a pre-existing Task. An additional Technique, suitable for agent support, has also been identified for inclusion in the OPF repository (and one that will need further extension – not discussed in detail here). Prometheus supplies a total of 5 new Work Products but no additional Roles or Stages.

Many of the tasks described in Prometheus are already incorporated into the method fragment library of OPEN, albeit sometimes under a different name. First we discuss the mappings to existing method fragments (Section 5.1) and then identify new components for addition to the OPF repository (Sections 5.2 to 5.4).

5.1 Existing Support and Mappings Between OPF and Prometheus

The Prometheus task of 'Identifying Percepts and Actions' maps to the Agent OPEN Tasks: 'Model the agent's environment'. Useful techniques here might be 'Context Modelling', 'CRC Card Modelling' and 'Event Modelling'. 'Identifying Systems Goals and Functionality' in Prometheus is paralleled by the set of Requirements Engineering tasks in OPEN that directly cover this Prometheus task (particularly OPEN's 'Identify Client's Vision' and 'Analyze Requirements'). The OPEN task: 'Use Case Modeling' corresponds directly to the Prometheus task of 'Specify Use Case Scenarios'.

The Prometheus task named 'Identifying Agent Types and Instances' leads to the need for a new OPF Task which we name 'Construct the Agent Model' (see Section 5.2). Similarly, Prometheus's 'Identifying and Specifying Shared Data Objects' identifies a gap which we fill with a new OPF Task: 'Specify shared data objects'. On the other hand, there is some high level support in Agent OPEN's Task: 'Model the agent environment' for both events and percepts. However, we recommend supporting these more substantially through the introduction of two new subtasks (see Section 5.2 for details).

For Prometheus's 'Specifying Agent Interaction', there is a good mapping to OPEN's Task: 'Construct the object model'/Technique: 'Interaction modelling' [15] plus Task: 'Determine agent interaction protocol' [33]; whereas the Prometheus's 'Designing Agent Internal Structure' requires the addition to the OPF repository of a new task called 'Design agent internal structure'.

These task mapping are summarized in Table 1.

Table 1. Mappings of tasks between Prometheus and OPF

Name in Prometheus	Name in OPF
1) Tasks	
Identifying percepts and actions	Model the agent's environment
Identifying systems goals and functionality	RE Tasks: especially Identify client's vision and Analyze requirements
Specify use case scenarios	Model use cases
Identifying agent types and instances	NEW: Construct the agent model
Identifying and specifying shared data objects	NEW: Specify shared data objects
Specifying agent interaction	Construct the object model and Determine agent interaction protocol
Designing agent internal structure	NEW: Design agent internal structure
2) Subtasks	
Identifying percepts and actions	NEW: Model percepts
Identifying events	NEW: Model events
	(both subtasks of Model the agent's environment

There are many existing OPF Techniques covering those required by Prometheus. Techniques to support Prometheus's 'Identifying percepts and actions' include 'Context modelling', 'CRC card modelling' and 'Event modelling'. For 'Identifying System Goals and Functionality', OPF already has 'Hierarchical task analysis'. For 'Specifying Use Case Scenarios', OPF offers Technique: 'Scenario development'.

For 'Identifying Agent Types and Instances' in Prometheus, the OPF has some support, although inadequate in parts. While existing Techniques of 'Cohesion measurement' and 'Coupling measurement' offer support, the existing Technique:

'Intelligent agent identification' covers only the need for agents and agent modelling notation and significant extension will be required. OPEN also offers various techniques for OO class identification/modelling (such as 'Abstract Class Identification' and 'Class Naming'), which can be extended/adapted for the identification of agent classes. The extension should take into account the major differences between OO classes and agent classes, for example, agent classes are generally more coarse-grained than OO classes (thus, the 'Granularity' Technique in the OPF repository should be extended to account for this difference).

For 'Identifying Events' in Prometheus, the OPEN Technique: 'Event Modelling' is directly applicable. OPEN currently offers no techniques for the Prometheus task of 'Identifying and Specifying Shared Data Objects'. Support for 'Specifying Agent Interactions' is partial through the OPF Techniques of 'Interaction modelling' and 'Collaboration analysis'. However, these need extension. The Agent OPEN [33] Techniques of 'Contract nets' and 'Market mechanisms' may also be useful. Finally, we need to propose a new Technique (Section 5.3) to support the Prometheus task of 'Designing Agent Internal Structure'. This we name 'Agent internal design'.

For work products, Prometheus uses a suite of diagrams that include both new diagrams and extensions of existing (often UML) diagrams. We therefore propose the addition of four new diagram types to the OPF method fragment repository. Those that can be classified as belonging to the suite of OPF Static Architecture Diagrams are Agent Model; Agent Acquaintance Diagram; Agent Overview Diagram.

The agent interaction model has two components: a standard Interaction Diagram and a new Protocol Diagram. Other new diagrams are the Functionality Descriptor and Capability Diagrams. The Capability Diagram is essentially the same as that proposed in Tropos – a diagram already been incorporated into the OPF repository [3]. The Agent Overview Diagram is essentially a Context Diagram so no new work product is proposed here for the OPF repository. Finally, there is a close mapping from the Prometheus Use Case Descriptor to the OPF Use Case Specification.

5.2 New Tasks

Although these tasks are a contribution to the OPF, commonly found in several AO methods, we itemize them here since they are currently missing from the repository.

TASK NAME: Construct the agent model
Focus: Static architecture
Typical supportive techniques: Intelligent agent identification, Control architecture
Explanation: An analogue of the "object model" as the main description of the static architecture needs to be constructed. This model shows the agents, their interfaces and how they are connected both with other agents and other objects.

TASK NAME: Design agent internal structure
Focus: Internal structure of agents
Typical supportive techniques: Agent internal design, 3-layer BDI model, Reactive reasoning
Explanation: Using an appropriate model for the internal agent architecture, such as the BDI model, the internal structure of each agent needs to be determined. If a hybrid architecture is used, then both ECA rules (event-condition-action rules) and I-

rules (inference rules) may be needed. If using a BDI architecture, then goals and plans will be needed (see Agent OPEN Tasks: 'Model goals' and 'Model plans' [3]. When using Prometheus, high level capabilities are identified and iteratively decomposed, finally resulting in plans, internal events and data.

TASK NAME: Specify shared data objects
Focus: Data storage
Typical supportive techniques: appropriate database-focussed techniques
Explanation: Synchronization is required if several agents write to the same data storage object. Appropriate data-sharing mechanisms are needed.

Finally, two subtasks are recommended for addition to the existing Task: Model the Agent's Environment

Subtask: Model Percepts. This task focuses on modelling the percept component of the agent's environment.

Subtask: Model Events. This task focuses on modelling the events that result from changes in the environment, which are then recognized by the agent itself as an input to its own internal reasoning.

5.3 New Technique

Although this is a contribution common to many AO methods, we itemize it here in the context of it being currently missing from the OPF repository.

TECHNIQUE NAME: Agent internal design
Focus: Internal features of an agent
Typical tasks for which this is needed: Design agent internal structure
Technique description: The fine detail of an individual agent must be described in terms of its attributes and operations (as for objects) but more importantly in terms of its goals, plans, capabilities, responsibilities, events responded to and pre- and post-conditions.
Technique usage: Document each of these internal characteristics (or features) of every agent in the system. The detail should be sufficient for coding to take place easily from these design specifications.
Deliverables: Capability diagram

5.4 New Work Products

Although these Work Products are not unique to Prometheus, they are currently missing from the OPF repository and are therefore documented here.

NAME: Functionality Descriptor
OPF CLASSIFICATION: Requirements set of work products
RELATIONSHIP TO EXISTING WORK PRODUCT: None
BRIEF DESCRIPTION: This is a textual template describing the functionality in terms of name, description, percepts, actions, data used/produced and a brief discussion of interactions with other functionality.

NAME: Agent structure diagram
OPF CLASSIFICATION: Static Architecture diagrams

RELATIONSHIP TO EXISTING WORK PRODUCT: extension of static structure diagram

BRIEF DESCRIPTION: This diagram describes the internal structure of an individual agent. It needs to explain how inputs are received (events), thus linking to the Functionality Descriptor, what goals and plans are possessed and how reasoning is accomplished. If using a BDI model for the agent architecture, modified following [36], then an extension to the UML class notation might look like the proposal in Figure 6 in which the additional boxes already supported in the UML are utilized here for agent, rather than object, concepts.

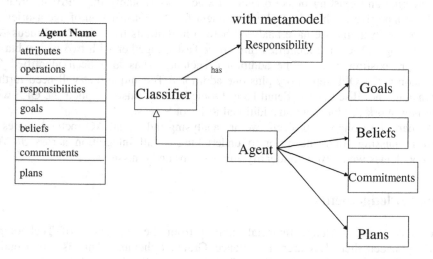

Fig. 6. One proposal for extended UML notation for an individual agent plus the underpinning metamodel fragment It is not yet clear whether the attributes and operations are valid features of an agent (e.g. [37]). Since these are derived from the UML Classifier, their rejection would negate the generalization relationship between Agent and Classifier

NAME: Agent acquaintance diagram
OPF CLASSIFICATION: Static Architecture diagrams
RELATIONSHIP TO EXISTING WORK PRODUCT: modification of a collaboration diagram
BRIEF DESCRIPTION: The agent acquaintance diagram is a simplified version of a UML V1.4 collaboration diagram. It shows the agents and connectivity without necessarily specifying directionality of connections.

NAME: Agent protocol diagram
OPF CLASSIFICATION: Dynamic Behaviour diagrams
RELATIONSHIP TO EXISTING WORK PRODUCT: None
BRIEF DESCRIPTION: Agent protocols are shown using a UML Sequence Diagram. This diagram complements a standard sequence diagram to show agent interactions. Together, these two diagrams constitute the Agent Interaction Model.

NAME: Agent overview diagram
OPF CLASSIFICATION: Static Architecture diagrams

RELATIONSHIP TO EXISTING WORK PRODUCT: extension of UML object model
BRIEF DESCRIPTION: A high level diagram showing capabilities of the agents, events between these capabilities and any internal data. This top level diagram forms the basis for further expansion (addition of detail) into a number of Capability Diagrams [1,3].

6 Summary and Conclusions

As part of an extensive research programme to combine the benefits of method engineering and existing object-oriented frameworks (notably the OPF) to create a highly supportive methodological environment for the construction of agent-oriented information systems, we have analysed here contributions from the Prometheus AO methodology. We have identified three new Tasks, together with two new subtasks for a pre-existing Task. One additional Technique has also been identified for inclusion in the OPF repository plus one additional Technique that will need further extension – not discussed in detail here. Prometheus has also supplied the OPF with four new Work Products but no additional Roles or Stages.

As part of an ongoing projects, we are analysing individual AO methodologies to identify missing fragments prior to undertaking a full integration across *all* AO methodologies where we will identify any overlaps and omissions.

Acknowledgements

We wish to acknowledge financial support from the University of Technology, Sydney under their Research Excellence Grants Scheme. This is Contribution number 04/03 of the Centre for Object Technology Applications and Research.

References

1. Bresciani, P., Giorgini, P., Giunchiglia, F., Mylopolous, J. and Perini, A., 2003, Tropos: an agent-oriented software development methodology, *Autonomous Agents and Multi-Agent Systems,* 8(3), 203-236
2. Henderson-Sellers, B., Giorgini, P. and Bresciani, P., 2003, Evaluating the potential for integrating the OPEN and Tropos metamodels, *Procs. SERP '03* (eds. B. Al-Ani, H.R. Arabnia, and Y.Mun), CSREA Press, Las Vegas, 992-995
3. Henderson-Sellers, B., Giorgini, P. and Bresciani, P., 2004, Enhancing Agent OPEN with concepts used in the Tropos methodology, *Engineering Societies in the Agents World IV. 4th International Workshop, ESAW 2003* (eds. A. Omicini, P. Pettra and J. Pitt), LNAI Volume 3071, Springer-Verlag, Berlin, 328-345
4. Wooldridge, M., Jennings, N.R. and Kinny, D., 2000, The Gaia methodology for agent-oriented analysis and design, *J. Autonomous Agents and Multi-Agent Systems,* 3, 285-312
5. Coleman, D., Arnold, P., Bodoff, S., Dollin, C. and Gilchrist, H., 1994, *Object-Oriented Development. The Fusion Method,* Prentice Hall, Englewood Cliffs, NJ, USA, 313pp
6. Bernon, C., Gleizes, M.-P., Picard, G. And Glize, P., 2002, The ADELFE methodology for an intranet system design, presented at AOIS2002, Toronto, 27-28 May

7. Kruchten, Ph., 1999, *The Rational Unified Process. An Introduction*, Addison-Wesley, Reading, MA, USA

8. Jacobson, I., Booch, G. and Rumbaugh, J., 1999, *The Unified Software Development Process*, Addison-Wesley, Reading, MA, USA

9. van Slooten, K., Hodes, B., 1996, Characterizing IS development projects, in *Procs. IFIP TC8 Working Conf. on Method Engineering: Principles of method construction and tool support* (eds. S. Brinkkemper, K. Lyytinen, R. Welke) Chapman&Hall, Great Britain, 29-44

10. Juan, T., Sterling, L., Martellis, M. And Mascardi, V., 2003, Customizing AOSE methodologies by reusing AOSE features, *Procs. AAMAS '03*, ACM Press, 113-120.

11. Kumar, K. and Welke, R.J., 1992, Methodology engineering: a proposal for situation-specific methodology construction, in *Challenges and Strategies for Research in Systems Development* (eds. W.W. Cotterman and J.A. Senn), J. Wiley, Chichester, 257-269

12. Brinkkemper, S., 1996, Method engineering: engineering of information systems development methods and tools, *Inf. Software Technol.*, **38(4)**, 275-280.

13. Ter Hofstede, A.H.M. and Verhoef, T.F., 1997, On the feasibility of situational method engineering, *Information Systems*, **22**, 401-422

14. Graham, I., Henderson-Sellers, B. and Younessi, H., 1997, *The OPEN Process Specification*, Addison-Wesley, UK.

15. Firesmith, D.G. and Henderson-Sellers, B., 2002, *The OPEN Process Framework. AN Introduction*, Addison-Wesley, Harlow, Herts, UK

16. Rolland, C. and Prakash, N., 1996, A proposal for context-specific method engineering, *Procs. IFIP WG8.1 Conf. on Method Engineering*, 191-208, Atlanta, GA, USA

17. Padgham, L. and Winikoff, M., 2002, Prometheus: A Methodology for Developing Intelligent Agents, **In** *Procs. Third International Workshop on Agent-Oriented Software Engineering, at AAMAS'02.*

18. Padgham, L. and Winikoff, M., 2002, Prometheus: A Pragmatic Methodology for Engineering Intelligent Agents. **In** *Procs.Workshop on Agent-oriented Methodologies at OOPSLA 2002*, November 4, 2002, Seattle.

19. Padgham, L. and Winikoff, M., 2004, *Developing Intelligent Agent Systems: A Practical Guide*, J. Wiley and Sons, Chichester, 240pp

20. Henderson-Sellers, B., Debenham, J. and Tran, Q.-N.N., 2004, Adding agent-oriented concepts derived from GAIA to Agent OPEN, *Advanced Information Systems Engineering. 16th International Conference, CAiSE 2004, Riga, Latvia, June 2004 Proceedings* (eds. A. Persson and J. Stirna), LNCS 3084, Springer-Verlag, Berlin, 98-111

21. Tran, Q.-N.N., Henderson-Sellers, B. and Debenham, J. 2004, Incorporating the elements of the MASE methodology into Agent OPEN, *Procs. ICEIS2004* (eds. I. Seruca, J. Cordeiro, S. Hammoudi and J. Filipe), INSTICC Press, **Volume 4**, 380-388

22. Ralyté, J. and Rolland, C., 2001, An assembly process model for method engineering, in K.R. Dittrich, A. Geppert and M.C. Norrie (Eds.) *Advanced Information Systems Engineering)*, LNCS2068, Springer, Berlin, 267-283.

23. Brinkkemper, S., Saeki, M. and Harmsen, F., 1998, Assembly techniques for method engineering. *Proceedings of CAISE 1998*, Springer Verlag, 381-400.

24. Rolland, C., Prakash, N. and Benjamen, A., 1999, A multi-model view of process modelling, *Requirements Eng. J.*, **4(4)**, 169-187

25. Nguyen, V.P. and Henderson-Sellers, B., 2003, Towards automated support for method engineering with the OPEN approach, *Procs. 7th IASTED SEA Conference*, ACTA Press, Anaheim, USA, 691-696

26. Saeki, M., 2003, CAME: the first step to automated software engineering, *Procs. OOPSLA 2003 Workshop on Process Engineering for Object-Oriented and Component-Based Development*, Centre for Object Technology Applications and Research, Sydney, Australia, 7-18

27. Henderson-Sellers, B. and Hutchison, J., 2003, Usage-Centered Design (UCD) and the OPEN Process Framework (OPF), *Performance by Design. Procs. forUSE2003* (ed. L.L. Constantine), Ampersand Press, Rowley, MA, USA, 171-196

28. Haire, B., Henderson-Sellers, B. and Lowe, D., 2001, Supporting web development in the OPEN process: additional tasks, *Procs. 25th Annual International Computer Software and Applications Conference. COMPSAC 2001*, IEEE Computer Society Press, Los Alamitos, CA, USA, 383-389.

29. Henderson-Sellers, B., Haire, B. and Lowe, D., 2002, Using OPEN's deontic matrices for e-business, *Engineering Information Systems in the Internet Context* (eds. C. Rolland, S. Brinkkemper and M. Saeki), Kluwer Academic Publishers, Boston, USA, 9-30.

30. Henderson-Sellers, B., 2001, An OPEN process for component-based development, Chapter 18 in G.T. Heineman and W. Councill (Eds.) *Component-Based Software Engineering: Putting the Pieces Together*, Addison-Wesley, Reading, MA, USA, 321-340

31. Henderson-Sellers, B. and Serour, M., 2000, Creating a process for transitioning to object technology, *Procs. Seventh Asia-Pacific Software Engineering Conference. APSEC 2000*, IEEE Computer Society Press, Los Alamitos, CA, USA, 436-440.

32. Serour, M., Henderson-Sellers, B., Hughes, J., Winder, D. and Chow, L., 2002, Organizational transition to object technology: theory and practice, *Object-Oriented Information Systems* (eds. Z. Bellahsène, D. Patel and C. Rolland), LNCS 2425, Springer-Verlag, Berlin, 229-241.

33. Debenham, J. and Henderson-Sellers, B., 2003, Designing agent-based process systems - extending the OPEN Process Framework, Chapter VIII in *Intelligent Agent Software Engineering* (ed. V. Plekhanova), Idea Group Publishing, 160-190.

34. Odell, J., Van Dyke Parunak, H. and Bauer, B., 2000, Extending UML for agents. In G. Wagner, Y. Lesperance and E. Yu (eds.), *Procs. Agent-Oriented Information Systems Workshop*, 17th National Conference on Artificial Intelligence (pp. 3-17). Austin, TX, USA.

35. AOS, 2000, *JACK Intelligent Agents User Guide*, AOS Technical Report, Agent Oriented Software Pty Ltd, July 2000. http://www.jackagents.com/docs/jack/html/index.html.

36. Henderson-Sellers, B., Tran, N. and Debenham, J., 2005, An etymological and metamodel-based evaluation of the terms "goals and tasks" in agent-oriented methodologies, *J. Object Technology*, **4(2)**, 131-150

37. Torres da Silva, V. and de Lucena, C.J.P., 2004, From a conceptual framework for agents and objects to a multi-agent system modeling language, *Autonomous Agents and Multi-Agent Systems*, **9(1-2)**, 145-189

A Preliminary Comparative Feature Analysis of Multi-agent Systems Development Methodologies

Quynh-Nhu Numi Tran[1], Graham Low[1], and Mary-Anne Williams[2]

[1] School of Information Systems, Technology and Management,
The University of New South Wales,
New South Wales, Australia
{numitran, g.low}@unsw.edu.au
[2] Innovation and Technology Research Laboratory,
Faculty of Information Technology, University of Technology Sydney,
New South Wales, Australia
Mary-Anne@it.uts.edu.au

Abstract. While there are a considerable number of software engineering methodologies for developing multi-agent systems, not much work has been reported on the evaluation and comparison of these methodologies. This paper presents a comparative analysis of five well-known MAS-development methodologies. The comparison is based on a feature analysis framework published previously. This framework allows the comparative analysis to be made on a variety of evaluation criteria, covering both agent-oriented aspects and system engineering dimensions. The analysis also compares the methodologies in terms of their support for the steps in the development process and for agent-oriented concept modeling.

1 Introduction

Compared to the preceding efforts in system engineering such as object-oriented (OO) paradigm, the work in agent-oriented (AO) system engineering is still under-developed. However, with the rapid growth and promise of the agent technology, a number of methodologies for developing MAS (denoted as "MAS methodologies") have been proposed in recent years. This has in turn led to the need to evaluate and compare them, thereby noting their strengths and weaknesses, and determining which methodology to use in a particular application.

In a previous publication, we have proposed an evaluation framework for assessing MAS methodologies [1]. Based on feature analysis approach, this framework provides a list of evaluation criteria or methodological features to be used as yardsticks to assess MAS methodologies from different dimensions and aspects. This paper presents an application of this framework to five well-known MAS methodologies: MASE [2], GAIA [3][4], methodology for systems of BDI agents [5], Prometheus [6], and MAS-CommonKADS [7]. The objective is to obtain a comparative analysis of the five methodologies, rather than a detailed analysis of each.

P. Bresciani et al. (Eds.): AOIS 2004, LNAI 3508, pp. 157–168, 2005.
© Springer-Verlag Berlin Heidelberg 2005

The remainder of the paper is organized as follows: section 2 provides an overview of the feature analysis framework while section 3 gives a summarized description of the five MAS methodologies. We present the comparative analysis in section 4, with some conclusions and perspectives in section 5.

2   Feature Analysis Framework

The framework proposed in [1] was developed from the synthesis of various existing feature analysis frameworks, including those for evaluating conventional system development methodologies – namely [8], [9], [10] and [11], and those for evaluating MAS methodologies – namely [12], [13], [14] and [15]. The framework therefore improves on the existing work by extensively assessing both agent-specific (or MAS specific) and generic system engineering dimensions. It also pays attention to all three major components of a system development methodology i.e. process, techniques and models. The framework's evaluation criteria are considered representative, case-generic and centred on the capabilities and usefulness of a MAS methodology. The criteria are grouped into [1]:

- *Process Related Criteria*: which assess a methodology's support for the MAS-development process (15 criteria);
- *Technique Related Criteria*: which examine the methodology's techniques to develop MAS (5 criteria);
- *Model Related Criteria*: which evaluate the capabilities of the methodology's models (21 criteria); and
- *Supportive Feature Criteria*: which evaluate various high-level methodological capabilities (8 criteria).

Each criterion in the framework is accompanied by an evaluation question (Table 1). Two criteria, *"Steps in the development process"* (in Process Related Criteria) and *"Concepts"* (in Model Related Criteria), which respectively examine the development steps supported by a MAS methodology, and the concepts that the methodology's models are capable of expressing, require a more comprehensive assessment. Tran *et al.* [1] proposed a list of "standard" process steps and concepts that serve as a checklist for this assessment. This list is presented in Tables 3 and 4 of this paper.

Table 1. Feature analysis framework for evaluating MAS-development methodologies [1]

Process Related Criteria
1. **Development lifecycle:** What development lifecycle best describes the methodology (e.g. waterfall)?
2. **Coverage of the lifecycle:** What phases of the lifecycle are covered by the methodology (e.g. analysis, design, implementation…)?
3. **Development perspective:** What development perspective is supported (i.e. top-down, bottom-up, or hybrid)?
4. **Application domain:** Is the methodology applicable to a specific or multiple application domains?
5. **Size of MAS:** What size of MAS is the methodology suited for?
6. **Agent nature:** Does the methodology support agents of any type (i.e. heterogeneous agents), or of a particular type (i.e. homogeneous agents)?
7. **Support for verification:** Does the methodology contain rules to allow for the verification and validation of correctness of developed models and specifications?

8. **Steps in the development process:** What development steps are supported by the methodology?
9. **Comments on the overall strengths/weaknesses of each step:** This criterion allows the evaluator to record any comments on a process step that cannot be recorded anywhere else.
10. **Notational components:** What models and diagrams are generated from each process step?
11. **Definition of inputs and outputs:** Are inputs and outputs to each process step defined, with possible examples?
12. **Ease of understanding of the process steps:** Are the process steps easy to understand?
13. **Usability of the methodology:** Are the process steps easy to follow?
14. **Refinability:** Do the process steps provide a clear path for refining the methodology's models through gradual stages to reach an implementation, or at least for clearly connecting the implementation level to the design specification?
15. **Approach towards MAS development:** what is the methodology's
    a. generic MAS development approach (e.g. OO-based or knowledge-engineering based)?
    b. approach towards using "role" in MAS development?
    c. approach in role identification, if the methodology uses "role" in MAS development?

Technique-Related Criteria

16. **Availability of techniques and heuristics:**
    a. What are the techniques to perform each process step?
    b. What are the techniques to produce each notational component (i.e. modeling techniques)?
17. **Ease of understanding of techniques:** Are the techniques easy to understand?
18. **Usability of techniques:** Are the techniques easy to follow?
19. **Provision of examples and heuristics:** Are examples and heuristics of the techniques provided?
20. **Comments on the strengths/weaknesses of the techniques:** This criterion allows the evaluator to record any comments on the techniques to perform each step or to produce each model.

Model-Related Criteria

21. **Concepts:** What concepts are the methodology's models capable of expressing?
22. **Expressiveness:** How well can each model express these concepts? (e.g. is each model capable of capturing the concept at a great level of detail, or from different angles?)
23. **Completeness:** Are all necessary agent-oriented concepts that describe the target MAS captured by the methodology's models?
24. **Formalization/Preciseness of models:** Are the notation (syntax) and semantics of models clearly defined?
25. **Model derivation:** Does there exist explicit process/logic and guidelines for transforming models into other models, or partially creating a model from information present in another?
26. **Consistency:**
    a. Are there rules and guidelines to ensure consistency between levels of abstractions within each model (i.e. internal consistency), and between different models?
    b. Are representations expressed in a manner that allows for consistency checking between them?
27. **Complexity:** is there a manageable number of concepts expressed in each model/diagram?
28. **Ease of understanding of models:** Are the models easy to understand?
29. **Modularity:** Does the methodology and its models provide support for modularity of agents?
30. **Abstraction:** Does the methodology allow for producing models at various levels of detail and abstraction?
31. **Autonomy:** Can the models support and represent the autonomous feature of agents (i.e. the ability to act without direct intervention of humans or others, and to control their own states and behaviours)?
32. **Adaptability:** Can the models support and represent the adaptability feature of agents (i.e. the ability to learn and improve with experience)?
33. **Cooperative behavior:** Can the models support and represent the cooperative behavior of agents (i.e. the ability to work together with other agents to achieve a common goal)?
34. **Inferential capability:** Can the models support and represent the inferential capability feature of agents (i.e. the ability to act on abstract task specifications)?
35. **Communication ability:** Can the models support and represent "knowledge-level" communication ability (i.e. the ability to communicate with other agents using language resembling human-like speech acts)?
36. **Personality:** Can the models support and represent the personality of agents (i.e. the ability to manifest attributes of a "believable" human character)?
37. **Reactivity:** Can the models support and represent reactivity of agents (i.e. the ability to selectively sense and act)?

38. **Deliberative behavior:** Can the models support and represent deliberative behavior of agents (i.e. the ability to decide in a deliberation or proactiveness)?
39. **Temporal continuity:** Can the models support and represent temporal continuity of agents (i.e. persistence of identity and state over long periods of time)?
40. **Human Computer Interaction:** Do the models represent human users and the user interface?
41. **Models Reuse:** Does the methodology provide, or make it possible to use, a library of reusable models?
Supportive Feature Criteria
43. **Software and methodological support:** Is the methodology supported by tools and libraries (e.g. libraries of agents, agent components, organizations, architectures and technical support)?
44. **Open systems and scalability**: Does the methodology provide support for open systems and scalability (e.g. the methodology allows for dynamic integration/removal of new agents/resources)?
45. **Dynamic structure**: Does the methodology provide support for dynamic structure? (i.e. the methodology allows for dynamic reconfiguration of the system)?
46. **Agility and robustness**: Does the methodology provide support for agility and robustness (e.g. the methodology captures normal processing and exception processing, provides techniques to analyze system performance for all configurations or provides techniques to detect/recover from failures)?
47. **Support for conventional objects**: Does the methodology cater for the use/integration of ordinary objects in MAS (e.g. the methodology models the agents' interfaces with objects)?
48. **Support for mobile agents**: Does the methodology cater for the use/integration of mobile agents in MAS (e.g. the methodology models which/when/how agent should be mobile)?
49. **Support for self-interested agents**: Does the methodology provide support for MAS with self-interest agents (whose goals may be independent or enter in conflict with other agents' goals)?
50. **Support for ontology**: Does the methodology cater for the use of ontology in MAS development process and/or the inclusion of ontology in MAS development models (i.e. ontology-based MAS development)?

3   MAS Development Methodologies

The five MAS methodologies selected for the comparative analysis are considered the most comprehensive, widely referenced and well-documented AO software engineering methodologies compared to other existing work. Each of these methodologies offers a set of steps, techniques and/or models for the analysis and design of MAS.

Multiagent Systems Engineering - MaSE [2]

This methodology has been applied to numerous graduate-level and research projects. Its process steps include identifying and organizing system goals, distilling use cases and elaborating them into sequence diagrams, identifying roles, identifying agent classes from roles, defining inter-agent conversations, designing agent internals and specifying MAS deployment details.

The GAIA Methodology [3][4]

GAIA adopts an organization-oriented approach towards MAS development. Its Analysis phase develops four major models: Preliminary Role Model, Preliminary Interaction Model, Environment Model (which describes MAS environment in terms of abstract resources) and Organizational Rule Model (which specifies rules that affect the whole MAS).

The Design phase then transforms these models into sufficiently low-level abstractions, including Complete Role and Interaction Models, Organizational Structure Model, Agent Model, Service Model (which specifies the services offered by each agent) and Acquaintance Model.

Methodology for BDI Agents – BDIM [5]
This methodology classifies models into *external* or *internal* levels. External models represent a system-level view of the system and include Agent and Interaction Models. At the internal level, each model describes an abstract internal component of the agent, including Belief Model, Goal Model and Plan Model.

The Prometheus Methodology [6]
Prometheus aims to provide a detailed, complete methodology for developing MAS with BDI-like agents. It consists of three phases:

- *System specification*: identifies the basic functionalities, percepts, actions and use case scenarios of the target MAS;
- *Architectural design*: identifies agents, events, interactions and shared data objects; and
- *Detailed design:* designs the internals of each agent. Each agent is composed of "capabilities", which are in turn made up of lower-level capabilities, plans, internal events and data.

The MAS-CommonKADS Methodology [7]
This methodology also extends from CommonKADS, although it takes advantage of many OO techniques. The guidelines for constructing each model are summarized as follows:

- *Agent Model*: Agents are identified using use cases, problem statements, RDD and CRC techniques.
- *Task Model*: Tasks are identified and decomposed as in CoMoMAS functional analysis.
- *Coordination Model*: Agent interactions are identified from use case scenarios. Coordination protocols are described by Event Flow Diagrams, State Transition Diagrams and Message Sequence Charts.
- *Expertise Model*: Different types of agent knowledge (e.g. domain knowledge, task knowledge, inference knowledge and problem-solving methods) are specified.
- *Organization Model*: MAS organization is described in terms of agent aggregation and inheritance.
- *Design Model*: Infrastructure facilities, agent architecture, software and hardware required for MAS implementation are specified.

4   Comparative Analysis

Using the feature analysis framework of Tran *et al.* [1], the comparative analysis of the above MAS methodologies was performed for Process Related, Model Related and Supportive Feature Criteria. The evaluation of Technique Related Criteria is not presented in this paper, as it entails an in-depth analytical discussion of each methodology, which is most relevant when the developer has decided on which particular methodology to use, or is choosing between a small number of methodologies that provide the same or similar process steps (thus requiring an investigation of techniques to determine which method is the best in performing these common steps for a particular application). An in-depth comparison of MAS methodologies' techniques will be presented in a future paper. Criteria 9, 10, 13, 22 and 27 are also not presented in this paper for the same reason. Criteria "Steps in the development process" and "Concepts represented by MAS models" will each be analyzed separately because each requires an extensive assessment (Tables 3 and 4 respectively).

Process-Related Analysis (Table 2)
Apart from BDIM which does not explicitly specify its lifecycle model, the other MAS methodologies adopt an iterative, incremental SDLC for their MAS development. The documentation of BDIM [5] actually does reveal the need for iterative refinements for its models (specifically, the refinement of internal models like Belief, Goal and Plan Models feeds back to the external models such as Agent and Interaction Models, and vice versa). All methodologies cover only the Analysis (A) and Design (D) phases of the SDLC, except for MAS-CommonKADS that touches on the issues of conceptualization (C) phases.

With regard to the development perspective, GAIA and MASE are top-down (TD), Prometheus is bottom-up (BU), while BDIM and MAS-CommonKADS are hybrid (H). We define an AOSE methodology as top down if it starts from the analysis of high-level elements such as system goals, major functionality, problem statement and organizational structure, and proceeds to identifying and designing agents as system components that realize these elements. In contrast, a bottom-up AOSE methodology begins by analyzing low-level behaviours or tasks of the system, which are then packaged to compose agents. A hybrid approach integrates both approaches by identifying agents from the consideration of both high-level system goals/organization, as well as low-level system tasks and responsibilities.

Most MAS methodologies are suitable to all types of application domains and heterogeneous agents, except for BDIM and Prometheus that target BDI-like agents. MaSE and Prometheus are considered supportive of the verification and validation process, since they provide rules or guidelines to assist the system developers in verifying and validating the developed models. For example, Prometheus suggests that a good MAS design will have a minimal number of shared data objects captured in its System Overview Diagram. MaSE, Prometheus and MAS-CommonKADS are also perceived to be easier to understand and to follow than GAIA and BDIM, thanks to their detailed instructions on the development process and on each process step. All methodologies provide a clear path for refining their models through gradual stages to reach an implementation (or at least for clearly connecting the implementation level to the design specification).

With regard to the approaches towards MAS development, our assessment is performed on three categories of approaches:

- *Generic approach*: including OO-based approach and Knowledge-Engineering (KE) based approach. The former either adapts or extends OO models and techniques, while the latter builds upon techniques from knowledge engineering [16].
- *The use of "role"*: A MAS methodology can be role-oriented (RO), i.e. using "roles" as the main abstraction for MAS analysis and design, or non-role-oriented (NRO), i.e. relying on other constructs such as use cases, enterprise/workflow models and interactions to develop agents and MASs.

- *Approach in role identification:* If a methodology is role-oriented, it can identify roles in the system by following a goal-oriented analysis approach (GO), behaviour-oriented analysis approach (BO) or organisation-oriented analysis approach.

The five investigated MAS methodologies can demonstrate the adoption of all of the above approaches, except for the behaviour-oriented analysis approach for role identification.

Model-Related Analysis (Table 2)

Compared to other MAS methodologies, MAS-CommonKADS can capture and represent the highest number and the most diverse AO concepts (i.e. criterion "Completeness") thanks to its comprehensive set of models. All five methodologies offer detailed explanations on their models' notation and semantics, except for MAS-CommonKADS which does not provide any notation for its Design model (i.e. criterion "Formalization/Preciseness"). All methodologies, except for MAS-CommonKADs, offer steps and related techniques to support the transforming of models into other models (i.e. "Model Derivation" criterion).

"Consistency" criterion is assessed in terms of two questions:

- whether there are rules and guidelines to ensure consistency between levels of abstractions of a model/diagram or between different models/diagrams; and
- whether the models/diagrams are expressed in a manner that allows for consistency checking between them.

As shown in Table 2, methodologies that offer the highest support for consistency assurance are MaSE and Prometheus. All methodologies, however, encourage their models to be developed at various levels of details and abstractions (i.e. "Abstraction" criterion).

Agent characteristics that all five MAS methodologies can support and model are modularity, autonomy, agent cooperative behaviour, "knowledge-level" communication ability, reactivity and deliberative behaviour. This finding is desirable, considering the significance of these constructs in MAS analysis and design. Constructs that most methodologies overlook are agent adaptability, agent personality, agent temporal continuity, and sub-system interactions.

All five methodologies make it possible to reuse the developed models, e.g. Expertise Models of MAS-CommonKADS can be reused by agents with similar task inference requirements [7].

Supportive Feature Analysis (Table 2)

The five investigated methodologies appear to focus merely on the development of typical, simple MASs, without paying much attention to add-on capabilities of MAS such as openness/scalability, software tool, agility and robustness. No methodologies address the use of mobile agents in MAS. Only GAIA explicitly supports the development of MASs with self-interested agents[1]. Despite its significance in MAS design and operation, ontology is not supported nor used by most MAS methodologies. Only MAS-CommonKADS briefly involves ontology in its development process, particularly in the modelling of agent "domain knowledge". It also acknowledges that ontology servers should be part of the infrastructure facilities to be designed for the agent network.

---

[1] This issue is addressed in the updated version of GAIA [4].

Table 2. Comparative analysis results

Evaluation Criteria	MaSE	GAIA	BDIM	Prome-theus	MAS-CommonKADS
Process Related Criteria					
Development lifecycle	Iterative across all phases	Iterative across all phases	Not specified	Iterative across all phases	Risk-driven & component-based
Coverage of the lifecycle	A & D	A & D	A & D	A & D	C, A & D
Development perspective	TD	TD	H	BU	H
Application Domain	Any	Any	Any	Any	Any
Size of MAS	≤ 10 agents	≤ 100 agents	Not specified	Not specified	Not specified
Agent nature	Hete.	Hete.	BDI agents	BDI agents	Hete.
Support for verification	Yes	No	No	Yes	Briefly mentioned
Ease of understanding of process steps	High	High	High	High	High
Usability of the methodology	High, except for internal agent modeling.	Medium. Missing many important steps	Medium, Lack of detailed instructions for each step	High	High
Refinability	Yes	Yes	Yes	Yes	Yes
Approach towards MAS development	• OO • RO • GO	• OO • RO • OO	• OO • RO • N/A	• OO • NRO • N/A	• KE • NRO • N/A
Model Related Criteria					
Completeness	High	Medium	Medium	High	High
Formalization/ Preciseness of models	High	High	High	High	Low
Model derivation	Yes	Yes	Yes	Yes	No
Consistency	• Yes • Yes	• Yes • Yes	• No • Yes	• Yes • Yes	• No • Yes
Ease of understanding	High	High	High	High	Medium
Modularity	Yes	Yes	Yes	Yes	Yes
Abstraction	Yes	Yes	Yes	Yes	Yes
Autonomy	Yes	Yes	Yes	Yes	Yes
Adaptability	No	No	No	No	No
Cooperative behaviour	Yes	Yes	Yes	Yes	Yes
Inferential capability	Yes	No	Yes	Yes	Yes
Communication ability	Yes	No	Yes	Yes	Yes
Personality	No	No	No	No	No
Reactivity	Yes	Yes	Yes	Yes	Yes
Deliberative behaviour	Yes	Yes	Yes	Yes	Yes
Temporal continuity	No	No	No	No	No
Human Computer Interaction	No	No	No	Yes	Yes
Models Reuse	Yes	Yes	Yes	Yes	Yes
Supportive Feature Criteria					
Software and methodological support	Yes	No	No	Yes	No
Open systems and scalability	No	Yes	No	No	No
Dynamic structure	No	Yes	No	No	No
Agility and robustness	No	No	No	Yes	No
Support for conventional objects	No	No	No	Yes	No
Support for mobile agents	No	No	No	No	No
Support for self-interested agents	No	Yes	No	No	No
Support for ontology	No	No	No	No	Yes

Table 3. Comparative analysis on support for steps in the development process

Steps	MaSE	GAIA	BDIM	Prometheus	MAS-CommonKADS
Problem Domain Analysis					
Identify system goals	3	0	0	0	0
Identify system roles	3	3	2A	0	0
Identify system functionality/tasks	3	3	1	3	2A
Develop use cases/scenarios	3	0	0	3	2B
Produce sequence diagrams	3	0	0	0	2B
Identify design requirements	0	0	0	0	0
Identify agent classes	3	3	3	3	3
Agent Interaction Design					
Specify agent interaction pathways	3	3	2A	3	3
Define exchanged messages	3	0	0	1	2B
Specify interaction protocols	3	0	0	3	3
Specify contracts/commitments	0	0	0	0	0
Specify conflict resolution mechanisms	0	0	0	0	0
Specify coordination/control regime (e.g. centralized or hierarchical)	1	0	0	0	0
Specify agent communication language	0	0	0	0	0
Agent Internal Design					
Define agent architecture	3	0	0	0	1
Define agent mental attributes (e.g. goals, beliefs, plans…)	0	0	3	3	3
Define agent behavioural interface (e.g. capabilities, services)	0	3	3	3	0
System/Environment Design					
Define system architecture/organisational structure	0	0	0	0	0
Specify dynamic agent group formulation / dissolution	0	0	0	0	0
Specify agent relationships (e.g. inheritance, aggregation & association)	0	3	3	0	2B
Specify co-existing non-agent entities	0	3	0	2A	0
Specify infrastructure/environment facilities	0	0	0	0	1
Specify agent-environment interaction mechanism	0	0	0	3	1
Instantiate agent classes	3	1	3	0	0
Specify agent instance location	3	0	0	0	0

Support for Steps in the Development Process (Table 3)

The list of standard MAS-development steps proposed by [1] is used as a checklist to compare the five MAS methodologies. The support of each methodology for each step is assessed on a 4-point scale:

0: no support is provided
1: the step is included but no techniques or examples are provided
2A: the methodology provides techniques for performing the step
2B: the methodology provides examples of how the step can be performed
3: the step is discussed with techniques and examples

This scheme of rating allows us to indirectly assess and compare the provision of techniques and heuristics by the methodologies. Methodologies that are most complete in terms of their support for the development steps are MaSE, Prometheus and MAS-CommonKADS.

Support for Concepts of MAS Models (Table 4)

We will use the list of standard MAS concepts proposed by [1] to compare the five MAS methodologies. If a MAS methodology can represent or capture a concept in its models, we can simply give it a tick ✓.

Most concepts in the categories of "problem domain", "agent properties", "agent relationships" and "agent interactions" are supported by most MAS methodologies. However, "deployment" concepts are overlooked by most methodologies, indicating their lack of support for MAS deployment issues.

Table 4. Comparative analysis on support for concepts of MAS models

Concepts	MaSE	GAIA	BDIM	Prometheus	MAS-CommonKADS
Problem Domain					
System goals	✓				
System roles	✓	✓	✓		
System functionality/Tasks	✓	✓		✓	✓
Task responsibilities/Procedures	✓	✓	✓		
Design requirements					
Use case/Scenarios	✓			✓	✓
Agent Properties					
Agent classes	✓	✓	✓	✓	✓
Agent instances (including cardinality)	✓	✓	✓	✓	✓
Agent's roles	✓	✓	✓		✓
Agent's functionality	✓	✓	✓	✓	✓
Agent's knowledge/Beliefs				✓	✓
Agent's plans				✓	✓
Agent's goals	✓			✓	✓
Agent's capabilities				✓	✓
Agent mobility					
Agent Interaction					
Interaction pathways	✓	✓	✓	✓	✓
Exchanged messages	✓		✓	✓	✓
Interaction protocols	✓			✓	✓
Interaction constraints					
Conflict resolution mechanisms					
Contracts/commitments					
Ontology					
Agent Relationships					
Inheritance				✓	✓
Aggregation		✓	✓	✓	✓
Association		✓	✓		✓
System/Environment					
Co-existing non-agent entities				✓	
Infrastructure/environment facilities		✓			
Organisational structure					
Agent-environment interaction				✓	✓
Environment characteristics					
Deployment					
Agent architecture	✓				✓
System architecture					
Location of agent instances	✓				
Sources of agent instances					

5 Conclusions

In this paper, we have compared five well-known MAS methodologies using the feature analysis framework proposed in [1]. The comparison takes into account a variety of evaluation criteria and methodological features, covering from process-related and model-related aspects to high-level MAS capabilities. We also assessed the capability of methodologies in terms of their support for steps in the development process, and for AO concept modelling. This assessment will help developers to decide on the most appropriate methodology to use in a specific application. However, it should be noted that, while this paper examines the features (and steps and concepts) of a methodology as independent from each other, some methodologies may offer the features (or steps or concepts) in combination. Thus, the developer may need to assess these constructs as a group rather than as independent entities. Future work includes extending the comparative analysis to many other existing MAS methodologies, in order to obtain an overall assessment of the current work in AO software engineering.

References

1. Tran, Q.N., Low, G., Williams, M.A.: A Feature Analysis Framework for Evaluating Multi-agent System Development Methodologies. In Zhong, N., Ras, Z.W., Tsumoto, S., Suzuki, E. (eds): Foundations of Intelligent Systems – Proc. of the 14th Int. Symposium on Methodologies for Intelligent Systems ISMIS'03 (2003) 613-617.
2. Wood, M.: Multiagent Systems Engineering: A Methodology for Analysis and Design of Multiagent Systems. MS Thesis, Air Force Institute of Technology, USA (2000).
3. Wooldridge, M., Jennings, N.R. and Kinny, D.: The Gaia methodology for agent-oriented analysis and design. Journal of Autonomous Agents and Multi-Agent Systems, 3 (2000) 285-312
4. Zambonelli, F., Jennings, N., Wooldridge, M.: Developing multiagent systems: the Gaia methodology. ACM Transaction on Software Engineering and Methodology (in press)
5. Kinny, D., Georgeff, M., Rao, A.: A Methodology and Modelling Technique for Systems of BDI Agents. Proc. of the 7th European Workshop on Modelling Autonomous Agents in a Multi-Agent World (1996) 56-71
6. Padgham, L., Winikoff, M.: Prometheus: a methodology for developing intelligent agents. Proc. of the 1st Int. Joint Conf. on Autonomous Agents and Multi-Agent Systems (2002).
7. Iglesias, C. A., Garijo, M., Gonzalez, J.C., Velasco, J.R.: Analysis and Design of Multi-agent Systems Using MAS-CommonKADS. In Singh, M.P., Rao, A., Wooldridge, M.J. (eds.). Intelligent Agents IV (ATAL'97). Springer-Verlag, Berlin (1998)
8. Wood, B., Pethia, R., Gold, L.R., Firth, R.: A Guide to the Assessment of Software Development Methods. Technical Report CMUSEI-88-TR-8, SEI, Software Engineering Institute, Carnegie Mellon University (1988)
9. Jayaratna, N.: Understanding and Evaluating Methodologies - NIMSAD A Systematic Framework. McGraw-Hill, England (1994)
10. Olle, T.W., Sol, H.G., Tully, C.J. (eds.): Information Systems Design Methodologies - A Feature Analysis. Elsevier Science Publishers, Amsterdam (1983)
11. The Object Agency Inc.: A Comparison of Object-Oriented Development methodologies. http://www.toa.com/smnn?mcr.html (1995)

12. Shehory, O., Sturm, A.: Evaluation of modeling techniques for agent-based systems. Proc. of the 5th Int. Conf. on Autonomous agents (2001) 624-631.
13. O'Malley, S.A., DeLoach, S.A.: Determining When to Use an Agent-Oriented Software Engineering Paradigm. Proc. of the 2nd Int. Workshop on Agent-Oriented Software Engineering (AOSE) (2001).
14. Cernuzzi, L., Rossi, G.: On the Evaluation of Agent-Oriented Modelling Methods. Proc. of the OOPSLA Workshop on Agent-Oriented Methodologies (2002)
15. Sabas, A., Badri, M., Delisle, S.: A Multidimentional Framework for the Evaluation of Multiagent System Methodologies. Proc. of the 6th World Multiconference on Systemics, Cybernetics and Informatics (SCI-2002), 211-216.
16. Iglesias, C.A., Garijo, M., & Gonzalez, J.C.: A survey of agent-oriented methodologies. Proc. of the 5th Int. Workshop on Intelligent Agents V: Agent Theories, Architectures, and Languages (1999)

CMRadar: A Personal Assistant Agent for Calendar Management

Pragnesh Jay Modi, Manuela Veloso, Stephen F. Smith, and Jean Oh

Department of Computer Science,
Carnegie Mellon University,
Pittsburgh PA 15213
{pmodi, mmv, sfs, jeanoh}@cs.cmu.edu

Abstract. Personal assistant agents have long promised to automate routine everyday tasks in order to reduce the cognitive load on humans. One such routine task is the management of a user's calendar. In this paper, we describe CMRadar, a calendar management system that is a significant step towards achieving the enduring vision of assistant agents. CMRadar is an implemented system with wide-ranging capabilities for supporting email exchange, multiagent negotiations and schedule optimization based on user preferences. The motivation is to develop an end-to-end system for use by real users to obtain data to facilitate learning. Having now completed an initial prototype which we believe is the first end-to-end agent for calendar management, we present as contributions our architecture design, the communication language used to tie system components together, and initial simulation experiments that isolate negotiation cost a key factor to be logged and predicted in order to improve performance.

1   Introduction

One of the more compelling visions for agents research is the development of "personal assistant agents" that are tasked with making people and organizations more efficient by autonomously handling routine tasks on behalf of their users [6] [7] [3]. Most recently, several researchers including ourselves have embarked on a large research project, called The Radar Project [10], whose overall goal is to develop a personalized agent that is able to assist its user in a wide range of everyday tasks. Within this larger project, we are concerned with the more focused task of managing a user's calendar. While aspects of calendar management have been investigated before [9] [11] [12] [5] [4], in this paper, we present CMRadar, a *complete* agent with capabilities ranging from natural language processing of incoming scheduling-related emails, to making autonomous scheduling decisions, to negotiating with other users, to user interfacing and visualization. Although many research issues remain, we believe CMRadar is the first end-to-end agent for automated calendar management.

A key contribution of the design of CMRadar is the specification of a basic representation, called a Template, for communicating calendar scheduling related information. The Template data structure is used as the language for the communication between the components in CMRadar and as the "glue" that binds them together. In addition,

P. Bresciani et al. (Eds.): AOIS 2004, LNAI 3508, pp. 169–181, 2005.
© Springer-Verlag Berlin Heidelberg 2005

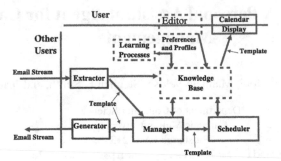

Fig. 1. Architecture of a single user's CMRadar

Templates are also used to normalize unformatted natural language emails into a machine readable format. We offer the Template data structure as a flexible approach to the general design of a meeting scheduling agent.

The CMRadar architecture contributes a modular design in which the core scheduling functions of the agent are separated from the multiagent aspects of calendar management. Rather than an approach that tightly couples schedule optimization and negotiation, CMRadar has a separate Manager component which handles the sending and receiving of messages from other agents and more generally, manages the negotiation with others. The Manager then communicates via Templates with a separate Scheduler component that handles the core optimization problems. We found that this modular architecture facilitates the integration of existing scheduling systems and indeed, a core component of CMRadar is the Ozone scheduler [13] originally designed for and used in several real-world logistics planning domains.

The primary underlying emphasis of the Radar project is to learn to improve performance, adapt to unexpected situations and to customize to different users. The emphasis on learning is reflected in our design of the CMRadar architecture in which all components read and write data to a central knowledge base that can be used by a separate learning process to provide feedback to the decision making components (see Figure 1). Indeed, it is the need to collect real-world data to support learning that drives our development of a complete end-to-end agent.

In anticipation of learning, this paper also presents simulation experiments in which we isolate negotiation cost as a key factor that should be logged in order to facilitate the construction of high quality schedules while avoiding high negotiation costs. We present empirical results in which an agent that remembers negotiation costs and takes them into account when deciding whether to bump a meeting outperforms simpler approaches.

2   The CMRadar Agent

CMRadar is developed as a personalized agent that interacts with other users or agents. Figure 1 shows the overall architecture of CMRadar with its functional modules. Dotted lines represent components not yet implemented. We present two main modules in the coming sections, namely the Manager and the Scheduler. In this section, we overview the complete architecture, briefly describing each of the modules.

duration: ["for" | "last"] <digits> ["hr(s)" | "min(s)"]
timeslots: ["at" | "before" | "after"] <time-exp>
       : <time-exp> "to" <time-exp>
       : <time-exp> "-" <time-exp> //ex: "10:00 - 11:00"
time-exp: <1-2 digits>":"<2 digits> //ex: "10:00", "6:00"
       : <1-2 digits>":"<2 digits> <tag>
       : <1-2 digits> <tag> // ex: "10 am", "1 pm"
tag: ["am" | "a.m." | "pm" | "p.m."]

Fig. 2. Example grammar rules for converting emails to Templates

Extractor: We assume that multiagent interaction in calendar meeting scheduling occurs through email message exchange. The Extractor is responsible for parsing email messages into a *template* normalized format representing the meeting request or reply to a request (see Section 4). The email messages can be sent directly by other Radar agents or by users in natural language. We have followed research on applying state-of-the-art natural language parsing techniques,[1] as well as successfully defining and applying special purpose parsing rules for language specific to meeting scheduling.[2] Figure 2 shows examples of such domain-specific language parsing rules.

Manager: Calendar management is in its essence a multiagent problem as meetings involve more than one person. The Manager module in CMRadar explicitly handles the multiagent aspects of calendar management, including flexible negotiation with other agents and control of email threads. Meeting scheduling is a complex process dependent on many factors, and different users schedule meetings with other users according to many different strategies. We view this variety of possible multiagent interactions similar to a *playbook* approach that we have previously developed in robot soccer [2]. The Manager can represent and reason about several different multiagent (team) strategies and learn to select the ones that are more effective when interacting with other specific agents.

Scheduler: The core task of meeting scheduling involves determining times for the meetings. The Scheduler module in CMRadar handles all the time analysis. It receives (or initiates) a specific request for a meeting and returns the user's time availability by considering the user's preferences and its calendar with different kinds of commitments. Calendar management is handled by the Scheduler under a rich set of soft and hard constraints, and agents can reason truthfully and rationally about their preferences towards optimizing the general social welfare. [3]

Calendar Data and Display: A human user is used to maintaining a calendar using the existing available COTS calendars. Our Calendar Data and Display module aims at having CMRadar use the same calendar programs. The current system is integrated with MS Outlook as shown in Figure 3. [4]

---

[1] We thank Donna Gates, Lori Levin, and Benjamin Han for their NLP work.
[2] We thank Kerry Hannan for her NLP work.
[3] We thank Elisabeth Crawford for her initial work on addressing this problem under a game theoretical approach.
[4] We thank Andrew Faulring and Brad Meyers for the integration of CMRadar with MS Outlook.

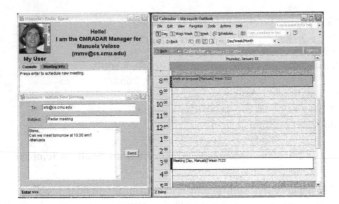

Fig. 3. A single user's CMRadar integrated with MS Outlook

Learning: Learning is necessary because obtaining ill-structured user preferences and customizing behavior to different users by hand is infeasible. The agent must acquire much of its required knowledge about its specific user over time through experience. Although learning is not yet part of the system, the current CMRadar as we present in this paper is the base step towards a complete CMRadar agent which will be truly a learning agent. Some initial work on an approach to learning user preferences by observing meeting scheduling episodes is reported in [8].

3   Template Data Format

A Template is a special-purpose language we have constructed for all the multiagent communication related to meeting scheduling in CMRadar. For communication with other agents or humans, templates are converted to and from natural language emails using the Extractor and Generator. We have found the Template representation to be extremely flexible for not only inter-agent communication but also for gluing components together within an agent.

As shown in Figure 4, a Template consists of a number of fields and we discuss three of the main ones: *timeslots*, *attendants* and *purposes*.

- **Timeslots:** This is a list of individual time slots, each of which contains a feasible scheduling window, denoted by earliest-start-time and latest-finish-time, and a specific desired slot denoted by start-time and finish-time. The priority field is the preference for this slot relative to other time slots in the template. Each time slot has an associated status field whose value is taken from {possible, impossible, pending, confirmed}. The "(im)possible" value is used to indicate the (un)availability of a time slot, "pending" indicates that a time slot is currently reserved by an on-going negotiation and finally, "confirmed" indicates that the meeting has been scheduled and the time slot cannot be used for another meeting without triggering a rescheduling negotiation.
- **Attendants:** This is a list of all participants of the meeting. Each attendee has an associated priority level that can be used to indicate the person's relative importance to the meeting.

```
(template
  (meeting-id MT5) (msg-id MGS1205)
  (timestamp 2003-12-17[15:04 -0500])
  (initiator sfs@cs.cmu.edu)
  (duration 3600) (location NSH1305)
  (time-slots
    (time-slot
      (earliest-start-time 2003-12-17[15:00 -0500])
      (latest-finish-time 2003-12-17[16:00 -0500])
      (start-time 2003-12-17[15:00 -0500])
      (finish-time 2003-12-17[16:00 -0500])
      (priority 1)
      (status confirmed)))
  (attendants
    (attendant (id sfs@cs.cmu.edu) (level 1.0))
    (attendant (id mmv@cs.cmu.edu) (level 1.0)))
  (purposes
    (purpose (predefined-kind project-meeting)
            (description "Radar project meeting")
            (special-note nil))))
```

Fig. 4. Example of a CMRadar template

- **Purposes:** This field is used to hold general text related to the meeting. Of note is the predefined-kind field which references an existing taxonomy of meetings in the knowledge base, e.g., project-meeting, faculty-meeting, advisor-meeting, etc. This field is used by the Scheduler to inform scheduling decisions, e.g., prefer to schedule faculty-meetings on Friday.

We have found in the development of CMRadar that this template-based communication is notable for its flexibility where a Template can be interpreted according to the context of the current negotiation. For example, when an agent receives a new template containing a time slot with status "pending", it is interpreted as a proposal to meet at that time. Conversely, when an agent receives a template that is a reply to a previous proposal containing a time slot with status "pending", the agent interprets it as an affirmative reply to its previous request. Templates are currently used for single occurrence meetings. Representation of *repeating* meetings, i.e., "Every Monday at 2:00 pm" is not yet available, but we envision extending the template to define a set of keywords such as "every", "every other", "monthly", etc, to represent this type of meeting.

4   Manager

The purpose of the manager is to interact with other users and agents in service of scheduling meetings. These interactions can be very complex requiring sophisticated decision making by the agent. To illustrate the complexity of the problem, we describe a meeting scheduling episode between four users shown in Figure 5 which highlights many of the key decisions to be made by an agent.

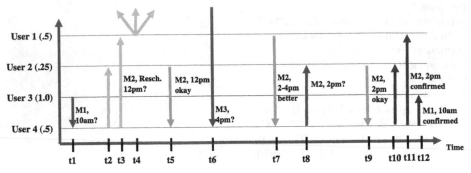

Fig. 5. Example of a complex negotiation

The Y-axis in Figure 5 shows four users each with a level of priority as shown in parentheses. The priority of a user represents his or her rank relative to others in the organization. At time t1, User 3 proposes (via an email message) to User 4 a meeting M1 at 10 am. Although the calendars of each agent are not shown, let us assume that User 4 has a meeting M2 already confirmed with Users 1 and 2 for 10 am. Because User 3 has a high priority, User 4 wishes to accommodate User 3's request and so tries to reschedule meeting M2 to another time. At t2 and t3, User 4 sends proposals to reschedule M2 for 12 pm. At t4, we see that User 1 enters into negotiations with others to attempt to accommodate User 4's request, while at t5, User 2 responds to User 4. At t6, User 4 receives a request for a new meeting. At t7, User 1 responds to User 4 by counter proposing a range of times, indicated preferences but not a hard constraint. User 4 chooses a time within the given range and re-proposes to User 2 (the other attendee of M2). At t9, User 2 responds affirmatively and at times t10,t11,t12 User 1 is able to finally confirm both meetings M1 and M2.

To successfully execute this scenario requires the following key competencies.

– **Multiple Thread Management:** A key challenge is the management of multiple inter-linked negotiation threads. Indeed, performing such "multi-linked negotiations" [14] effectively is an outstanding research issue in multiagent systems. As illustrated by the interactions between meeting M1 and M2 in our scenario, the decision to accept a meeting proposal for a given time may depend on the result of other negotiations. Furthermore, others may not respond immediately to requests or may never respond at all. The agent must be able to keep track of the status of different negotiation threads and their interactions and make timely decisions.

– **Context-Dependent Negotiation Strategies:** The agent must be flexible and able to adapt its decision making depending on the context of the current meeting negotiation and its participants. For example, we saw that User 4 chose to accommodate User 3's request by bumping meeting M2 which resulted in a renegotiation with others. In other scenarios, it may be better to refuse User 3's proposal. Indeed, this type of decision cannot be a static one but must take into account the current context. The appropriate strategy to use in a given situation depends on very rich context information including local user preferences, the other participants of the meeting, the history of the negotiations with those people, and the history of the current negotiation itself.

– **Explanation:** The agent must be able to keep the user informed of the status of on-going negotiations and explain scheduling decisions when asked. For example in our scenario, if User 4 queries her agent as to why meeting M2 has been rescheduled, the agent should be able to respond that it was due to request for a meeting M1 from User 3. This competency is crucial for usability and trust by humans.

In our current system, the Manager responds to requests for meetings on its user's behalf by querying the Scheduler (described in the next section) for free time slots. The Manager can display and update the status of meetings via the MS Outlook Calendar interface. The Manager currently uses a simple fixed negotiation strategy in which an initiator always proposes a single time slot and a receiver either accepts it or rejects it in which case the initiator re-proposes. Limited forms of rescheduling decisions are made where lower priority meetings are bumped in favor of higher priority ones. In next steps, we will expand these capabilities with more sophisticated negotiation strategies and learn to adaptively choose the appropriate negotiation strategy using a playbook strategy [2].

5   Scheduler

The Scheduler is the component within CMRadar responsible for representing and managing the user's calendar. Whereas the Manager handles the negotiation with other calendar agents, the scheduler reasons about the user's constraints and preferences to determine the best options in a given meeting context. The CMRadar Scheduler has been built using the Ozone [13], an incremental, constraint-based scheduling framework previously used to develop a number of complex logistics planning applications [1]. Ozone is designed specifically from a continuous scheduling mindset, where schedules evolve incrementally over time as new requirements are received, priorities change and unexpected conflicts arise. This orientation makes it ideally suited for the problem of calendar management.

Within CMRadar, the Scheduler provides basic support for both (1) responding to meeting requests and (2) assisting in initiation of meeting requests. In both cases, the action of the Scheduler is to generate options that are consistent with the constraints specified in the triggering message and maximize satisfaction of known user preferences. In more detail, the Scheduler's response to a meeting request (originating either from another agent or the user herself) proceeds in three steps (see Figure 6):

– **Generate feasible meeting options:** The input meeting request template specifies a set of acceptable time periods (in the simplest case, an earliest start time est_m and a latest finish time lft_m) together with any constraints on meeting duration. By default, a feasible option is any time slot that satisfies these constraints and is currently not booked for another purpose. If these constraints yield no options, the Scheduler will relax the constraint that existing meetings must be respected, and consider pre-emption of lower priority meetings (currently a function of attendees and meeting type). Other more complex resolution strategies (e.g., shrinking the durations of one or more existing meetings) are also possible.

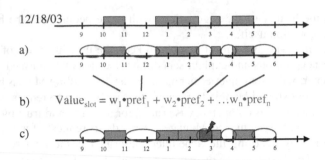

Fig. 6. Responding to a Request

- **Collect and evaluate preferences:** The scheduler maintains representations of various meeting attendants (including the user) , meeting groups, meeting types, etc., which provides a backbone for organizing known meeting preferences. Using the parameters of the template as indicies into this representation, the set of preferences relevant to the request are collected. Each option is then evaluated and assigned a rating (discussed in more detail below), indicative of how well each satisfies this set of preferences.

- **Select option(s):** According to the current response strategy in force, the highest valued option or the n highest valued options are returned.

As suggested above, a preference assigns a *utility* to a given meeting option, reflective of how well it is satisfied. Utilities are defined to span the range $[-1, 1]$, with 1 implying that the preference is completely satisfied, 0 that it is neutral, and -1 indicating that the option is intolerable. A preference also has an intrinsic *importance* in relation to other preferences, a number between 0 and 1. In a given option evaluation context, the importance values of all relevant preferences are normalized to produce the set of weights for computing the overall rating of a given option (see Figure 6). One aspect of this normalization involves striking a balance between those preferences held by the user and those held by other meeting participants.

The set of preferences that must be accounted for in meeting scheduling are quite diverse, and we have devised representations that allow specification of several broad classes. In addition to simple interval preferences (e.g., I prefer to meet from 2:00PM to 3:00PM, piece-wise linear curves can be used to specify more complex time-of-day preferences (e.g., afternoon is best, late morning is acceptable but never before 9:00 AM). More interesting are so-called *dynamic* preferences, which depend on the current state of the user's calendar and change as the calendar schedule evolves.

Figure 7 gives an example of a dynamic scheduling preference - a preference for scheduling meetings back to back. On the left, the utility curve of the preference is shown, indicating the level of satisfaction of the preference to be a function of the percentage of total meetings over a given horizon that fall adjacent to the option (i.e., time slot) under consideration. (In this case, adjacency is defined to tolerate some, presumably small, time gaps.) On the right of Figure 7, a three meeting schedule is displayed to show the preference's utility for different options. The preference value for the time

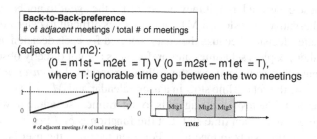

Fig. 7. Back-to-Back Preference

slot between Meeting 1 and Meeting 2 is highest because it will make all four meetings back to back.

6   Empirical Results in Simulation

We investigate the effect of different scheduling strategies on system performance in a simulation setting. The purpose of these experiments is to provide guidance in further developing the CMRadar system by answering the question: What data should be logged by a deployed CMRadar agent in order to help it learn? Although a working prototype of CMRadar is completed as described in this paper, we use simulations for our investigation because it allows large numbers of experiments to be done efficiently. Furthermore, CMRadar has not yet been deployed to users so that in-situ studies may be done.

In the next section, we describe the experimental setup and the results obtained. The results show that a scheduling strategy that explicitly takes into account negotiation costs outperforms other simpler strategies assuming that these costs can be perfectly known. Of course, predicting negotiation costs can be a difficult challenge in the real world and is one of the key issues that we will investigate next. However, the results presented in this section are significant because they show that recording past negotiation costs and learning to predict them would be valuable since they can be used to improve system performance.

6.1   Experimental Setup

While CMRadar is responsible for making many different calendar management decisions, this section focuses on one key decision related to meeting scheduling in which the agent must decide in which time slot to put a particular meeting. This decision is complicated by the fact that multiple meetings may compete for the same time slot. For example as we saw in Figure 5, M2 occupied a time slot (10 am) that was desired by a new higher priority meeting M1. The agent must decide whether to assign the time slot to M1 and "bump" M2 and reschedule it, or keep M2 where it is and put M1 somewhere else. The decision to bump M2 incurs cost because it requires sending messages to the other attendees with a request to reschedule and waiting for responses. These responses may not come immediately because the other attendees may in turn need to bump other meetings. If these costs are large, it may be better for the agent to not bump M2 and instead find an alternative time slot for M1. Note that it is difficult to determine in advance which is the better decision because the costs incurred for each decision are not known and because other people's schedules and preferences are not directly observable.

To investigate this issue, we use the following model. Let $calendar = \{slot_1, slot_2, ..., slot_n\}$ be the set of time slots in a user calendar and $M = \{M_1, M_2, ..., M_m\}$ be a set of meetings. The task of the agent is to determine a schedule in which no more than one meeting is in a given time slot. Let the function $sched : calendar \rightarrow M$ be a schedule that maps time slots to meetings. For each meeting, the user has a preference ordering over all time slots. Let $V_p^i(M_j)$ denote the user preference for putting meeting M_j in $slot_i$. For a given schedule $sched$, let $V_p(sched) = \sum_{slot_i \in calendar} V_p^i(sched(slot_i) = M_j)$ denote the total quality of the schedule. Finally, the assignment of a meeting to a time slot incurs some negotiation cost which can be a complex function of the other attendees of the meeting and the time slot. Let $C_n^i(M_j)$ be the cost for putting meeting M_j in $slot_i$. We assume that each meeting has a unique desired slot where there is zero cost if it is scheduled in that slot. The "desired slot" models a time that is proposed by other attendees. That is, when an agent receives a request "Can you meet at 10 am?", there is no negotiation cost for scheduling at 10 am because presumably the requester is free at that time. So we assume $C_n^i(M_j) = 0$ if $slot_i$ is the desired slot for M_j. Finally, the total cost of a schedule is given by $C_n(sched) = \sum_{slot_i \in calendar} C_n^i(sched(slot_i) = M_j)$. While this model is clearly limited in many respects, it provides a simple yet effective approach for investigating alternative decision-making strategies.

6.2   Evaluating Strategies

Using the above model, we now present empirical results for three different decision-making strategies: *Greedy, Bumping* and *Ncost*. In the simplest Greedy strategy shown in Figure 8, an agent only inserts meetings into free slots and never backtracks on these decisions. If the desired slot for a particular meeting is already taken, the meeting is inserted into an alternative time slot that is both free and highest-ranked according to local preferences. For not putting the meeting in the desired slot, the agent incurs a negotiation cost as shown in line 6 of Figure 8.

```
procedure GreedyStrategy(Mᵢ, desiredSlot)
(1)     if desiredSlot is not null and is free:
(2)         put Mᵢ into desiredSlot
(3)     else:
(4)         timeslot ← best free slot for Mᵢ
                according to preferences
(5)         put Mᵢ into timeslot
(6)         cᵢ ← actual cost of negotiating with
                other attendees for Mᵢ
(7)         Cₙ = Cₙ + cᵢ
```

Fig. 8. Greedy Meeting Scheduling

```
procedure BumpingStrategy(Mᵢ, desiredSlot)
```
(1)   if desiredSlot is free:
(2)   put M_i into desiredSlot
(3)   else:
(4) $M_j \leftarrow$ current meeting in desiredSlot
(5) $v_j \leftarrow$ preference for M_j in desiredSlot
(6) $v_i \leftarrow$ preference for M_i in desiredSlot
(7)   if $v_i > v_j$: // *bump* M_j
(8)   put M_i into desiredSlot
(9)   GreedyStrategy(M_j, null)
(10)   else:
(11)   GreedyStrategy(M_i, null)

Fig. 9. Scheduling with Bumping

The Bumping strategy shown in Figure 9 is more complex because it bumps meetings out of their desired slots if a new meeting is more preferred. However, the decision to bump or not is made exclusively using local preferences and does not take into account negotiation costs that may be incurred.

Finally, the NCost strategy shown in Figure 10 takes into account both local preferences and predicted negotiation costs. As shown in line 9, an existing meeting M_j is bumped in favor of meeting M_i only if the preference for M_i minus the cost for renegotiating for M_j is greater than preference for M_j minus the cost for renegotiating for M_i.

Figure 11 shows the empirical results averaged over 100 runs. In each run, we use a calendar consisting of 9 one hour time slots (from 8 am to 5 pm) initialized with 25% of the slots full. The agent is tasked with iteratively scheduling meetings as they arise over time. The negotiation cost for a particular meeting is modeled as a random number taken from [0,100]. The user preference $V_p^i(M_j)$ is calculated as the priority of M_j divided by the distance of $slot_i$ from $slot_{pref}$, where priority is a random number taken from

```
procedure NCostStrategy(Mᵢ, desiredSlot)
```
(1)   if desiredSlot is free:
(2)   put M_i into M_i
(3)   else:
(4) $M_j \leftarrow$ current meeting in desiredSlot
(5) $v_j \leftarrow$ preference for M_j in desiredSlot
(6) $v_i \leftarrow$ preference for M_i in desiredSlot
(7) $c_i \leftarrow$ predicted cost of negotiating with
                other attendees for M_i
(8) $c_j \leftarrow$ predicted cost of negotiating with
                other attendees for M_j
(9)   if $v_i - c_j > v_j - c_i$: // *bump* M_j
(10)   put M_i into desiredSlot
(11)   GreedyStrategy(M_j, null)
(12)   else:
(13)   GreedyStrategy(M_i, null)

Fig. 10. Scheduling with consideration of negotiation costs

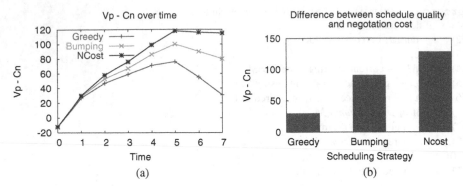

Fig. 11. The NCostStrategy, which trades off local preference (V_p) with negotiation cost (C_n), outperforms a strategy that schedules only in free slots (Greedy) and one that only uses preferences (Bumping). (b) shows the final V_p - C_n for the time series data shown on (a)

[0,100] and $slot_{pref}$ is a random slot in the calendar. Thus V_p and C_n range from zero to 100 times the number of meetings in the calendar. Figure 11 (a) shows how performance varies as 7 meetings are scheduled in sequence, while Figure 11 (b) shows that the final schedule obtained using NCost strategy is superior in performance to the others as measured by the quality of the resulting schedule (V_p) minus the negotiation costs for obtaining that schedule (C_n). These results indicate that logging past negotiation costs and using them to predict future costs can be used to improve performance.

7   Conclusion

We presented CMRadar, an implemented system for calendar management. CMRadar is a complete agent in the sense that it is able to facilitate meeting scheduling across the entire spectrum from initiation to confirmation to rescheduling. While we have thus far concentrated on breadth of functionality, in future work we will develop more sophisticated reasoning within each component along the dimensions of the key challenges discussed. CMRadar indeed presents a challenging road map for future research in effective learning personal assistant agents.

Acknowledgments

This work is supported by the Defense Advanced Research Projects Agency (DARPA) under Contract No. NBCHC030029. We thank the following people for their work on CMRadar: Andrew Faulring, Brad Meyers, Kerry Hannan, Lawrence Lee, Akiva Leffert, Elisabeth Crawford, Donna Gates, Benjamin Han, and Lori Levin.

References

1. M.A Becker and S.F Smith. Mixed-initiative resource management: The amc barrel allocator. In *Proceedings of the Fifth International Conference on Artificial Intelligence Planning and Scheduling (AIPS-00)*, pages 32–41, Breckenridge CO, April 2000. The AAAI Press.

2. Michael Bowling, Brett Browning, and Manuela Veloso. Plays as effective multiagent plans enabling opponent-adaptive play selection. In *Proceedings of the International Conference on Automated Planning and Scheduling (ICAPS'04)*, 2004.
3. H. Chalupsky, Y. Gil, C.A. Knoblock, K. Lerman, J. Oh, D.V. Pynadath, T.A. Russ, and M. Tambe. Electric elves: Applying agent technology to support human organizations. In *Proceedings of Innovative Applications of Artificial Intelligence Conference*, 2001.
4. Leonardo Garrido and Katia Sycara. Multi-agent meeting scheduling: Preliminary experimental results. In *Proceedings of the First International Conference on Multi-Agent Systems (ICMAS'95)*.
5. N. R. Jennings and A. J. Jackson. Agent based meeting scheduling: A design and implementation. *IEE Electronics Letters*, 31(5):350–352, 1995.
6. Pattie Maes. Agents that reduce work and information overload. *Communications of the ACM*, 37(7), 1994.
7. Tom M. Mitchell, Rich Caruana, Dayne Freitag, John McDermott, and David Zabowski. Experience with a learning personal assistant. *Communications of the ACM*, 37(7):80–91, 1994.
8. J. Oh and S.F. Smith. Learning user preferences for distributed calendar scheduling. In *Proc. 5th International Conference on Practice and Theory of Automated Timetabling (PATAT)*, Pittsburgh, PA, 2004.
9. T. R. Payne, R. Singh, and K. Sycara. Calendar agents on the semantic web. In *IEEE Intelligent Systems*, volume 17(3), pages 84–86, 2002.
10. The Radar Project. "www.radar.cs.cmu.edu", 2004.
11. Sandip Sen and Edmund H. Durfee. On the design of an adaptive meeting scheduler. In *Proc. The Tenth IEEE Conference on Artificial Intelligence for Applications*, pages 40–46, 1994.
12. Sandip Sen and Edmund H. Durfee. A formal study of distributed meeting scheduling. In *Group Decision and Negotiation*, volume 7, pages 265–289, 1998.
13. S.F. Smith, O. Lassila, and M.A. Becker. Configurable, mixed-initiative systems for planning and scheduling. In A. Tate, editor, *Advanced Planning Technology*. AAAI Press, Menlo Park, 1996.
14. Xiaoqin Zhang and Victor Lesser. Multi-linked negotiation in multi-agent systems. In *Proceedings of the first international joint conference on Autonomous agents and multiagent systems*, 2002.

Agents as Catalysts for Mobile Computing

G.M.P. O'Hare[1], M.J. O'Grady[2], R.W. Collier[2], and S. Keegan[2]

[1] Adaptive Information Cluster (AIC),
Department of Computer Science, University College Dublin (UCD),
Belfield, Dublin 4,Ireland
gregory.ohare@ucd.ie
[2] Practice & Research in Intelligent Systems & Media (PRISM) Laboratory,
Department of Computer Science, University College Dublin (UCD),
Belfield, Dublin 4, Ireland
{michael.j.ogrady, rem.collier, stephen.keegan}@ucd.ie

Abstract. Agent-Oriented Programming (AOP) offers an alternative and radical approach to the development of information systems in various domains. However, one domain that AOP has only minimally affected, at least up until now, is that of mobile computing. Until recently, the use of strong intentional agents in such a domain has been considered impractical and, indeed, computationally intractable. In this paper, Agent Factory, a system for the fabrication of strong intelligent agents, is reviewed in the light of agent deployment on mobile devices. As an illustration of the potential of agents in mobile applications, two archetypical mobile computing applications, realised through Agent Factory, are described.

1 Introduction

This paper explores one particular genre of Agent-Oriented Information Systems (AOIS), namely mobile and ubiquitous computing. Such systems are typified by devices that are computationally challenged in terms of screen, memory and processor real estate, as well as networks that are resource-bounded and bandwidth restricted. Users expect content relevance, timeliness and a degree of personalization to their individual needs. These demands are significant and demanding, and necessitate systems that exhibit the ability to anticipate the content and service needs of users.

Until recently, the use of strong intentional agents in such a domain would have been considered impractical, and, indeed, computationally intractable. In this paper, Agent Factory, a system for the fabrication of strong, intelligent, mobile and agile agents is utilized. In particular, its strategies for realising such agents in the computationally-constrained world of mobile computing are outlined. We illustrate the successful deployment of agent technology generally and Agent Factory specifically via two archetypical mobile computing applications. The first, EasiShop, a ubiquitous commerce (uCommerce) application, enables shoppers to seek out good deals while wandering an arbitrary shopping mall or high street. The second, Gulliver's Genie, is a mobile context-sensitive tourist guide that focuses on the delivery of personalised multimedia content in a just-in-time basis.

P. Bresciani et al. (Eds.): AOIS 2004, LNAI 3508, pp. 182–197, 2005.

2 Agent Factory

Agent Factory (AF) [1] [2] [3] is a cohesive framework, illustrated in Figure 1., for the development and deployment of agent-oriented applications that has been developed by the authors. Central to this framework is the Agent Factory Agent Programming Language (AF-APL), an Agent-Oriented Programming (AOP) language that supports the fabrication of agents that are autonomous, situated, socially able, intentional, rational and mobile. However, Agent Factory differs from other AOP offerings in that AF-APL has been embedded within a distributed FIPA-compliant [4] Run-Time Environment, and supports the development and deployment of agents through an integrated development environment, and an associated software engineering methodology. Details of these layers are presented in the following sections.

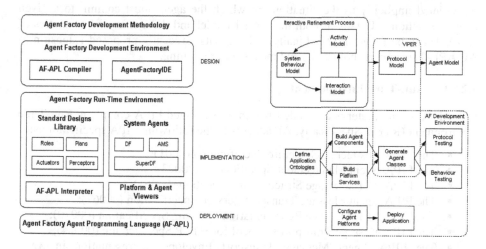

Fig. 1. The Agent Factory Framework and its associated Development Methodology

A key concern in the design of AF has been to ensure that AF-APL agents can be deployed on Personal Digital Assistants (PDAs). This has been achieved by ensuring that the Run-Time Environment, which includes the AF-APL Interpreter, is compliant with version 1.1.8 of the Java SDK (a.k.a. Personal Java for Mobile Devices). To check compatibility with future versions of Java, J2ME-compliant versions of the Run-Time Environment have also been developed. However, due to incompatibilities between Personal Java and J2ME, and as a result of our wish to ensure that AF can be deployed on the most prevalent operating system / JVM configuration for PDAs (e.g. MS PocketPC and Jeode), AF is currently not J2ME-compliant.

2.1 AF-APL

AF-APL is a declarative Agent-Oriented Programming (AOP) language that supports the programming of agent behaviours. The basic premise behind AF-APL is the view that complex agent behaviours can be more naturally modelled by viewing agents to be mental entities that maintain an internal *mental state* that is comprised of mental attitudes, in this case: *beliefs* and *commitments*. Beliefs describe, using a first-order logic representation language, the current state of the agent and its environment, and commitments describe the current (and future) activities that the agent has decided to perform. These will be illustrated further in Sections 3.3 and 4.4 respectively. Finally, decisions are modelled through a set of commitment rules that map situations (a conjunction of positive and negative beliefs) onto commitments. These rules are checked repeatedly within a sense-deliberate-act cycle.

As with other similar offerings, such as Goal-Directed 3APL [5] and AgentSpeak(L) [6], the syntax and semantics of AF-APL have been formally specified. In particular, AF-APL is based upon a logical model of reasoning that is centred about the notion of commitment. This contrasts with the more traditional Belief-Desire-Intention (BDI) architecture [7] on which these other approaches are based. In our model, intentions are synonymous with commitments, while goals are represented implicitly as the situations in which the agent must commit to a given course of action. Details of both the formal model and the syntax and semantics of AF-APL can be found in [2]. Finally, [8] presents a recently proposed extension to AF-APL that supports both goals and means-end reasoning.

2.2 The Run-Time Environment

The AF-APL interpreter is embedded within a distributed FIPA-compliant Run-Time Environment (RTE). Specifically, AF adheres to the following FIPA specifications:

- The FIPA Abstract Architecture Specification (0001);
- The FIPA Agent Management Specification (00023);
- The FIPA ACL Message Structure Specification (00061);
- The FIPA Agent Message Transport Service Specification (00067);
- The FIPA ACL Message Representation in String Specification (00070);
- The FIPA Message Transport Protocol for HTTP Specification (00084);
- The FIPA Agent Message Transport Envelope Representation in XML Specification (00085).

Within the context of these specifications, the RTE is organised as a collection of *agent platforms*. An Agent Platform (AP) provides the basic infrastructure that is necessary to deploy agents. Specifically, each AP implements a number of *platform services*, which provide various mandatory and optional infrastructure services. One platform service is the Agent Management System (AMS) service. This service is mandatory and is responsible for the creation, termination, suspension, resumption, registration, deregistration and execution of agents that are residing on the AP. A second service is the optional HTTP Message Transport Service, which provides a HTTP-based message-passing infrastructure for the Run-Time Environment. Other services include directory facilitator services (i.e. yellow pages services), persistence services, migration services and cloning services. During the development of agent-oriented applications, developers are required to identify and implement an appropriate set of platform services.

In addition to the platform services, the RTE also implements a number of System Agents, the most important being the AMS and DF agents. In essence, both these agents are agent wrappers that envelop the associated AMS and DF platform services respectively. Both agents control access to the relevant service on the AP.

2.3 The Development Methodology

Methodological support for the fabrication of agent-oriented applications using Agent Factory is provided through a software engineering process that supports the design, implementation, testing and deployment phases of the software engineering lifecycle and utilizes the UML as its modelling language. A diagrammatical overview of this process, details of which can be found in [9], is presented in Figure 1. It can be seen that the design stage of the process focuses around the development of five models:

1. The **System Behaviour Model (SBM)** is used to identify the main roles that agents will play within the system, and to associate those roles with the key system behaviours. Visually, this model is formalised using a customised UML Use Case Diagram where actors are stereotyped as roles, and use-cases are stereotyped as system behaviours.
2. The **Interaction Model (IM)** expands on the SBM through the modeling of the interactions that occur within each of the system behaviors. Visually, this model is formalized using a customized UML Collaboration Diagram.
3. The **Activity Model (ActM)** complements the IM, in that it expands on the SBM through the modeling of the set of activities that occur within each of the system behaviors. Visually, this model is formalized using a customized UML Activity Diagram where swimlanes are employed to represent roles.
4. The **Protocol Model (PM)** represents the transition point where the focus turns from understanding the system behaviors to the formalization of those behaviors as a set of protocols and agent-classes. Visually, these protocols are represented using Agent UML Sequence Diagrams.
5. Finally, the **Agent Model (AgtM)** completes the design by switching the focus from roles, interactions and activities to a more agent-centric view of the target system in which roles and agent classes become the constituent components.

2.4 The Development Environment

Support for the development of agents is realized through a number of toolsets. The Agent Factory Integrated Development Environment (IDE) provides a standard programming environment in the vein of NetBeans and JBuilder. Specifically, the editor includes features such as syntax highlighting, code compilation and application execution.

In addition, VIPER [10] is a graphical tool suite that allows the user to compose the Agent UML Sequence Diagrams that sit at the heart of the Protocol Model. VIPER is comprised of two tools: a Protocol Editor that provides a visual tool for generating Agent UML Sequence Diagrams and a Rule Editor that further supports the user by guiding them through the step of implementing the protocols in AF-APL.

In addition to the tools that have been provided to support the development of AF-APL agents, the Agent Factory Development Environment also includes a suite of tools that facilitate the testing and debugging of agent-oriented applications. These tools are associated with the Agent Platform component of the Run-Time Environment and include:

- the **Agent Viewer Tool**, which allows the developer to monitor and modify the agents internal state;
- the **Message Sender**, which allows the developer to interact with other agents as if they were themselves an agent; and
- the **Community Monitor**, which allows the developer to monitor interactions between a specified set of agents.

3 EasiShop

Delivering a real-time shopping solution is regarded as a litmus test for intelligent mobile agent technologies. Attempts to deliver such a mechanism on the web are well documented. Some insights revealed by these attempts hold a certain relevance to our

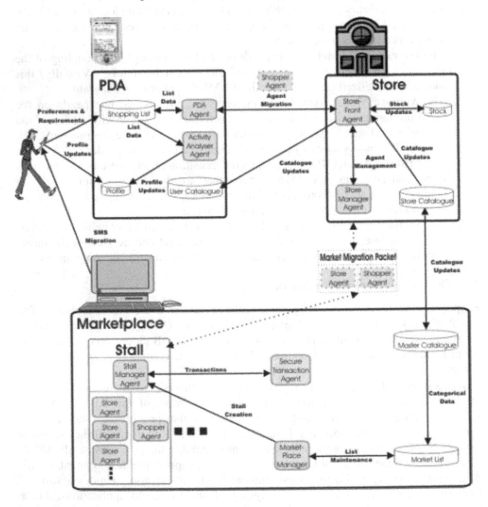

Fig. 2. Overview of EasiShop

domain. Ringo [11] for example, incorporated a collaborative filtering mechanism. This approach has since been adopted in the commercial realm by vendors such as Amazon. ShopBot [12] was an agent that could learn how to submit queries to e-commerce sites and interpret the resulting dataset to identify lowest-priced items. ShopBot automated the process of building wrappers to parse semi-structured HTML documents and extract features such as product descriptions and prices. Tete@Tete agent technology [13] strives to deliver integrated product brokering, merchant brokering and negotiation, thus encompassing three stages of the consumer buying behavior model as documented by Howard and Sheth [14].

Research into the role of intelligent mobile shopping systems is less mature. The Impulse project [15] developed at MIT augments GPS with agent technologies to provide context-sensitive information to the user. The main objective of the MyGrocer [16] project is to enable interactivity, personalisation and automation of home replenishment activities for products in the grocery retail sector. The Shopper's Eye experiment [17] introduces the concept of location-based filtering to assist the shopper. In contrast to all of these, however, EasiShop [18] [19] adopts a user-centric approach, realised through a suite of strong intentional agents. Its principal objective is the delivery of a scalable architecture that permits the partial automation of the shopping process while maximizing the opportunity for a prospective shopper to avail of optimum consumer conditions, for example, price, geographical proximity, after-sales service and so on.

3.1 The EasiShop Scenario

To envisage the modus operandi of EasiShop, let's assume the situation whereby the shopper is in possession of a PDA with the onboard client-side EasiShop system. To initiate the system, the shopper provides a composite set of preferences, profile and shopping list information. This is accomplished using the standard input of the PDA – stylus or virtual keyboard. The EasiShop architecture is complemented by another aspect of the system – the server-side components. It is envisaged that each participating retailer will make provision for an EasiShop Hotspots (EH). The EH is an active bluetooth broadcast area, strategically positioned at the foyer of the store. This zone provides a channel by which negotiation and trade can occur between the PDA Agent and the representative Store Agent. Figure 2 illustrates the main components of EasiShop.

The architecture is completed by the EasiShop Marketplace. This is a remote server containing software implementing an agent-based auction protocol. Using a specially adapted auction protocol (based on the Vickrey model), the system permits expedient and Pareto-efficient negotiation in real-time. The Marketplace also contains a secure datasink in which user profile information is retained. This information can be utilized to provide the shopper with more appropriate product offerings as well as providing Store Agents with valuable information as to what type of potential customer is in the proximity. It can be seen that the EH acts as a conduit between the shopper, represented by a personal PDA Agent, and the Marketplace.

3.2 Implementation

The EasiShop system was realised as a seven layer architecture, as illustrated in Figure 3. These layers are now considered briefly:

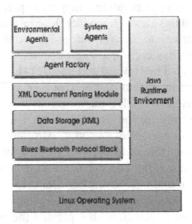

Fig. 3. The EasiShop Architecture

Agent Factory. System intelligence is delivered through Agent Factory.

Data Structures (XML). An adaptation of the Contract Net Protocol as proposed by Davis and Smith [20] has been proven to be the most appropriate mechanism for EasiShop. Agents utilise the protocol to make contracts which are binding for sales and purchases. For each bidding cycle, the communication involves four message types: Task announcement, Bidding, Awarding and Report Messages. In implementing the Contract Net Protocol, a suitable product description ontology is necessitated. For EasiShop, the UNSPSC [21] has been proven to be the most appropriate. XML was selected to represent the product information because of its inherent portability and for the fact that it becoming a de facto standard. It is extensible and separates content from presentation. Each time the shopper passes an EasiShop Hotspot, the difference (if any) between the product database on the EasiShop server and the PDA is sent to the PDA. In essence, all that is sent is the *diff* of the two files.

Auction Protocol. There are several existing protocols for multiple seller/single buyer auctions. English, Dutch and Vickrey are some examples. Each has a set of inherent advantages and drawbacks. When compared to other auction protocols, Vickrey auctions have the advantage that their duration is known prior to the auction taking place (each interested party bids only once). This factor holds particular relevance to the EasiShop domain, where, due to the fact that users are mobile and typically moving at a walking pace, real-time auction resolution is imperative. Furthermore, since the dominant bidding strategy of the Vickrey protocol is to bid to one's true evaluation, counter-speculation is avoided and a realistic psuedo-marketplace can be realised. Dutch auctions, on the other hand, have been shown to provide more revenue for the seller than Vickrey auctions in situations with three or more bidders, while both English and Vickrey auctions provide higher revenue for the auctioneer than their Dutch and first-price sealed bid counterparts.

BlueZ Bluetooth Protocol Stack. BlueZ is the official Linux Bluetooth protocol stack. It is an Open Source project distributed under GNU General Public License (GPL). To facilitate EasiShop, a module that accesses and utilises the BlueZ core was developed. As part of this process, it was necessary to construct an interface to permit information flow between the BlueZ module and the JRE.

Java Runtime Environment (JRE). The Blackdown JRE 1.3.1 RC1 for the Linux/ARM architecture is utilised on the PDA. Kaffe, a clean room implementation of the Java virtual machine, plus the associated class libraries needed to provide a JRE is used at the Store and Marketplace hosts. Blackdown is the JRE of choice for implementation on the PDA since it offers sophisticated GUI functionality. This includes the Swing components like JTree and JEditPanel, which allow for complex XML document display and manipulation techniques.

Linux Operating System. The Server-side components reside on a Linux 2.4.18-3 server. The PDA (an IPAQ 3870) runs the familiar v0.6.1 Linux build (2.4.18-3) from handhelds.org. Many of the inherent benefits of Linux are applicable to the EasiShop implementation. These are widely documented and encompass stability, security, open source, network orientation, speed and efficiency.

3.3 Agents @ Work in EasiShop

To demonstrate how agents support the EasiShop vision, consider the following series of events. In the typical EasiShop scenario, the shopper, equipped with a PDA, is situated in a busy shopping street. The shopper enters an EasiShop hotspot when passing within bluetooth broadcast range of a participating retailing outlet. Upon entering the hotspot, agent collaboration ensues. Activity is initiated by the PDA Agent (housed on the user's PDA) when it (having briefly liaised with the StoreFront Agent) uploads a shopping list to the shop. At this point, the Store Manager agent determines that one of the products on the list is currently in stock here. The PDA Agent is informed of this and may choose at this point to initiate the migration of the Shopper Agent from the PDA to the shop. The commitment rule that specifies this behavior is as follows and is further illustrated in Figure 4.

```
BELIEF(ShopHasProduct(?product)) &
BELIEF(inHotspot(?thestore)) =>
COMMIT(Self,Now,BELIEF(true),Migrate2Store(?thestore));
```

In general, the Agent Factory IDE proved to be invaluable during the delivery of EasiShop. The Agent Viewer Tool, the Message Sender and the Community Monitor were seen to be essential in debugging and optimizing agent states and interactions. The Agent Viewer Tool in particular enables a convenient means of visualizing real-time inter-agent communications. At present, the VIPER tool has been integrated to a lesser degree with the overall system when compared with the other tools. However, the potential of this tool, particularly in terms of delivering efficient inter-agent activity protocols, became apparent during the implementation and full integration would undoubtedly be of great benefit.

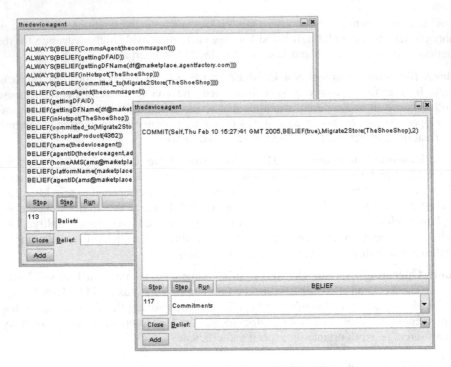

Fig. 4. A commitment is triggered in EasiShop

4 Gulliver's Genie

Gulliver's Genie [22] [23] is an application developed with the primary intention of delivering services to mobile users. Though it currently concentrates on the tourist domain, we expect it to evolve into a generic and customisable application that will deliver various services to mobile users. In addressing the needs of tourists, it is not unique, as several research disciplines have found the tourist domain a fertile testbed for theories and applications. Projects that come closest to the Genie in objectives and scope include GUIDE [24], a context-sensitive tourist guide for the city of Lancaster, and CRUMPET [25], developed for the city of Heidelberg. Examples of commercial products include Vindigo [26] and Portable Guide [27]. However, it is its use of BDI agents that differentiates the Genie from all other efforts in this area. Indeed, it may be regarded as a Multi-Agent System (MAS), the context of which envelops the Internet, a wireless data network and PDAs, and comprising a suite of agents all collaborating to obtain the Genie's goal: the timely distribution of information to roaming tourists.

4.1 Genie Services

At present, services provided by the Genie fall into two categories:

1. Navigation: Navigation support is a service that mobile users, and tourists in particular, find useful. Such a service can range from simple to sophisticated

with the Genie lying somewhere in between. An electronic map, scaled to street level and with all the relevant attractions highlighted, constitutes the initial component of the Genie's navigation support service. However, this is augmented with a real-time position determination facility that ensures that the tourist's position and orientation are always highlighted on the map. In this way, the tourist can see their location at any given instance.

2. Cultural Information: Though the motivation of individual tourists may vary considerably, experiencing the culture of a new environment is a common goal. The Genie seeks to facilitate this experience by delivering concise multimedia presentations on the various tourist attractions within the region in question. The presentations are dynamically assembled to account for the tourist's position, orientation and, particularly, their individual cultural interests. As tourists come within a predefined range of an attraction, a presentation is automatically activated.

4.2 Genie Architecture

The Genie architecture is illustrated in Figure 5, and comprises the following agents:

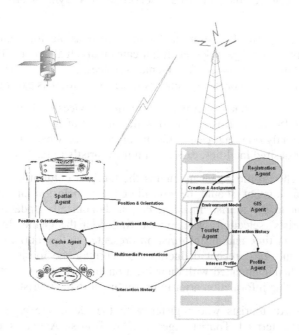

Fig. 5. The Architecture of the Genie

Spatial Agent. As its name suggests, the Spatial Agent monitors the tourist's movement and draws some inferences about what their activity is at any point in time. It continuously monitors the position sensor, in this case GPS, and extracts both position and orientation. After verifying that the readings are accurate and consistent (a history of the tourist's position readings is also maintained), it updates the display and notifies the Cache Agent. It then proceeds to review this new information in the light of its goals or objectives. Obviously, one of its primary goals is to keep the agents on the server up-to-date. Therefore, if the tourist has moved a significant distance since the last update, the server agents may be notified. If not, then the agent may decide not to dispatch any messages thus conserving bandwidth. Alternatively, if the server agents have not been notified of a new position reading within a certain time frame, the agent may decide that an update is appropriate.

Cache Agent. This agent manages the multimedia cache on the PDA, a critical task given the bandwidth limitations of wireless networks as well as the memory restrictions on current PDA models. Again, the Cache Agent works in close co-operation with the Spatial Agent and the agents on the server. It relies on the server-side agents for updates to its model of the tourist's environment as well as the actual multimedia files. It also relies on regular updates from the Spatial Agent concerning the tourist's current position and orientation. By comparing this reading with its model of the attractions in the tourist's vicinity, it can fulfil its fundamental objective of displaying information that has been customised to the tourist's interest profile, at the appropriate time and place. It is assured that the individual tourist's cultural interests have been catered for when server agents dynamically assemble the presentation.

Registration Agent. The Registration Agent is responsible for administrating the agent community on the Agent Server. It allocates individual agents (Tourist Agents) to tourists seeking to register for Genie services. It also performs standard maintenance tasks and reallocates system resources upon tourists exiting the system.

GIS Agent. Providing what we term GIS - related services to Tourist Agents is the function of the GIS Agent. It is equipped with a model of the environment in which the tourist is currently roaming. Using this, it can advise on what tourist attractions, or indeed any other desired facilities, exist within the tourist's immediate vicinity.

Profile Agent. The Profile Agent maintains the tourist's cultural interest profile and advises on what content should be considered for inclusion in any multimedia presentation sent to the tourist. In particular, it dynamically updates the model in response to tourists' selections when interacting with the Genie. In this way, the model evolves over time and all information presented to the tourist is assured to be compliant with the most recent deductions concerning the tourist's interests. The user's profile, when augmented with their location and orientation, provide a rich set of filters for adapting information prior to presenting it to the tourist.

Tourist Agent. All tourists who register with the Genie are assigned their own individual agents, termed Tourist Agents. The Tourist Agent is essentially the tourist's gateway to the services provided by the Genie and maintains a snapshot of the tourist's activities at any given time. This agent, acting on information received from the Spatial Agent, collaborates with both the GIS Agent and the Profile Agent to ensure that the Cache Agent's model of the tourist's immediate environment is valid. Secondly, it ensures that all cultural presentations that may be required as the tourist continues to roam are pre-cached on the server, awaiting a download request from the Cache Agent. This content has been adapted in light of input from the Profile Agent concerning the tourist's interests. Adaptivity of information content ensures that different users may well be presented with very different content even though they are in the same vicinity! In the case of the Genie, adaptivity manifests itself in a variety of forms. For example, a presentation could display different images dependent upon an individual tourist's direction of approach.

4.3 Implementation

The initial version of Gulliver's Genie has been realised on an IPAQ H3660 running Pocket PC. The IPAQ is equipped with a dual slot expansion sleeve that hosts the PCMCIA cards for GPS (position recovery) and GPRS (data communications) respectively. GPRS (General Packet Radio Service) is the first step in the evolution of GSM data services to 3G. In contrast to its predecessor, it is a packet-switched system and supports the IP protocol. It also supports dynamic bandwidth allocation thus making the prediction of download times impossible. While it supports data speeds of up to 30 kb/s on average, our experience indicates that these can vary quite considerably and even drop down to 9.6 kb/s, the standard rate supported by GSM. All data communications with the server use the standard Internet protocol HTTP and the Jakarta Servlet engine is used to interface with the server. In each case, Java is the programming language of choice. At present, the Java client is implemented using Jeode, a commercial implementation of a JVM for devices running Pocket PC. Sound playback is achieved using a customised version of the Java Media Framework (JMF).

4.4 Agents @ Work in Gulliver's Genie

Before discussing some examples of commitment rules that the Genie uses, it is instructive to reflect on some of the pertinent issues concerning the deployment of strong intentional agents of mobile devices. The first issue of note is that such agents are computationally expensive when considered in the light of the limited resources on PDAs. Therefore, the task(s) assigned to the agent needs careful consideration. However, at some point a trade-off will occur. Ideally, each task would be assigned a different agent. From a design perspective, this is appealing and intuitive for all the obvious reasons. In practice, this could well mean assigning what might be considered relatively trivial tasks to agents. However, as the number of agents increases, system performance will decrease in something that would be quite noticeable on a PDA. Therefore the designer must, early in the design process, make a judicious decision concerning the number of agents that can be deployed without degrading performance.

Two agents have been incorporated into the Genie MAS for deployment on the PDA. Given the importance of position to the successful operation of the Genie, the task of interfacing with the GPS device and interpreting the GPS signals has been assigned to the Spatial Agent. While the autonomous nature of the agent makes it ideal for this task, its reasoning engine is not unduly stressed. In essence, it periodically polls the device to assess the health of the signal and determine the user's new position and orientation. By recording the most recent positions, it can of course make certain deductions concerning the user's movement, for example, whether they are walking or standing. Although another approach could have been adopted, the use of an agent ensured that this vital task could be performed in an integrated manner without affecting system performance adversely. A secondary consideration was the possibility that an alternative position determination mechanism might be used at some future point, either one based on wireless telecommunications network or one that augmented the basic GPS signal via some Satellite-Based Augmentation System (SBAS). In which case, the basic agent functionality would be the same but its logic for interfacing with the appropriate device would be different.

In the case of the Cache Agent, it has responsibility for implementing the Genie's intelligent precaching mechanism, the details of which may be found elsewhere [22]. However, as an example, consider the scenario where the agent must trigger a presentation for the user. To do this, it must first precache a presentation for the exhibit in question. Then, if the exhibit is the nearest exhibit, which can be determined from its model of the local environment, and the tourist is with in a certain predefined distance of the exhibit, calculated from the current position as indicated by the Spatial Agent, then the Cache Agent is in a position to trigger a presentation. An example of a commitment rule that achieves this is as follows:

```
BELIEF(NearestExhibit(?exhibit)) &
BELIEF(ExhibitDistance(?delta) < (activation_radius)) &
BELIEF(CachedPresentation(?exhibit)) => COMMIT(Self,
Now, BELIEF(true), DisplayPresentation(?exhibit));
```

An illustration of an agent's mental state that would give rise to the activation of this commitment rule is illustrated in Figure 6.

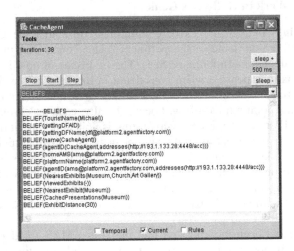

Fig. 6. Example of the mental state of a Cache Agent that triggers the display of a presentation

Finally, it's useful to reflect on the use of the Agent Factory IDE when developing the Genie, in particular those tools provided for testing and debugging. The Agent Viewer Tool proved indispensable for ensuring that the agents' mental state remained consistent. In particular, its ability to track the adoption of commitments facilitated the quick identification of those parts of the system that were functioning incorrectly. Though Message Sender Tool was used less frequently, it proved useful for interactively testing various scenarios whenever an agent's mental state was inconsistent and the immediate cause of this was unclear. The Community Monitor was not used to any great extent as the number of agents did not warrant its extensive use.

5   Conclusion

This paper has explored one particular genre of Agent-Oriented Information Systems (AOIS), that of mobile and ubiquitous computing. Specifically, we have commissioned Agent Factory, a system for the fabrication of strong, intelligent, mobile and agile agents, in the realization of two archetypal mobile computing applications: EasiShop and Gulliver's Genie. Our experiences have shown the feasibility of supporting mobile intentional agents within a mobile computing context. Both EasiShop and Gulliver's Genie have successfully harnessed intentional agents in the delivery and deployment of location-aware and context-aware services. These systems have served as case studies vindicating the efficacy of the approach, the methodology utilised and the Agent Factory development environment.

Mobile computing applications present some particular problems from which agent based systems are typically shielded. The first is that of the heterogeneity of mobile devices, ranging from processor specification, memory availability, screen real estate, peripherals, operating system, available battery power and many more. All present specific decisions ranging from the use of J2ME or Personal Java, to the feasibility of a single or multi-threaded approach. Further to this are the restrictions and limitations of network bandwidth and latency. Where multimedia content is dynamically assembled and fetched from a remote server, these are critical performance issues. Within Gulliver's Genie, agents can and have been used in the creation of the illusion of limitless bandwidth through intelligent precaching. Within EasiShop the migration of agents to the market place gives rise to further network demands.

In conclusion, agents offer intriguing possibilities in the new ubiquitous and mobile application space. Part and parcel of this are the associated challenges that this sector presents necessitating agile, mobile agents that can potentially exhibit autonomic and self adaptive capabilities.

Acknowledgements

Michael O'Grady gratefully acknowledges the support of the Irish Research Council for Science, Engineering & Technology (IRCSET) though the Embark Initiative postdoctoral fellowship programme. Gregory O'Hare gratefully acknowledges the support of Science Foundation Ireland under Grant No. 03/IN.3/1361.

References

1. O'Hare G.M.P., Agent Factory: An Environment for the Fabrication of Multi-Agent Systems, in Foundations of Distributed Artificial Intelligence (G.M.P. O'Hare and N. Jennings eds) pp449-484, John Wiley and Sons, Inc., 1996

2. Collier., R., Agent Factory: A Framework for the Engineering of Agent-Oriented Applications, PhD Thesis, Dept. Computer Science, University College Dublin, 2001.
3. Collier, R., O'Hare, G. M. P. Lowen, T. D., and Rooney, C. F. B., Beyond Prototyping in the Factory of Agents, In Proc. 3rd Int. Central and Eastern European Conference on Multi-Agent Systems (CEEMAS), Prague, Czech Republic, 2003.
4. FIPA, The FIPA 2000 Specifications, FIPA Website URL: http://www.fipa.org
5. Dastani, M., van Riensdijk, B., Dignum, F., Meyer, J.J., A programming language for cognitive agents: Goal directed 3APL, In: Proc. AAMAS2003, Melbourne, Australia, 2003.
6. Rao, A., *Agentspeak(L)*: BDI agents speak out in a logical computable language, In de Velde, W., Perram, W.J.V., eds.: Proceedings of the 7th International Work-shop on Modeling Autonomous Agents in a Multi-Agent World, Eindhoven, The Netherlands, 1996
7. Rao, A.S., Georgeff, M.P.: Modelling Rational Agents within a BDI Architecture. In: Principles of Knowledge Representation. & Reasoning, San Mateo, CA. 1991.
8. Ross, R., Collier, R., O'Hare, G.M.P.: AF-APL – Bridging Principles & Practice in Agent-Oriented Languages. In: Proceedings of the 2nd International Workshop on Programming Multi-Agent Systems Languages and Tools (PROMAS-2004), New York, July, 2004.
9. Collier, R., O'Hare, G., Rooney, C.: A UML-based Software Engineering Methodology for Agent Factory. In: Proc. 16th Int. Conf. on Software Engineering and Knowledge Engineering (SEKE), Banff, Alberta, Canada, 2004.
10. Rooney, C.F.B., Collier, R.W., O'Hare., G.M.P.: VIPER: Visual protocol editor. In: Proceedings of COORDINATION 2004, Pisa, Italy, 2004.
11. Shardanand, U., Maes, P.: Social information lettering: Algorithms for automating word of mouth. In: Conference on Human Factors in Computing Systems: Mosaic of Creativity (CHI'95), New York, USA, 1995, 210-217.
12. Doorenbos, R. B., Etzioni, O., Weld, D. S.: A Scalable Comparison-Shopping Agent for the World-Wide Web. In: Proceedings of the First International Conference on Autonomous Agents (Agents'97), Marina del Rey, CA, USA, 1997, 39-48.
13. Maes, P., Guttman, R., Moukas, A.: Agents that Buy and Sell: Transforming Commerce as We Know It. In: Communications of the ACM, 42 (93), 1999, 81-91.
14. Howard, J. A., Sheth, J. N..: The Theory of Buyer Behavior. New York, John Wiley & Sons, Inc., 1969.
15. Youll, J., Morris, J., Krikorian, R., Maes, P.,: Impulse: Location-based Agent Assistance. In: Software Demos, Proceedings of the Fourth International Conference on Autonomous Agents, Barcelona, Spain, June, 2000.
16. Kourouthanasis, P., Spinellis, D., Roussos, G., Giaglis, G.: Intelligent cokes and diapers: MyGrocer ubiquitous computing environment. In: Proceedings of the First International Mobile Business Conf., 2002, 150-172.
17. Fano, A.: SHOPPER'S EYE: Using Location-based Filtering for a Shopping Agent in the Physical World. In: Proc. 2nd Int. Conf. on Autonomous Agents, Minnesota, 1998, 416-421.
18. Keegan, S., O'Hare, G.M.P.: EasiShop - Agent-Based Cross Merchant Product Comparison Shopping for the Mobile User. In: Proc. of 1st Int. Conf. on Information & Communication Technologies: From Theory to Applications (ICTTA '04), Damascus, Syria, 2004.
19. Keegan, S., O'Hare, G.M.P.: EasiShop: Enabling uCommerce through Intelligent Mobile Agent Technologies. In: Proceedings of 5th International Workshop on Mobile Agents for Telecommunication Applications (MATA'03), Marrakesh, Morocco, 2003.

20. Davis, R., Smith, R.G.: Negotiation as a Metaphor for Distributed Problem Solving. In: Bond, A., Gasser, L. (eds.): Readings in Distributed Artificial Intelligence, 1988, 333-356.
21. United Nations Standard Products and Services Code: http://www.unspsc.org.
22. O'Grady, M. J., O'Hare, G. M. P.: Just-in-Time Multimedia Distribution in a Mobile Computing Environment, IEEE Multimedia, vol. 11, no. 4, pp. 62-74, 2004.
23. O'Hare, G. M. P., O'Grady, M. J.: Gulliver's Genie: A Multi-Agent System for Ubiquitous and Intelligent Content Delivery, Computer Communications, 26 (11), 2003, 1177-1187.
24. Cheverst, K., Mitchell, K., Davies, N.: The Role of Adaptive Hypermedia in a Context-Aware Tourist Guide, Communications of the ACM. Vol. 45 (5), 2002, 47-51.
25. Poslad, S., Laamanen, H., Malaka, R. Nick, A., Buckle, P., Zipf, A.: CRUMPET: Creation of User-friendly Mobile Services Personalised For Tourism. Proceedings of the 2nd International Conference on 3G Mobile Communication Technologies, London, UK, 2001.
26. Vindigo, Inc. New York. http://www.vindigo.com.
27. 27.Port@ble Internet, Inc. New Jersey, http://www.portableinternet.com.

A Systematic Approach for Including Machine Learning in Multi-agent Systems

José A.R.P. Sardinha, Alessandro Garcia, Carlos J.P. Lucena,
and Ruy L. Milidiú

TecComm Group (LES), Computer Science Department, PUC-Rio,
Rua Marques de São Vicente 225, Gávea, Rio de Janeiro, Brazil
{sardinha, afgarcia, lucena, milidiu}@inf.puc-rio.br

Abstract. Large scale multi-agent systems (MASs) in unpredictable environments must use machine learning techniques to perform their goals and improve the performance of the system. This paper presents a systematic approach to introduce machine learning in the design and implementation phases of a software agent. We also present an incremental implementation process for building asynchronous and distributed agents, which suppors the combination of machine learning strategies. This process supports the stepwise building of adaptable MASs for unknown situations, improving their capacity to scale up. We use the Trading Agent Competition (TAC) environment as a case study to illustrate the suitability of our approach.

1 Introduction

Multi-Agent Systems (MASs) [1] [2] is a new technology that has been recently used in many simulators and intelligent systems to help humans perform several time-consuming tasks. Applications for e-commerce, information retrieval and business intelligence use MAS technology to build distributed systems over the Internet. In this context, machine learning algorithms are crucial to providing well-known strategies to support the construction of adaptable agents, especially in unpredictable, heterogeneous environments such as the Internet.

However, the incorporation of learning techniques into large scale multi-agent systems is not a trivial task. Software engineers who design and implement realistic MASs are faced with recurring learning concerns, such as: (i) How to evaluate if the goal of a multi-agent system has been achieved? (ii) How to define the individual goal of each agent in the system and evaluate it? (iii) How the knowledge of each individual agent is going to be modelled? (iv) How this agent will acquire the knowledge? (v) How to combine the multiple used learning techniques and to distribute them to the different agents in a MAS, (vi) How to associate the learning issues with typical abstractions in agent-based software engineering? and (vii) How to specify the learning issues at an early design stage and support a smooth transition of those issues to the implementation stages?

Unfortunately, software engineers have largely relied on their experience and intuition to address the questions above during the development of realistic adaptable MASs. Research on agent-based software engineering has focused on the

P. Bresciani et al. (Eds.): AOIS 2004, LNAI 3508, pp. 198–211, 2005.

development of new methodologies and implementation frameworks. However, these approaches do not provide guidelines to support the incorporation of learning issues into the system in the early stage of design. Implementation frameworks [3][4] provide object-oriented APIs for MAS development, but they do not assist the handling and structuring of the learning design in a systematic way. In addition, most proposed methodologies [5] [6] are at too a high level and do not indicate how to master the complexity of these learning concerns through the design and implementation steps.

This observation provides the rationale for investigating how to integrate learning issues neatly within agent-oriented software engineering. This paper presents a systematic approach to support a disciplined introduction of machine learning techniques in MASs from an early stage of design. The proposed approach encompasses guidelines to both the design and implementation phases of an agent-based system. It is based on an incremental development strategy that largely relies on simulation and testing techniques.

This systematic approach emerged from our extensive experience on the development of distinct and heterogeneous MAS applications, including: (a) a multi-agent system [7][8] that uses evolutionary techniques to build offerings in a retail market, (b) an agent-based system [9] that learns to play Tic-Tac-Toe with no prior knowledge, (c) a multi-agent system [10] for the Trading Agent Competition (TAC) [15], and (d) a multi-agent system [11] for managing the paper submission and selection process in workshops and conferences.

The remainder of this paper is organized as follows. Section 2 presents a case study that involves a multi-agent system for the TAC Competition. Section 3 presents our approach to support the introduction of machine learning techniques in large scale multi-agent systems. Section 4 presents our conclusions and directions for future work.

2 The Trading Agent Competition MAS – A Case Study

The Trading Agent Competition [12] (TAC) is designed to promote and encourage high quality research into the trading agent problem. Figure 1 presents the architecture of *LearnAgents* [10], a multi agent system with modular entities that are asynchronous, distributed, reusable and easy to interoperate. We define agent types that tackle sub-problems of trading, such as price prediction, bid planning, goods allocation, bidding, among others. The system's goal is to acquire travel packages for clients with as much profit as possible. This profit is defined as the sum of the utilities of the eight clients in the TAC game, minus the costs of acquiring the travel goods in the auctions.

The Hotel Sensor Agent, Flight Sensor Agent and Ticket Sensor Agent are responsible for the market sensory and knowledge building of the system. These agents collect price information from auctions and store them in the knowledge base. The sensor agents also receive all the events from the environment and are responsible for notifying other agents in the system with these events. The Flight and Hotel Price Predictor Agent is also responsible for knowledge building. This agent predicts hotel and flight auction prices for the knowledge base. The price predictor agent uses the price history in the knowledge to forecast auction quotes.

The agent types responsible for bid planning are the Allocator Master Agent and the Allocator Slave Agents. The slave agents calculate different scenarios based on the prices in the knowledge base. These scenarios define travel good types and quantities, and characterize a list of different strategies for the system. The Allocator Master Agent is responsible for combining all the scenarios generated from the other slave agents. These scenarios are then stored in the knowledge base.

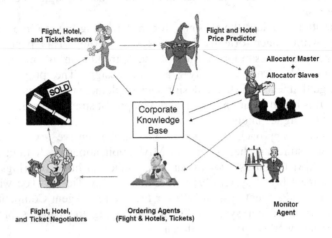

Fig. 1. The *LearnAgents* Architecture

The Ordering Agent is responsible for good allocation. It also decides the quantity of the required travel goods based on the scenarios in the knowledge base. This decision is based on a scenario with a high profit and a low risk. The Hotel Negotiator Agent, Flight Negotiator Agent and Ticket Negotiator Agent are responsible for negotiating travel goods in the auctions based on the decision from the Ordering Agent. The negotiators have the goal of buying all the requested goods with the minimum expenditure. The Monitor Agent is responsible for saving data from the environment and evaluating the performance of the multi-agent system.

There was a need to introduce machine learning techniques in the Flight and Hotel Price Predictor Agent, the Allocator Master and Slave Agents, as well as in the Hotel Negotiator Agent. For reasons of brevity, we will only illustrate in Section 3 the design decisions of the Flight and Hotel Price Predictor Agent. However, we present results of the performance gain obtained with the process of including machine learning algorithms in the *LearnAgents* system based on our stepwise approach.

3   Introducing Learning Techniques in Multi-agent Systems

Mitchell [13] defines machine learning as follows: "A computer program is said to learn from experience E with respect to some class of tasks T and performance measure P, if its performance at tasks in T, as measured by P, improves with experience E". Consequently, machine learning techniques are normally used when performance gain is required in a system. The main goal of the proposed approach is to support a disciplined introduction of machine learning techniques into a multi-agent system. The process also permits in the implementation phase a disciplined integration of disparate machine learning algorithms in agent-based systems and their performance assessment. This systematic approach has four phases:

(i) *Systemic Goal & Performance Measure Selection*, where a systemic goal is defined and a measure of performance is selected;

(ii) *Agent Selection & Agent Learning Goal Definition*, where agents with complex plans are selected and goals are defined for the learning algorithm;

(iii)*Agent Machine Learning Design*, where code design is defined; and

(iv)*Incremental Implementation & Performance Measurement*, where an incremental implementation is proposed with training, testing and evaluation.

Figure 2 depicts all the phases of the process. The following subsections describe in detail each of the process phases and present the application of the approach to our case study.

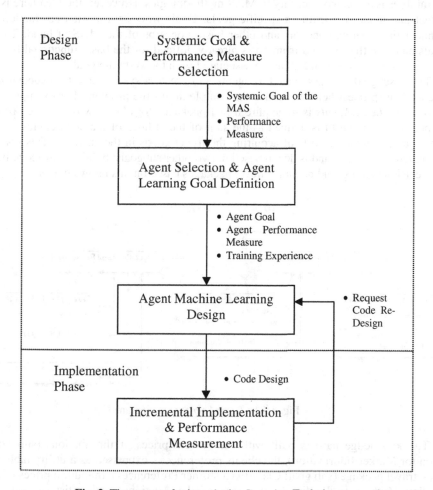

Fig. 2. The process for introducing Learning Techniques

3.1 Systemic Goal and Performance Measure Selection

Software engineers must define in this phase two central elements related to learning issues: (i) the *Systemic Goal*, SG, and (ii) the *Systemic Performance Measure*, SP, which measures the system's performance gain. The systemic goal is the highest-level goal of the system, which is usually captured in the initial phase of a typical development process of multi-agent system. The systemic performance measure is the mechanism to evaluate the goal achievement. As a consequence, it is directly derived from the systemic goal. For example, these elements are defined in *LearnAgents* as: (i) SG: acquire travel packages for clients with as much profit as possible; (ii) SP: average score. The average score counts how much profit is being achieved in the system.

The goal abstraction is central in our approach since it is essential to determine the performance measures for each software agent (Section 3.2) and the learning techniques in later design stages (Section 3.3). As a consequence, we must also decompose the systemic goal in many subgoals. Note that the modeling of goal hierarchies is a common activity in MAS methodologies. However, the idea here is to detect and model the learning-specific goals. Goals work as a unified abstraction to connect the learning concerns and other basic concerns of the MAS at hand. These goals can be either derived from goals already defined for the basic functionalities of the agents or from new ones that are associated with the systemic goal.

These subgoals are associated to agents and create a system based on specialized agents. This process helps to reduce the complexity of the problem. For example, the goal of the *LearnAgents* is to acquire travel packages for clients with as much profit as possible. This profit is defined as the sum of the utilities of the eight clients in the TAC game, minus the costs of acquiring the travel goods in the auctions. This goal is presented in Figure 3, and is decomposed in two other subgoals: build a knowledge base for decision making; and negotiate travel packages based on this knowledge base.

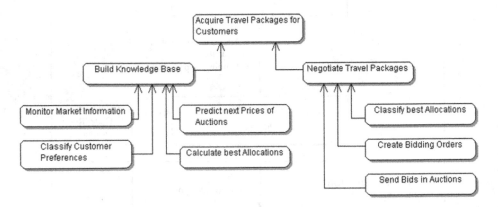

Fig. 3. The *LearnAgents* goal diagram

The knowledge base is built with the current prices of the auctions (sub goal: Monitor Market Information), the clients preferences - expressed as a utility table for each travel package (sub goal: Classify Customer Preferences), the future prices of the auctions (sub goal: Predict Next Prices of the Auctions) and a list of different scenarios based on the prices and client's preferences (sub goal: Calculate Best Allocations).

The negotiation of travel goods depends on the following actions: selection of a scenario with a high profit and a low risk (sub goal: Classify Best Allocations), definition of the number and type of travel goods to be bought based on the selected scenario (sub goal: Create Bidding Orders) and the price definition of the bids for the auctions (sub goal: Send Bids in Auctions).

In the agent identification process, we associate a sub goal in the goal diagram to one or more agents in the system. Table 1 illustrates the mapping of the sub goals to agent types in figure 1. We will select agents in the following phase that use machine learning to achieve its individual goal and the systemic goal defined above.

Table 1. Mapping of the sub goals to agents

Sub Goal	Agent
Monitor Market Information	Hotel Sensor Agent, Flight Sensor Agent, Ticket Sensor Agent
Classify Customer Information	Hotel Sensor Agent
Predict Next Prices of the Auctions	Price Predictor Agent
Calculate Best Allocations	Allocator Master, Allocator Slaves
Classify Best Allocations	Ordering Agent
Create Bidding Orders	Ordering Agent
Send Bids in Auctions	Hotel Negotiator Agent, Flight Negotiator Agent, Ticket Negotiator Agent

3.2 Agent Selection and Agent Goal Definition

The Agent Selection and Agent Goal Definition phase selects the agents in the system that perform complex plans and need a machine learning technique to improve the performance of the system. The goal of this phase is to establish a well-defined *Agent Learning Problem* and defines three features for each selected agent: (i) *Learning Goal*, G; (ii) *Performance Measure*, P, which measures the performance improvement of the agent; and (iii) a *Training Experience*, E, which defines the knowledge acquisition process in learning.

The Flight and Hotel Price Predictor Agent is one of the agents selected for receiving a machine learning technique in the *LearnAgents*. The *Agent Learning Problem* for this agent is:

- G : predict future auction quote prices for hotel rooms;
- P : error between the predicted and real price; and
- E : use history of quote prices to build prediction knowledge.

3.3 Machine Learning Design

We present in this section a straightforward design that enables reuse and an easy maintenance. The process of maximizing the performance measure defined in the prior phases, normally requires the test of different algorithms. Figure 4 presents a class diagram of the Flight and Hotel Price Predictor Agent using an object-oriented design pattern [14]. This design can be reused and refined to different contexts and applications.

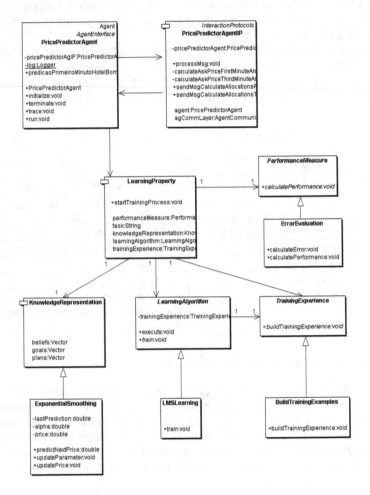

Fig. 4. The Class Diagram of the Price Predictor Agent

The classes *PricePredictorAgent* and *PricePredictorAgentIP* are specialized classes that code the software agent's basic services, such as sensory of the environment, event handling, message handling etc.

The class called *KnowledgeRepresentation* is an abstract class of the data structure of the agent's knowledge. The monitor of the agent's performance measure (defined in Section 3.2) is coded as an abstract class called *PerformanceMeasure*. The learning algorithm is an abstract class called *LearningAlgorithm*. The example generator of the agent's training experience (defined in section 3.2) is modeled as an abstract class called *TrainingExperience*.

The concrete classes *ExponentialSmoothing*, *ErrorEvaluation*, *LMSLearning* and *BuildTrainingExamples* are the classes that respectively implement the abstract classes *KnowledgeRepresentation*, *PerformanceMeasure*, *LearningAlgorithm* and *TrainingExperience*.

Several events can trigger the agent learning [13], including the execution of internal agent actions, throwing of exceptions, messages exchanged between agents and events sensed in the external environment. The concrete classes *PricePredictorAgent* and *PricePredictorAgentIP* access the class *LearningProperty* to trigger the agent learning, and this class is the main interface to the learning pattern.

3.4 Implementation, Training, Testing and Evaluation

We are normally faced with three key aspects in the implementation phase of the selected software agents in section 3.2: (i) knowledge representation; (ii) learning algorithm; and (iii) training set used by the learning algorithm.

The first decision determines exactly what type of knowledge will be learned. This knowledge can be modeled as a function F that receives a state S and determines an action A, or $F: S \rightarrow A$. However, it may be very difficult in general to perfectly learn this function (representation of the knowledge), and normally we reduce the complexity and transform the problem to only learn some approximation of this selected function. We must then choose a reasonable representation of this knowledge for the agent. This best representation can be described as a linear weighted function, a collection of rules, a neural network or a quadratic polynomial function. This design choice normally involves an important tradeoff because we would like to pick a representation that is as close as possible to the ideal knowledge. However, an expressive function requires more training data in the training phase.

The knowledge representation for the Price Predictor Agent is also modeled as a function called *NextAskPrice* that accepts the ask price A of the last game instances and produces the next ask price N (*NextAskPrice:A→N*). The Price Predictor Agent uses a simple representation to describe the approximate knowledge. The following formula called Exponential Smoothing [15] is used to predict the next price: *PredictedAskPrice(n)= α*AskPrice(n-1) + (1 - α)*PredictedAskPrice(n-1)*, where α is a number between 0 and 1; and n is the n-th game instance. This formula is coded in the class *ExponentialSmoothing* in figure 4. A Least Mean Squares (LMS) algorithm is used to adapt the value of α: *α(n)=α(n-1)+β*(AskPrice(n-1)-PredictedAskPrice(n-1))*, where β is a learning rate. This algorithm is coded in the class *LMSLearning* in figure 4.

A training set is required to build the knowledge of the agent, and we must select a process that selects this training set. Training examples can be obtained through a direct or indirect experience. In the direct experience, the designer can carefully select the best training examples that lead to a good approximate knowledge. In the indirect experience, the approximate knowledge must suggest actions that will lead to already known states that improve the performance of the system, and unknown states that guide to new experiences. The exploration is important for indirect learning agents that are willing to discover much better actions for the long run. The class *BuildTrainingExamples* has code that executes a query in a database with auctions prices for games already played, and implements the *Training Experience* defined in section 3.2. The *ErrorEvaluation* class implements the performance measure also defined in section 3.2.

3.4.1 Incremental Development, Testing and Integration of Intelligent Agents

Instead of building the multi agent system with all intelligent agents in a single stage, we propose an incremental development. The first version of the multi agent system is composed of simple agents that do not use a machine learning algorithm. This first step is important to test the communication of the agents and the interaction with the environment. The phases depicted in figure 5 illustrate the process of integration of the selected agents in section 3.2 in order to improve the *Systemic Performance Measure* defined in section 3.1.

The incremental development starts with the code removal of one of the agents selected in the section 3.2. This agent code is built with the classes defined in section 3.3. We then test the agent individually to measure the *Performance Measure* defined in section 3.2, before re-integrating it back in the system. This test is built by the system engineer and normally comprises small software modules that generate test cases. Code errors of the intelligent module are found at this point.

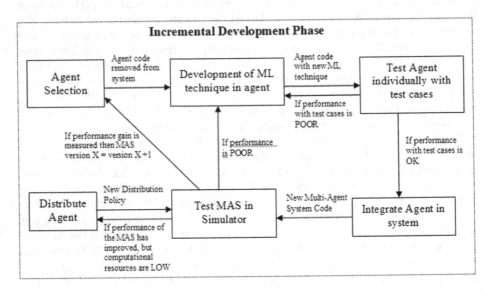

Fig. 5. The Incremental Development Phase

The re-integration of the agent is done after the test cases confirm that the machine learning algorithm works correctly. These tests cases do not guarantee any performance improvement of the system. Therefore, a performance test is done with the multi agent system and the new intelligent agent. A simulator of the environment is required for this phase, and we only give a new version to the multi agent system if the *Systemic Performance Measure* defined in section 3.1 has improved. When performance gain is not achieved, the system engineer must take one of the two decisions: (i) Modify the code and test again; or (ii) Re-model the design as shown in figure 2.

However, there are cases when a performance gain is achieved but the new intelligent agent starts to use too much computational resources such as CPU and memory. This slows down the system and the responses of the system are delayed. Consequently, we propose the distribution of this new agent to another CPU in the network.

3.4.2 Incremental Development of the *LearnAgents*

The first version of the *LearnAgents* was built with only reactive agents [1]. Our main goal at this point was to test the communication between the agents and the execution of the system in the environment. Although we were not expecting a good average score, a benchmark was executed to measure the evolution of the performance gain as shown in table 2. The benchmark used in table 2 is calculated against 7 simulated competitors called dummy agents [12]. The system plays 100 games in the benchmark against the dummies in order to evaluate the average performance and to smooth the variations in client preferences. The simulator of the real competition can be downloaded in the TAC web site[12].

The first selected agent was the Allocator Agent (version 1.0 in Table 1). The agent calculates different scenarios based on the prices in the knowledge base. These scenarios are travel good allocations (only flights and hotels) that are calculated using an integer programming solver called XPRESS [16]. The solver is executed not only in search of the optimal allocation, but as many best allocations as the solver can optimize in 25 seconds. After testing the new Allocator Agent with the test cases, we also modified the Ordering Agent with a new heuristic. The Ordering Agent had to decide the quantity of the required travel goods and the maximum price of the bids based on the allocations produced by the Allocator Agent. The multi agent system obtained a score of 1372 in the benchmark against 7 dummies.

The Negotiator Agent was the next selected agent for adding of an intelligent module. This module uses a min-max procedure [17] and an evaluation function calculated by a neural network [13] and a reinforcement learning [13] technique. The Negotiator Agent's goal is to send optimal bids to the auctions with the minimum expenditure. Therefore, the agent adapts the weights of the neural network and searches for an evaluation function that produces these optimal bids. The benchmark of the version 2.0 was 1752.

The next selected agent to include the intelligent module was the Price Predictor Agent. This agent uses a price history in the knowledge base to forecast ask prices. The technique implemented in the intelligent module is called moving average [15]. This agent is important for the system because it helped to deal with uncertainty of the auction prices. Consequently, the Allocator Agent could now calculate scenarios based on these predicted prices. This version 3.0 now scored 2224 in the benchmark.

We then decided to improve the Allocator Agent in the version 4.0 of the system. The flight and hotel goods were the only allocations calculated by the integer programming solver. We extended the model and included the entertainment tickets, and then modified the Ordering Agent heuristic to decide the quantity of tickets to buy based on these new allocations. We executed the benchmark and achieved a score of 2856. This agent improved the overall score but the system started to present delays in some responses to the market. This was clear evidence that CPU resources were low, so we created an Allocator Slave to solve the problem. This new agent also used an integer programming solver that calculated the tickets allocation and was now executing in another CPU.

Table 2. The Evolution of the MAS and the Performance Gain

LearnAgents Version	Agent Selected / Intelligent Module	Average Score	Games Played
0.0	---	-1855	100
1.0	Allocator / Solver – Integer Programming Model, Ordering Agent / Heuristic	1372	100
2.0	Hotel Negotiator / Minimax, N.N. and Reinforcement Learning	1752	100
3.0	Price Predictor (hotel) / Moving Average	2224	100
4.0	Allocator (Ticket) /Solver - Integer Programming Model, Ordering Agent / Heuristic	2856	100
5.0	Allocator / Solver – Integer Programming Model (second version)	3370	100
6.0	Price Predictor (flight) / Maximum Likelihood	3705	100

The Allocator Agent was again selected for improvements in version 5.0. The integer programming model was modified to include some parameters for tuning purposes. The travel good allocations are now calculated based on these parameters. We can select parameters that produce allocations with more hotel rooms from Shoreline Shanties [12] (the bad hotel) then the Tampa Towers [12] (the good hotel) in this version. The benchmark with the best parameter configuration produced a score of 3370.

Our last selected agent was the Price Predictor. This agent was only predicting hotel auction prices and we now wanted the prediction of flight auction prices. The flight auction prices are modified according to a stochastic function. The process uses a random walk that starts between $250 and $400 and is perturbed every 10 seconds. We included an intelligent module based on a technique called maximum likelihood [13] to predict a parameter of the stochastic function that was not revealed directly to the agents. The predicted parameter is then used to define the expected value of the flight auction prices. This benchmark achieved a score of 3705 in this 6.0 version.

4 Final Comments

The importance of the learning property in today's software systems is reflected by the support provided for this property in existing tools [18][19] and implementation frameworks [3]. However, software engineers have largely relied on their experience and intuition in order to develop adaptable MASs. This paper presents a systematic approach for building intelligent agents with machine learning techniques. These agents are now able to perform complex plans, adapt their beliefs and achieve predefined goals. In complex and open environments with many cooperating agents, it is important to have a system that is able to adapt to unknown situations. Learning techniques are crucial to the development of multi-agent systems since they provide well-known strategies to support the construction of adaptable agents.

The incremental development was extremely important for the development process of the *LearnAgents*. If all the techniques were added at once, we would never be able to evaluate the individual performance gain of each technique. This step-by-step process also prevents the development of agents that deteriorate the performance because we only include techniques that present improvements. The process presents an easy method to add new agents with different techniques and minimizes error development in concurrent and distributed agents.

Scores for competition TAC 2004 Finals (game 6084 - 6118)

Competition started at 2004-07-22 13:00:00 and ended at 2004-07-22 19:57:00. Final Scores.

Position	Agent	Avg Score	Games Played	Zero Games
1	whitebear04	4122.11	35	0
2	Walverine	3848.97	35	0
3	LearnAgents	3736.62	35	0
4	SICS02	3708.24	35	0
5	NNN	3665.97	35	0
6	UMTac-04	3281.43	35	0
7	Agent@CSE	3262.51	35	2
8	RoxyBot	2015.02	35	0

Scores last updated after game 6118 on server tac1.sics.se version 1.0 beta 10

Fig. 6. The Scores for the Finals of the TAC 2004

Figure 6 presents the final results of the *LearnAgents* in the 2004 TAC Classic tournament. The tournament had 14 participants from universities, research institutes and technology companies from around the world (USA, Brazil, France, Sweden, Netherlands, Israel, Macau, China, Japan etc.). The *LearnAgents* finished the tournament in the third place. An interesting observation is the similarity between the best score in the simulation process (3705) and the score in the final round of the competition. Although dummy agents use very naïve strategies, our system presents a strategy that is able to adapt to different competitors in an efficient manner.

This process emerged from the long-term application of our method to different multi-agent systems. We believe there is a need for a software engineering process for the disciplined introduction of learning properties in software agents through different development stages. This systematic approach helps the development team of a MAS to include machine learning techniques in adaptive environments and, consequently, leverage the performance of the system.

References

1. Wooldridge, M.: Intelligent Agents. In: G. Weiss. Multiagent systems: a modern approach to distributed artificial intelligence. The MIT Press, Second printing, 2000.
2. Ferber, J.: Multi-Agent Systems: An Introduction to Distributed Artificial Intelligence. Addison-Wesley Pub Co, 1999.
3. Telecom Italia Lab. JADE Programmer's Guide. http://sharon.cselt.it/ projects/ jade/ doc/ programmersguide.pdf, Feb. 2003.
4. Kendall, E.; Krishna, P.; Pathak, C.; Suresh, C.: A Framework for Agent Systems. In: Implementing Application Frameworks – Object-Oriented Frameworks at Work, M. Fayad et al. (editors), John Wiley & Sons, 1999.
5. Zambonelli, F.; Jennings, N. R.; Wooldridge, M.: Developing multiagent systems: the Gaia Methodology. ACM Transactions on Software Engineering and Methodology, 12 (3) 317-370, 2003.
6. Giunchiglia, F.; Mylopoulos, J.; Perini, A.: The tropos software development methodology: processes, models and diagrams. Proceedings of the first international joint conference on Autonomous agents and multiagent systems, 2002.
7. Milidiu, R.L.; Lucena, C.J.; Sardinha, J.A.R.P.: An object-oriented framework for creating offerings. 2001 International Conference on Internet Computing (IC'2001) June 2001.
8. Sardinha, J.A.R.P.: VGroups – Um framework para grupos virtuais de consumo. Master's dissertation – Departamento de Informática – PUC-Rio. March 2001.
9. Sardinha, J.A.R.P.; Milidiú, R. L.; Lucena, C. J. P.; Paranhos, P. M.: An OO Framework for building Intelligence and Learning properties in Software Agents. Proceedings of the 2nd International Workshop on Software Engineering for Large-Scale Multi-Agent Systems (SELMAS 2003) at ICSE 2003, Portland, USA, May 2003.
10. Sardinha, J.A.R.P.; Milidiú, R.L.; Lucena, C.J.P.; Paranhos, P.M.; Cunha, P.M.: LearnAgents - A multi-agent system for the TAC Classic. Poster Session at The Third International Joint Conference on Autonomous Agents & Multi Agent Systems (Trading Agent Competition), July 2004, New York, USA.
11. Garcia, A.: From Objects to Agents: An Aspect-Oriented Approach. Doctoral Thesis, PUC-Rio, Computer Science Department, Rio de Janeiro, Brazil, April 2004.
12. TAC web site.: http://www.sics.se/tac.
13. Mitchell, T. M.: Machine Learning. McGraw-Hill, 1997. ISBN 0070428077.

14. Sardinha, J.A.R.P.; Garcia, A.F.; Milidiú, R.L.; Lucena, C.J.P.: The Agent Learning Pattern. Fourth Latin American Conference on Pattern Languages of Programming, SugarLoafPLoP'04. August, 2004, Fortaleza, Brazil.
15. Bowerman, B. L.; O'Connell, R. T: Forecasting and Time Series: An Applied Approach. Thomson Learning, 3rd edition, 1993. ASIN: 0534932517.
16. Dash Optimization. http://www.dashoptimization.com
17. Russell, S.; Norvig, P.: Artificial Intelligence. Prentice Hall, 1995. ISBN 0-13-103805-2.
18. Computer Associates (CA) CleverPath web site: *http://www.ca.com/*
19. DB2 Business Intelligence web site: http://www-306.ibm.com/software/data/db2bi/

Agents to Foster Conscious Design and Reuse in Architecture

Daniel Pinho[1], Adriana S. Vivacqua[1], Sérgio Palma[1],
and Jano M. de Souza[1, 2]

[1] Department of Computer Science, Graduate School of Engineering (COPPE),
[2] Institute of Mathematics (DCC-IM), Federal University of Rio de Janeiro,
Rio de Janeiro, RJ, Brazil
dpinho@centroin.com.br
{avivacqua, palma, jano}@cos.ufrj.br

Abstract. In architecture companies, work is very often performed by several individuals. From conceptual design to the construction of a final product, the object passes through many hands, each one adding bits and pieces until it is completed. Often, though, these different groups of people who work on a design don't interact much, which generates problems at later phases. There is little reuse of materials and time may be wasted in exceedingly complex designs. The processes and problems exhibited by the company studied are quite common and can easily be found in other companies. We present an agent framework to improve process awareness in an architecture company. Based on user activities and previous designs, agents identify possibilities for reuse and provide information to the conceptual designer so that their designs take construction difficulties and possibilities for reuse into account. The agents instrument the process to produce global awareness, so that the designers design to facilitate later steps and optimize the process as a whole. In this paper we present the agent architecture, as well as each agent's general functioning and reasoning rules.

1 Introduction

Technology changes at a fast pace. For many companies, these changes motivate organizational changes. It has become easier to establish communication, exchange information and be aware of previously hidden processes. For many companies, however, it has been hard to keep up with the new technological demands and to adapt to new work or organizational formats that may improve their performance, without impacting their current business. Companies struggle to change with as little impact as possible, so as not to compromise their businesses.

In this fashion, even though organizations may adopt technology in their daily work environment, this technology hasn't been integrated in such a way as to produce organizational changes and enable improvements. Most companies still adopt strict organizational models and, in many cases, information flows only in one direction, causing breaks in communication. In many cases, technology automates the information flow as it exists, not introducing any change.

In a case study of an architecture company, we identified some problem areas that should be addressed and that are present in other segments and companies. The main

P. Bresciani et al. (Eds.): AOIS 2004, LNAI 3508, pp. 212–226, 2005.

problem in this type of company is that there are disjoint work groups, and, even though work done by one group (design) defines the work that will be done by the other (physical project), there is little communication between them. There is no feedback from the second group as to what could be improved or what has generated problems for them. This lack of awareness of the project as a whole stems from the company's organizational structure and difficulty in communication between teams and often generates waste, delays and problem difficulties.

We have devised agent-based system to integrate the different teams involved and promote information exchange and awareness of the process as a whole. Agents work with available information on the users' tasks and their current work and provide information about potential problems of the current design. The intent is to cause as little impact as possible on the way designers work, but to promote changes in their way of designing. Agents working in the background can provide a seamless integration between the different design teams. Ideally, designers would learn about the consequences of their design choices and about the potential problems these choices may cause during the later stages of the project, and design in a more informed way. This system will be implanted in our case study company and we'll verify if the new knowledge brought about changes in the designs produced and the designers' way of thinking.

We begin by presenting some background work and then go on to describe a case study of an architecture company, H Camargo Promotional Architecture and Landscaping, examining its processes and information flow, whose problems we are attempting to solve. We then go on to describe our approach and the communication agents we are implementing. We then present a scenario to illustrate how the system functions and wrap up with a brief discussion and conclusions in section 5.

2 Related Work

In this section we present some related research that has inspired and guided our, in particular, agent and awareness systems. Computer-supported design systems have been the object of much research in the past: ranging from expert and case-based reasoning systems to distributed agent approaches, many alternatives have been proposed. A good review of agent-based engineering systems can be found in Shen et al. [1].

2.1 Agent Systems

Russel and Norvig define Intelligent Agents as entities that perceive its environment through sensors and act upon it [2]. Agent-oriented techniques are being increasingly used in a range of telecommunication, commercial and industrial applications, as developers and designers realize its potential [3]. Agents are especially suited to the construction of complex, peer-to-peer systems, because they permit parallelization and easy reconfiguration of the system.

It is currently believed that Multi-Agent Systems (MAS) are a better way to model and support distributed, open-ended systems and environments. A MAS is a loosely-coupled network of problem solvers (agents) that work together to solve a given problem [4]. A comprehensive review of agent systems applied to cooperative work can be found in Ellis and Wainer [5].

2.2 Awareness Systems

Awareness has received a lot of attention among researchers in the past few years, as they start to realize the importance of being aware of collaborators and the environment while working. Initial awareness work focused on video and audio support for cooperation as, for instance in Fish et al. [6] or Isaacs et al. [7], but other tools and methods have appeared since.

The most basic form of awareness is the one provided by messenger systems (such as Yahoo or MSN Messenger, AOL Instant Messenger etc.), which have become widely accepted and adopted. A more specialized collaborative tool, GROOVE, introduces the concept of "shared spaces" to increase the scope of personal awareness. Within GROOVE's shared spaces, users can be aware of what others are doing and on what spaces' objects they are working.

Other researchers have focused on document- or task-based awareness and on providing information to users about who is working on the same document or performing similar tasks at a given moment, as in Moran et al. [8]. Many recent papers address awareness in mobile computing environments, where location awareness is a central issue for collaboration, as in Aldunate et al. [9] and Esborjörnsson et al. [10].

More interestingly, some proposals involve motivation, incentives and support for cooperation, such as described in Pinheiro et al. [11]. They propose a framework to provide past event awareness, where users are informed of past occurrences, results and work history of each other (which includes evolution of shared data, members' actions and decisions etc.), so as to better collaborate in the present.

Closer to our ideas, Hoffman and Hermann [12] propose a prospect awareness system that allows individuals to envision the potential benefits of collaboration, in an attempt to motivate collaboration. Our system provides potential problem information, in an effort to generate better and more cost-effective designs, avoiding problems in future steps.

3 Communication Problems in an Architecture Company

H. Camargo Promotional Architecture and Landscaping has been a leader in its segment since 1971. It develops custom-made architectural projects for fair and exhibit stands. It is housed in a large pavilion (with space for administration, workshops and stocks) and has a permanent team of 120 employees. As in any large company, communication problems have started to arise, generating difficulties during project development.

There are four main divisions in the company, as seen in Fig 1.

- Sales: finds potential clients and their needs.
- Design: creates proposals for these potential clients, establishing the overall designs and some of the materials to be used.
- Project: further details the project, defining the physical specification: measurements, quantity of materials, how these are to be put together etc., only for accepted proposals.
- Execution: executes the physical specification, building the actual stand and whatever components may be necessary.

The company essentially functions as two entities: the first one "Sales and Design divisions" is responsible for finding new potential clients and designing solutions for those. The second one "Project and Execution divisions" is responsible for seeing the

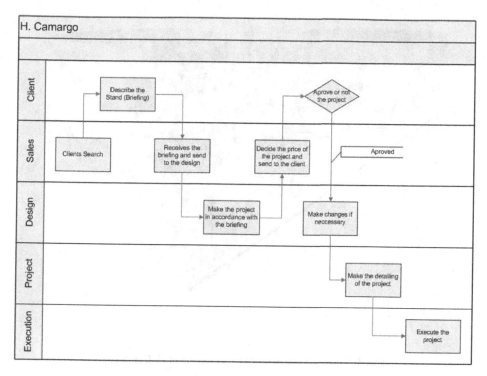

Fig. 1. H Camargo current information workflow

project through, effectively building the stand to the design initially specified. Stands are all built in–house and then taken to the event site and put together. Stands already used are either sent to another event or returned to the company for storage.

Project proposals need to be created quickly, be original and innovative. The Design department designs projects for the stands based on briefings sent by potential clients. These initial designs are not charged for, and the company will get paid if the project is accepted (and executed). It is important to note that communication flows almost exclusively in one direction: from the Design division, a design (a 3D Studio drawing) is handed on to the Project division and then to Execution. Given that these last two have no say whatsoever in the actual design, oftentimes problems are generated.

In an effort to rapidly create new and interesting designs, architects employ materials that may not be in stock (and possibly be hard to purchase) or define shapes that are difficult (if not impossible) to execute, which generates problems for the Project and Execution Teams. Some designs are harder to implement, which translates to more time spent on the physical specification and difficulties in construction. A sample design is shown in Fig 2.

The construction of a stand, from initial conception to the moment it is mounted at a fair, involves a series of processes and materials: after approval, a project has to be detailed (further specified) so that it can be mounted in the originally designed way. This specification may lead to the use of in-stock materials, and it also creates transformation processes to reuse materials (wood, aluminum and impressions). Some of these transformations are cutting, painting, silk screening and assembling. In the end,

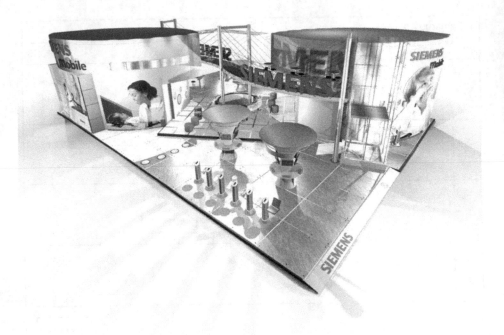

Fig. 2. Sample design created by designers at H. Camargo

all the pieces have to be arranged in trucks and taken to the fair, where it has to be mounted in exactly the same way as initially designed.

Furthermore, this lack of global awareness and communication increases the possibility of delays in the project (due to difficulties with physical specification and construction), materials waste (if the design includes materials or shapes that cannot be reused), storage of old (used) stands and increase in costs. Naturally, completed projects must be delivered on schedule, which may also lead to a need for overtime or hiring extra personnel to help with construction.

Currently, each division uses computers to perform their part of the process and hands down files with specifications to the next one. A knowledge base with all the designs created (executed or not) by the company is under construction and will be used to furnish information to our agents.

In the current model there is a total lack of communication between the teams that design and the teams that build the stand. In many cases this lack of communication and global awareness on the part of the architects generates serious quality problems and make it hard to reuse of the existing materials in stock.

The majority of problems are generated when the designer develops a project that demands materials that are not in stock. In this in case, extra costs will be incurred in purchasing materials so that the project is properly executed. In many cases problems occur because the stand is designed without any concern for the way in which it will be constructed. This is an even worse problem because the project cannot be built in the way it was designed, causing serious quality problems and issues with clients.

Given these issues, we can see that a major problem source is the lack of awareness and consciousness in relation other phases of the process. A good designer should be cogniscent of all the project phases. Lack of information is a cause of many problems.

4 Approach

We have envisioned an agent-based system to inform designers about similar projects in the knowledge base and potential problems during the conceptual design phase, based on previous problems. The agents also present ideas based on the information in the briefing to the designers, so they can consider previous similar needs and what solutions were given. Agents also extract information from each designer's current design and verify the feasibility of this design given previous designs, materials in stock and shapes being utilized. Agents are especially well suited because they can work pro-actively in the background, managing and exchanging information. Agents can also monitor users' actions and work progress, to display information to the user when necessary. Autonomous agents can work in parallel with the user, keeping track of their work and automatically providing information.

Our main goal is to provide designers with information on the possible consequences of their choices (for instance, if a certain type of material is out of stock and hard to come by, there is a good chance the ordering process will cause a delay in construction). We expect that, given this information, designers will make different decisions, which will benefit the company as a whole.

Information related to the project is delivered to the designers before and during its execution. Agents have access to the knowledge base, stock, processes and existing design objects. This information is used to assess the feasibility, determine possible problems with a project as it is designed and to estimate project cost, important factor when designing a proposal.

Agents analyze the information, linking it to other sources of information, establishing possible problems and displaying this information to the designer as they work on designing a new stand. Potential problems are: non-existence of materials, waste, cost, impossibility of reuse and time to construction. Agents have four main functions: filtering, processing and distributing information and project management. Fig 3 shows how the agents fit into the existing workflow.

- Filtering agents are in charge of presenting similar projects and extracting the necessary information from the 3d Studio drawing that is being worked on by the designers.
- Processing agents verify whether there are materials in stock or on order that match the information extracted by the filtering agents, and whether some of the old projects or objects can be reused for this one.
- Information distribution agents are in charge of informing the designers about the possible problems with the project and the purchasing department about the possible need to buy certain materials so that the project can be built as it has been designed.
- Agents for project management are activated from the moment a project is approved. They monitor all of the construction stages up to the opening of the stand in the fair and its breakdown afterwards.

The agent system is being implemented using IBM's Aglets library. The Aglets library supplies a standard template for agent creation. As mentioned before, there are four types of agents: filtering, processing, distribution and process management agents. These are further detailed below.

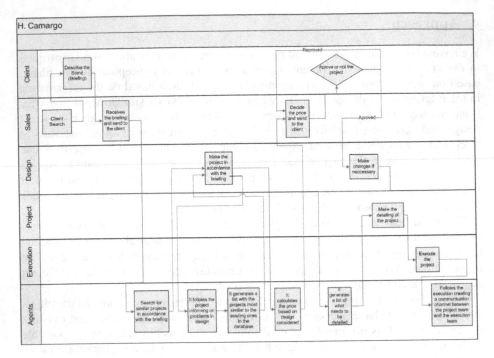

Fig. 3. Envisioned information workflow

4.1 Filtering Agents

Filtering agents initiate their work as soon as data from the project briefing becomes available. This is initially done by hand, and the designers feed the data into the system in a structured form. The information on the briefing usually includes: size of the stand, location, mandatory items, cost and others information about purpose and about the company. Given this information, a search on the knowledge base provides the previous stands that resemble more closely the briefing at hand. This would create a set of information that would enable the architects to design projects reusing some ideas, shapes and objects and still remain free to experiment with variations on these themes. In the near future, we will be collecting this information from the briefing through textual analysis.

Filtering agents also work on 3d Studio files. These files have lots of information about the design: they list objects used and their location and indicate the vertices for complex shapes. The agent extracts from this file what objects are being used, calculates sizes and recognizes shapes from the given vertices.

The following information is extracted from the design file and analyzed by the agents:

- Materials List: a list of all materials that will be used in the construction of the stand. These can be matched against existing materials (in stock) to determine the probability of delays due to lack of material. Note that it is not enough to check with materials currently in stock, but the processing agent has to take into account other designs currently under construction.

- Objects: pre-existing objects (for instance, chairs, desks or stools) that are part of the design. Some of the furniture items may already be in use by other stands. Agents need to verify not only the current snapshot of the information, but take into account the stands in construction.
- Shapes: shapes used in the construction of each stand or object of the stand. Agents perform shape analysis to see if parts of previous designs can be reused in the current one.

Information collected by the filtering agents is stored as XML in the knowledge base and then passed on to the processing agents so can be analyzed. A sample XML information file is shown below.

Table 1. XML representation of 3D Studio objects

```
<xml>
  <nmesh>1</nmesh>
  <mesh>
   <name>Box01</name>
   <nvertex>8</nvertex>
   <nface>12</nface>
   <vertex>
    <vert n="0">
     <x>-34.615379</x>
     <y>-21.005919</y>
     <z>0.000000</z>
     <u>382989452596352960000000000000000.000000</u>
     <v>183776526117779500000000000000000.000000</v>
     <nx>0.200000</nx>
     <ny>0.400000</ny>
     <nz>0.400000</nz>
    </vert>
    <vert n="1">
     <x>-34.615379</x> ...
   </vertex>
   <faces>
    <face n="0">
     <v1>0</v1>
     <v2>2</v2>
     <v3>3</v3>
     <n1>0.000000</n1>
     <n2>0.000000</n2>
     <n3>1.000000</n3>
    </face>
    <face n="1">
     <v1>3</v1> ...
   </faces>
  </mesh>
</xml>
```

From this file, all the necessary information can be extracted. The file contains all the objects as a mesh. A mesh has a name, the vertex numbers and the face numbers. Each vertex has coordinates x, y, z and the normal vectors. Each face is formed by a triangle and indicates which vertex from the list is being used. In this fashion it is easier for the processing agents to determine the area and volume from each object and it's still possible to reconstruct the object separately from the others.

4.2 Processing Agents

Processing agents evaluate items that exist in stock and shapes under construction. They work with the filtering agents to determine, in real time, if an object or shape can be used in that project, given the expected date of completion. We will be using shape analysis algorithms to assess the viability of the construct. These algorithms are currently under study. This agent is also responsible for determining costs of materials used and generating a list of materials that will need to be purchased.

The following inferences are made:

- Difficulty in specifying a project or in building certain shapes can be inferred from the time spent on previous similar tasks. Tasks that take longer, demand more individuals' work or must be reviewed several time can be considered more complex than others.
- Possibility for using parts of older stands can be found through shape analysis.
- Furniture reuse can be encouraged by suggesting alternative, already existing furniture that complies with the overall design (established through shape and color analysis and project history).

The initial list of materials will also help the physical specification teams, as one of their tasks is to generate a complete list of materials, with sizes and quantities. This team also determines which parts from other projects can be reused and what transformations should be made on previous designs.

4.3 Distribution Agents

Distribution agents are the interface with the designer. They pass the information analysis to the designers. They display messages on the designers' screen, offering useful information during the project.

We have a smaller window showing the design and highlighting the problems. There are some icons that display how many problems and of what types (structural, materials, time, cost) have been detected. This window also shows the cost of the project during its design. This is important information for the designer because it allows him to evaluate if his project is in accordance with the briefing. However, it is also important not to draw the designer's attention away from his or her current work too much, for that could compromise his or her work. We found an interface that is, at the same time, expressive and unobtrusive.

This agent is also able to create a direct communication link between the design and stock team so that faster, joint analysis can be performed. The agent also provides a communication link between designers and the execution department, to clear doubts and create an experience base. This communication is asynchronous, as the questions inserted in an issue base are answered during the course of the project. These issues will have an answer date limit and a priority order. They are sent by email (simple and fast method of communication) to individuals according to the type of issue. All the answers are stored for future consultations of similar issues.

4.4 Project Management Agents

As soon as the project is approved, the project accompaniment agents start to follow it. These agents work on the information received from the processing agents, following the workflow from the beginning of stand construction to its boarding on the truck for delivery.

Initially, a list is generated, containing all the materials that need to be bought and shapes that need to be built. For each shape, there is a registry of when construction on it was started, when it was finished and a text field for entering difficulties encountered during construction. All these data are inserted by the production teams. After the purchase of each material and the construction of each shape, these items are removed from the list, so that the team stays up to date on the items that still need to be constructed. A countdown on the days until shipping is always visible so the production team is aware of the schedule. Finally, another list is created to verify which materials have already been expedited in the trucks. This list is necessary because a very common problem that occurs is that certain parts are forgotten, which causes a great deal of trouble and cost increase.

5 Scenario

To illustrate, we present a case study: the Siemens stand built by H. Camargo for a telecommunications fair. Initially, Siemens supplied a briefing detailing the requirements for the stand. The following paragraphs present excerpts from the briefing text, drafted by the Sales team with the client, in an effort to understand their needs.

- The stand will sit in a 17x23 metre area, between two corridors. It needs to have two floors as described below. The greatest emphasis must be given to the cell phones, since the stand will be between two competing cell phone stands. They should be displayed in cells or "islands" and no longer on desktops as in previous stands.
- On the top floor, they envisioned two large blocks for meeting rooms. These would be connected by a deck, where a bar with tables and chairs could be placed. To get to the mezzanine, a large ramp could be used in place of stairs, since it would provide good movement, allow people going up and down to be seen, enable disabled access to the second floor and have and innovative design. An alternative idea would be to use a pantographic elevator, bringing in new ideas in relation to this aspect. This is an important differential.
- The lower level needs special treatment. The physical part should be the same that has been used in other stands this year. The differentiation should be in the lounge, which will be located beneath the deck and completely open. A bar integrated with the cell phone window displays should be the main draw of the stand.

- Cell phone displays should once again be innovative. As before, allow individuals to manipulate each model, so there should be a safety chord and also space for accessories. In some cases, a desktop for a notebook (same numbers as usual). This division from Siemens will be paying for 50% of the stand. Some of the displays should be integrated with the lounge and windows with the products on the floor can be used, since they were well received previously.
- As a whole, they are imagining a stand with scenic lighting or even floor lighting, using a cover for a high-impact stand and scenic lighting as a means of differentiation. The stand will contain an entertainment space that has not been thought through yet.

From this briefing, several bits of information can be extracted that serve as input for our agents to search the knowledge base. The items shown in **Table 2** can be extracted.

Table 2. Data from the briefing

Client	Siemens
Neighbors	None
Floors	2
1st floor area	391 m2
2nd floor area	Undefined
Length	23 m
Width	17 m
Price	Undefined
Spaces	Bar, Meeting Room, Deck, Ramp, Elevator, Lounge, Window Displays, Mezzanine, Computer, Notebook and Plasma TV.

These elements are used to search a case base of previous designs. As can be observed on the screenshot in Figure 4, the search yields several stands that are somehow similar to what is being designed at the moment. In this manner, the architect can re-use some ideas from previous designs to generate a new one or even reuse something that had previously been designed.

From the search results, one can also easily and quickly establish a price estimate for the stand, given the price tags on the similar stands. In this fashion, the commercial department can rapidly generate a cost estimate that can be given to the client.

During stand creation using 3D Studio, the architect receives several warnings with relation to the complexity of the stand and reuse of materials. One of the main issues relates to two curved walls created for the stand. These would be impossible to build using "Octanorm", a system for quick and easy construction and complete reuse, which means they would have to be constructed using wood, which means extra cost, time and risks.

Despite all the warnings, architects chose to keep the curved walls as planned. This generated a series of extra costs and problems, for they had to be specified and then cut from pieces of wood that had to be pre-built at the company site. This special operation happened because the stand needed to be ready within two days.

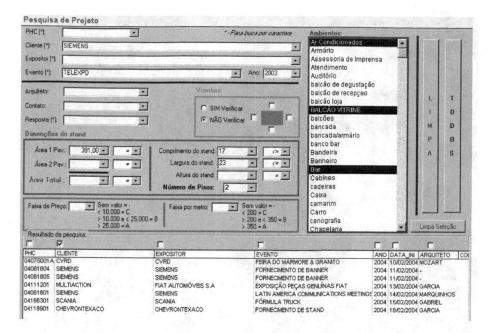

Fig. 4. Knowledge Base Screenshot

Another issue relates to the bar: the architect allocated objects that were already in use at another stand during the same period. The agent provides options to the architect, who accepts the suggestions. In this fashion the project can be altered before being sent for approval, with the "optimized" bar. If that had not been done, costs would have risen steeply, since a whole new bar would have to be built as specified in the project.

Another warning generated by the agents related to the floors. According to the briefing, the floor would have to be lit. To fulfil this requirement, the architect created a floor made of glass panes. However, the company didn't have that quantity of glass in stock. In this case, the purchase was inevitable but, given the early warning, better purchasing conditions could be negotiated.

After stand design approval, lots of messages were generated between the execution and design teams and the issue base became an important resource used by both parties, since the designers couldn't be available full time to help the builders. Through it asynchronous communication was made possible, which allowed both teams to answer questions in their own time.

A serious discussion point was the mushroom-shaped display window. Since it was a completely new design, the project and execution teams had to draw several technical drawings to fulfil the designer's drawings.

At the end of a long process, the stand was completely built within schedule, without errors or failures. The architects' approval was practically 100%, as several problems were avoided. The designers' creativity wasn't compromised at any moment, which enabled the generation of a beautiful project, as can be seen on the photo in Figure 5.

Fig. 5. Photo of the final stand being constructed at the fair site. This stand was considered the best in the fair

It is important to note that this is an illustration of how the system would work, and where the agents would chime in with suggestions and communication. This was an actual (successful) project that was undertaken in 2003, but without agent or knowledge base support. We are envisioning a number of improvements upon the process, and hope to test out the system using this case as the first test case, since it is highly complex and has the potential for generating several problems. The agents and knowledge bases are under construction and we hope to have them built soon to start testing.

6   Conclusions

With these agents we expect to change the way in which designers work: by providing them with data to inform their designs, they will be able to make better design choices, leading to more reuse and fewer errors.

It is important to note that the agents are not meant to restrict the design and never force the designer into any one solution at any moment. We mean for the agent to provide awareness so that the designer can make conscious choices. The designer may still choose to build all-new modules and complicated shapes that won't be reused, but he or she will be aware of what is being done (it will be a conscious choice). We will be investigating the consequences of the introduction of this information at a later time.

The global Knowledge Base under construction will hold information on previous designs (such as time spent on construction, objects and materials, spent on assembly, time spent on physical specification etc.), it will also establish, when possible, a design history and difficulties. This history will be automatically captured by the agents from this point on: the agents store all new information into the knowledge base, creating a case history that can serve as a basis for future inferences.

One addition we would like to make is to provide builders with tools for logging their problems, so that their knowledge can be disseminated throughout the company. Through these, builders would be able to document and create a history of each project. This history would be particularly useful for reflection on the process.

Agents are well suited for this type of application and also for triggering certain types of organizational changes: they can be easily integrated with other applications, doing their work without interfering with the designers' work, and they can work proactively and autonomously in the background, assisting the user as he or she works. Displaying information as users work is potentially more effective than expecting designers to study or learn about each other's designs or work, given they're always working under time constraints. Having the information available in its context, when it is relevant can have a greater impact than studying and trying to remember it all.

This approach has potential benefits, as it starts to generate a company-wide consciousness that did not exist, and does so from the bottom up, provoking thought, promoting information exchange and increasing process understanding by designers and architects, instead of imposing new organizational directives from the top down. Initial discussions with stakeholders have provided us with some useful insights and general approval of the idea and potential outcomes.

This approach is much more effective than the imposition approach, for individuals can see the consequences of their work and the benefits and problems raised by each design choice. This would generate a greater level of engagement with the process. One issue we are especially concerned with is that the application does not limit the designers' creativity, leading to repetitive designs. We will be watching how the introduction of this technology reflects of the designs produced. We hope that designers will still search for novel, creative solutions but that these will be more cost effective.

Acknowledgements

This work was partially supported by CAPES and CNPq. We would also like to thank H. Camargo Promotional Architecture and Landscaping for their support in the development of this project.

References

1. Shen, W., Norrie, D.H. & Barthès, J.P; Multi-Agent Design Systems for Concurrent Intelligent Design and Manufacturing. Taylor & Francis, London, 2001.
2. Russell, S. and Norvig, P. Artificial Intelligence - A Modern Approach. Prentice Hall, Englewood Cliffs, NJ, 1995.
3. Jennings, N.R. An Agent-Based Approach for Building Complex Software Systems. Communications of the ACM, April 2001/Vol. 44, No. 4

4. Wang, A., Conradi, R., Liu, C. A Multi-Agent Architecture for Cooperative Software Engineering Proceedings of the Third International Conference on Autonomous Agents, 1999Root, R. Design a Multi-Media Vehicle for Social Browsing. Proceedings CSCW, 1988.

5. Ellis, C.A. e Wainer, J. Groupware and Computer Supported Cooperative Work. In Weiss, G. (Ed.) Multiagent, Systems, MIT Press, 1999.

6. Fish, R. S., Kraut R. E. and Chalfonte, B. L. The VideoWindow System in Informal Communications. Proceedings CSCW, 1990.

7. Isaacs, E.A., Tang, J.C. and Morris, T. Piazza: A desktop Environment Supporting Impromtu and Planned Interactions. Proceedings of CSCW'96, Cambridge, MA, 1996

8. Morán, A. L., Favela, J., Martínez-Enríquez, A. M. and Decouchant, D. Before Getting There: Potential and Actual Collaboration. In: Haake, J. M. and Pino, J. A. (Eds.) CRIWG 2002, LNCS 2440, pp. 147 - 167, Spring-Verlag, 2002

9. Aldunate, R. Nussbaum, M. and González, R. An Agent Based Middleware for supporting Spontaneous Collaboration among Co-Located, Mobile and not Necessarily Known People. Workshop on Ad hoc Communications and Collaboration in Ubiquitous Computing Environments, CSCW 2002

10. Esborjörnsson, M. and Östergren, M. Issues of Spontaneous Collaboration and Mobility. Workshop on Supporting Spontaneous Interaction in Ubiquitous Computing Settings, UBICOMP'02, Göteberg, Sweden, 2002

11. Pinheiro, M.K., Lima, J.V. and Borges, M.R.S. A Framework for Awareness Support in Groupware Systems. Proceedings of the 7th International Conference on Computer Supported Cooperative Work in Design - CSCWD'2002, Rio de Janeiro, Brazil, September 2002, pp.13-18

12. Hoffman, M and Herrmann, T. Prospect Awareness - Envisioning the Benefits of Collaborative Work. Available online at: http://iundg.informatik.uni-dortmund.de/iug-home/people/MH/Prospect Awareness/PAhome.html

Author Index

Lecture Notes in Artificial Intelligence (LNAI)

Vol. 3230: J.L. Vicedo, P. Martínez-Barco, R. Muñoz, M. Saiz Noeda (Eds.), Advances in Natural Language Processing. XII, 488 pages. 2004.

Vol. 3229: J.J. Alferes, J. Leite (Eds.), Logics in Artificial Intelligence. XIV, 744 pages. 2004.

Vol. 3228: M.G. Hinchey, J.L. Rash, W.F. Truszkowski, C.A. Rouff (Eds.), Formal Approaches to Agent-Based Systems. VIII, 290 pages. 2004.

Vol. 3215: M.G.. Negoita, R.J. Howlett, L.C. Jain (Eds.), Knowledge-Based Intelligent Information and Engineering Systems, Part III. LVII, 906 pages. 2004.

Vol. 3214: M.G.. Negoita, R.J. Howlett, L.C. Jain (Eds.), Knowledge-Based Intelligent Information and Engineering Systems, Part II. LVIII, 1302 pages. 2004.

Vol. 3213: M.G.. Negoita, R.J. Howlett, L.C. Jain (Eds.), Knowledge-Based Intelligent Information and Engineering Systems, Part I. LVIII, 1280 pages. 2004.

Vol. 3209: B. Berendt, A. Hotho, D. Mladenic, M. van Someren, M. Spiliopoulou, G. Stumme (Eds.), Web Mining: From Web to Semantic Web. IX, 201 pages. 2004.

Vol. 3206: P. Sojka, I. Kopecek, K. Pala (Eds.), Text, Speech and Dialogue. XIII, 667 pages. 2004.

Vol. 3202: J.-F. Boulicaut, F. Esposito, F. Giannotti, D. Pedreschi (Eds.), Knowledge Discovery in Databases: PKDD 2004. XIX, 560 pages. 2004.

Vol. 3201: J.-F. Boulicaut, F. Esposito, F. Giannotti, D. Pedreschi (Eds.), Machine Learning: ECML 2004. XVIII, 580 pages. 2004.

Vol. 3194: R. Camacho, R. King, A. Srinivasan (Eds.), Inductive Logic Programming. XI, 361 pages. 2004.

Vol. 3192: C. Bussler, D. Fensel (Eds.), Artificial Intelligence: Methodology, Systems, and Applications. XIII, 522 pages. 2004.

Vol. 3191: M. Klusch, S. Ossowski, V. Kashyap, R. Unland (Eds.), Cooperative Information Agents VIII. XI, 303 pages. 2004.

Vol. 3187: G. Lindemann, J. Denzinger, I.J. Timm, R. Unland (Eds.), Multiagent System Technologies. XIII, 341 pages. 2004.

Vol. 3176: O. Bousquet, U. von Luxburg, G. Rätsch (Eds.), Advanced Lectures on Machine Learning. IX, 241 pages. 2004.

Vol. 3171: A.L.C. Bazzan, S. Labidi (Eds.), Advances in Artificial Intelligence – SBIA 2004. XVII, 548 pages. 2004.

Vol. 3159: U. Visser, Intelligent Information Integration for the Semantic Web. XIV, 150 pages. 2004.

Vol. 3157: C. Zhang, H. W. Guesgen, W.K. Yeap (Eds.), PRICAI 2004: Trends in Artificial Intelligence. XX, 1023 pages. 2004.

Vol. 3155: P. Funk, P.A. González Calero (Eds.), Advances in Case-Based Reasoning. XIII, 822 pages. 2004.

Vol. 3139: F. Iida, R. Pfeifer, L. Steels, Y. Kuniyoshi (Eds.), Embodied Artificial Intelligence. IX, 331 pages. 2004.

Vol. 3131: V. Torra, Y. Narukawa (Eds.), Modeling Decisions for Artificial Intelligence. XI, 327 pages. 2004.

Vol. 3127: K.E. Wolff, H.D. Pfeiffer, H.S. Delugach (Eds.), Conceptual Structures at Work. XI, 403 pages. 2004.

Vol. 3123: A. Belz, R. Evans, P. Piwek (Eds.), Natural Language Generation. X, 219 pages. 2004.

Vol. 3120: J. Shawe-Taylor, Y. Singer (Eds.), Learning Theory. X, 648 pages. 2004.

Vol. 3097: D. Basin, M. Rusinowitch (Eds.), Automated Reasoning. XII, 493 pages. 2004.

Vol. 3071: A. Omicini, P. Petta, J. Pitt (Eds.), Engineering Societies in the Agents World. XIII, 409 pages. 2004.

Vol. 3070: L. Rutkowski, J. Siekmann, R. Tadeusiewicz, L.A. Zadeh (Eds.), Artificial Intelligence and Soft Computing - ICAISC 2004. XXV, 1208 pages. 2004.

Vol. 3068: E. André, L. Dybkjær, W. Minker, P. Heisterkamp (Eds.), Affective Dialogue Systems. XII, 324 pages. 2004.

Vol. 3067: M. Dastani, J. Dix, A. El Fallah-Seghrouchni (Eds.), Programming Multi-Agent Systems. X, 221 pages. 2004.

Vol. 3066: S. Tsumoto, R. Słowiński, J. Komorowski, J.W. Grzymała-Busse (Eds.), Rough Sets and Current Trends in Computing. XX, 853 pages. 2004.

Vol. 3065: A. Lomuscio, D. Nute (Eds.), Deontic Logic in Computer Science. X, 275 pages. 2004.

Vol. 3060: A.Y. Tawfik, S.D. Goodwin (Eds.), Advances in Artificial Intelligence. XIII, 582 pages. 2004.

Vol. 3056: H. Dai, R. Srikant, C. Zhang (Eds.), Advances in Knowledge Discovery and Data Mining. XIX, 713 pages. 2004.

Vol. 3055: H. Christiansen, M.-S. Hacid, T. Andreasen, H.L. Larsen (Eds.), Flexible Query Answering Systems. X, 500 pages. 2004.

Vol. 3048: P. Faratin, D.C. Parkes, J.A. Rodríguez-Aguilar, W.E. Walsh (Eds.), Agent-Mediated Electronic Commerce V. XI, 155 pages. 2004.

Vol. 3040: R. Conejo, M. Urretavizcaya, J.-L. Pérez-de-la-Cruz (Eds.), Current Topics in Artificial Intelligence. XIV, 689 pages. 2004.

Vol. 3035: M.A. Wimmer (Ed.), Knowledge Management in Electronic Government. XII, 326 pages. 2004.

Vol. 3034: J. Favela, E. Menasalvas, E. Chávez (Eds.), Advances in Web Intelligence. XIII, 227 pages. 2004.

Vol. 3030: P. Giorgini, B. Henderson-Sellers, M. Winikoff (Eds.), Agent-Oriented Information Systems. XIV, 207 pages. 2004.

Vol. 3029: B. Orchard, C. Yang, M. Ali (Eds.), Innovations in Applied Artificial Intelligence. XXI, 1272 pages. 2004.

Vol. 3025: G.A. Vouros, T. Panayiotopoulos (Eds.), Methods and Applications of Artificial Intelligence. XV, 546 pages. 2004.

Vol. 3020: D. Polani, B. Browning, A. Bonarini, K. Yoshida (Eds.), RoboCup 2003: Robot Soccer World Cup VII. XVI, 767 pages. 2004.

Vol. 3012: K. Kurumatani, S.-H. Chen, A. Ohuchi (Eds.), Multi-Agents for Mass User Support. X, 217 pages. 2004.

Vol. 3010: K.R. Apt, F. Fages, F. Rossi, P. Szeredi, J. Váncza (Eds.), Recent Advances in Constraints. VIII, 285 pages. 2004.

Vol. 2990: J. Leite, A. Omicini, L. Sterling, P. Torroni (Eds.), Declarative Agent Languages and Technologies. XII, 281 pages. 2004.